INTERNATIONAL JOURNAL OF RELIGION

ISSN: 2633-352X (Print)
ISSN: 2633-3538 (Online)

International Journal of Religion (IJOR) is a multidisciplinary peer-reviewed journal aiming to offer a venue for scholarly discussion on religion in reference to the social sciences and humanities. International Journal of Religion aims to fulfil the need for critical discussion on how religion affects economics, society, politics, international relations, geography, anthropology, education, business and management, health, and the arts.

International Journal of Religion is currently under review by various indexing and abstracting services

International Journal of Religion is published twice a year in May and November.

International Journal of Religion is published by Transnational Press London, UK.

Addresses:
URL: journals.tplondon.com/ijor
Email: admin@tplondon.com

International Journal of Religion | ISSN: 2633-352X (Print) | ISSN: 2633-3538 (Online)

INTERNATIONAL JOURNAL OF RELIGION

ISSN: 2633-352X (Print) | ISSN: 2633-3538 (Online)

Volume 1 | Number 1 | November 2020

Special Issue: Politics of Religious Dissent

Edited by Jeffrey Haynes, Ahmet Erdi Öztürk, and Eric M. Trinka

International Journal of Religion
ISSN: 2633-352X (Print) | ISSN: 2633-3538 (Online)
journals.tplondon.com/ijor

TRANSNATIONAL PRESS®
LONDON

International Journal of Religion
November 2020
Volume: 1 | Number 1 | pp. 1 – 3
ISSN: 2633-352X (Print) | ISSN: 2633-3538 (Online)
journals.tplondon.com/ijor

TRANSNATIONAL PRESS®
LONDON

First Received: 6 November 2020
DOI: https://doi.org/10.33182/ijor.v1i1.1221

Editorial:

Launching the International Journal of Religion

Jeffrey Haynes[1], Ahmet Erdi Ozturk[2], Eric M. Trinka[3]

Introduction

The *International Journal of Religion* (IJOR) was founded to fill a gap: to discover more about how religion impacts on society and politics both within and between countries. IJOR will examine how and why religion influences national and international politics, society, and economics. IJOR will be comprehensive, inter-disciplinary and researched-based. IJOR will do all it can to be a respected social scientific journal of high academic quality. IJOR invites scholars, researchers, thinkers and practitioners working on and interested in these issues to contribute, in what the journal intends to be a conducive environment to stimulate critical and independent thinking.

IJOR's *raison d'être* is the long running and continuing debate about how secularisation influences the public roles of religion. The debate has lasted half a century or more. It was stimulated in the 1960s by the prediction of the sociologist, Peter Berger, that both industrialised and hence modernised, as well as industrialising and hence modernising, countries would *inevitably* become secular over time, implying that religion's influence would decline significantly. Today, while it is widely agreed that the public role of religion is variable in countries around the world, overall it has not lost influence to the extent that Berger and other believed it would. Instead, its influence has evolved in ways that often significantly affects our lives (Fox 2019). As evidence, we can mention some important events, including: Iran's Islamic Revolution (1979), the USA's Carter Doctrine which influenced international religious freedom, the emergence of religious political parties around the world, including in the 'secular' West and, tragically, the 9/11 attacks (on 11 September 2001) which killed 3,000 people directly. These events underline that religion has not gone away – instead, its influence is often very great on politics and society around the world (Haynes 2011; Thomas 2005; Sandal and Fox 2013).

Debates about religion's public role include (1) how central is religion to political outcomes, both domestically and in international relations, especially in relation to conflict? (Philpott 2007; Norris and Inglehart 2011; Haynes 2008; Fox 2018; Bettiza 2019). (2) How do we theoretically explain religion's involvement in politics and society? (Sandal and James 2011) (3) How does religion affect our understanding of economics? (Gill 2019) (4) What is the social impact of religion in public spaces, for example, in the controversial issue in many Western countries of Muslim women wearing face

[1] Jeffrey Haynes, PhD, Emeritus Professor, School of Social Sciences, London Metropolitan University, Department of Political Science and International Relations, London, UK. E-mail: tsjhayn1@londonmet.ac.uk

[2] Ahmet Erdi Ozturk, PhD, Lecturer, Department of Political Science and International Relations, London Metropolitan University, London, UK. E-mail: e.ozturk@londonmet.ac.uk

[3] Eric M. Trinka, PhD, Lecturer, James Madison University, United States. E-mail: trinkaem@jmu.edu

coverings? (Casanova 2011) (5) How does shared religious belief affect diasporic groups around the world? (Vertovec 2004) (6) What is the relationship between religion and our understanding of gender in both 'modern' and 'modernising' countries? (Nynas 2016), and (7) How do certain religious traditions, such as Islam, affect a country's economic, political and social development? (Kuru 2019). Aside from these specific questions, scholars and researchers interested in the public role of religion also ask how and to what extent conflicts, including those associated with terrorism, migration and inter-ethnic disputes, are linked to religion (Haynes 2005; Cesari 2019; Henne 2016; Trinka 2019; Gürses and Öztürk 2020). Stimulated by recent developments in Europe, the USA, India, Brazil and elsewhere, scholars and researchers now examine how and why religion impacts on populism and nationalism (Ozturk 2019; Koesel 2014). Finally in addition to these longstanding issues, another has emerged in recent years: how does religion affect the 'clash of civilizations', a paradigm advanced originally by the political scientist, Samuel Huntington (1996; see Haynes 2019 for an up to date analysis of the 'clash of civilizations').

These issues have received much attention in both popular and scholarly fora. In addition, think tanks and research centres around the world investigate the impact of religion on politics and society. Book series and dedicated academic journals also cover them in depth. With all this attention and coverage why do we need another journal? While there are already several important academic journals examining religion and related issues in social scientific contexts, none focuses on the multiple issues that IJOR does. But no journal can develop without its contributors: Please join us. We invite you to enter the world of the journal, and contribute to its debates, discussions and research findings.

References

Bettiza, G. (2019). *Finding Faith in Foreign Policy: Religion and American Diplomacy in a Postsecular World*. Oxford: Oxford University Press.

Casanova, J. (2011). *Public religions in the modern world*. Chicago: University of Chicago Press.

Cesari, J. (2019). Civilization as Disciplinization and the Consequences for Religion and World Politics. *The Review of Faith & International Affairs* 17(1): 24-33.

Fox, J. (2019). A world survey of secular-religious competition: state religious policy from 1990 to 2014. *Religion, State & Society* 47(1): 10-29.

Fox, J. (2018). *An introduction to religion and politics: Theory and practice*. London: Routledge.

Gill, A. (2019). A Great Academic Re-awakening: The Return to a Political Economy of Religion. In: J. Carvalho, S. Iyer, J, Rubin(eds.) *Advances in the Economics of Religion*, pp. 361-376. Cham: Palgrave Macmillan.

Gurses, M. and A. E. Ozturk (2020). Religion and Armed Conflict: Evidence from the Kurdish Conflict in Turkey. *Journal for the Scientific Study of Religion*, 59(2): 327-340.

Haynes, J. (2011). *Religion, politics and international relations: Selected essays*. London: Taylor & Francis.

Haynes, J. (2019). *From Huntington to Trump: Thirty Years of the Clash of Civilizations*. New York: Lexington Books.

Haynes, J. (ed.) (2008). *Routledge handbook of religion and politics*. London: Routledge.

Haynes, J. (2005). Religion and international relations after '9/11'. *Democratization*, 12(3): 398-413.

Henne, P. (2016). *Islamic politics, Muslim states, and counterterrorism tensions*. Cambridge: Cambridge University Press.

Koesel, K. J. (2014). Religion and authoritarianism: Cooperation, conflict, and the consequences. Cambridge: Cambridge University Press.

Kuru, A.T. (2019). *Islam, authoritarianism, and underdevelopment: A global and historical comparison*. Cambridge: Cambridge University Press.

Norris, P., and R. Inglehart. (2011). *Sacred and secular: Religion and politics worldwide*. Cambridge: Cambridge University Press.

Nynäs, P. (2016). *Religion, gender and sexuality in everyday life*. London: Routledge.

Öztürk, A. E. (2019). An alternative reading of religion and authoritarianism: the new logic between religion and state in the AKP's New Turkey. *Southeast European and Black Sea Studies* 19(1): 79-98.

Philpott, D. (2007). Explaining the political ambivalence of religion. *American Political Science Review*, 505-525.

Sandal, N. A., and P. James (2011). Religion and International Relations theory: Towards a mutual understanding. *European Journal of International Relations*, 17(1): 3-25.

Sandal, N., and J. Fox (2013). *Religion in international relations theory: interactions and possibilities*. London: Routledge.

Thomas, S. (2005). *The global resurgence of religion and the transformation of international relations: The struggle for the soul of the twenty-first century*. Springer.

Trinka, E. M. (2019). The End of Islands: Drawing Insight from John's Apocalypse to Respond to Prisoner Radicalization and Apocalyptically-Oriented Terrorism. *Religions* 10(2): 1-14. DOI:10.3390/rel10020073

Vertovec, S. (2004). Religion and diaspora. *New approaches to the study of religion* 2, 275-304.

International Journal of Religion

ISSN: 2633-352X (Print) | ISSN: 2633-3538 (Online)

journals.tplondon.com/ijor

TRANSNATIONAL PRESS®
LONDON

International Journal of Religion
November 2020
Volume: 1 | Number 1 | pp. 5 – 7
ISSN: 2633-352X (Print) | ISSN: 2633-3538 (Online)
journals.tplondon.com/ijor

TRANSNATIONAL PRESS®
LONDON

First Received: 2 November 2020
DOI: https://doi.org/10.33182/ijor.v1i1.1215

From the Editorial Desk

Eric M. Trinka[1]

Introduction

For this inaugural issue of the *International Journal of Religion* the editorial team sought to gather an array of papers that demonstrate substantive engagement with the questions of religious dissent as a political endeavor within and beyond religious frameworks. We solicited essays that would probe the following areas of study: historical and contemporary elasticities of religious traditions; internal tensions regarding the boundaries of acceptable belief and practice; the management and ethical treatment of dissent within particular religious traditions; whether religious faiths prescribe clear ways to manage dissent; religious reactions to dissent from feminist and queer activists; and reflections on the broader consequences of dissent in the political sphere. The papers assembled in this first issue have exceeded our expectations.

Although often understood as a compartmentalized element of one's personal cultural assemblage, religion is immanently a political enterprise. Power, exercised over and by persons, lies at the core of religious concerns. Dissent is a response to power and to the structural apparatuses that substantiate that which passes as the *status quo* in political and religious arenas. Acting in particular times and places, the bodies of religious practitioners are thus sites of political and religious negotiation. Insomuch, dissent is not simply a rejection of normativity, but rather a strategic set of subversive responses to entrenched ways of being or knowing. In the forms of thought and action, dissenters can simultaneously utilise and undermine the hierarchies promoting particular ontologies and epistemologies. Investigating the confluence of agency, power, and identity leads the discussion into the realms of ethics, where we inquire what humans can or ought to do with their bodies as instruments of dissent.

Within religions, we observe acts that contest belief and praxis. Internal debates regarding access to superhuman power(s), structures of leadership and power, as well as over different registers of religiosity create flashpoints. In such contexts, dissent is a means of initiating and negotiating conflict. In considering the increasing global reach of religious institutions, we also note that local and international systems of influence can be proactively and reactively constructed to inspire or maintain cultural and political homogeneity; leading to new forms of dissent. Beyond the realms of internal debate, we observe the extension and negotiation of religious identities in other parts of the public sphere, through activism, electoral processes, and even violent contestation.

From the fundamental need to answer questions of who gets to identify actors as dissidents—and what kinds of baggage such a label might carry—to discussion of the internal and external dimensions of dissent, the papers of this issue showcase the embodied intersectionality of dissent across different

---

[1] Eric M. Trinka, PhD, Lecturer, James Madison University, United States. E-mail: trinkaem@jmu.edu

scales of analysis. The authors represent a range of methodological approaches, including historical reflection, ethnographic analysis, international relations, political analysis, gender studies, and textual studies. Together, they attend to the dynamics of dissent in kaleidoscopic form, with essays that serendipitously overlap and illuminate one another.

The issue begins with Ronald Hatzenbuehler's essay, which takes up the topics of religious ethics and political choice. Hatzenbuehler investigates historical voting patterns as a form of dissent among lay adherents in the Church of Jesus Christ of Latter-Day Saints. His analysis captures an historical moment while also providing a cipher to interpret present-day political decision-making among LDS voters. Hendrik Johannemann continues the conversation with his examination of gender, sexuality, and internal religious dissent among South Korean Protestants. Johannemann identifies patterns of enemy-creation among anti- and pro-LGBT religious activists, demonstrating the power of "internal enemy" constructs in interreligious discussions of sexual identity and ethics. Luca Ozanno and Fabio Bolzonar's paper investigates dissent at the junctures of right-wing populism and LBTQ+ rights in France and Italy. Their inquiry leads them ask how discussions of religious dissent factor into the appropriation of religion by political parties.

T. Sultan Tepe's contribution to the issue elucidates the power of influence that political systems— namely, the U.S. court system—wield over public perceptions of religion. In her case study of the Nation of Islam, Tepe reveals how the intersection of race, religion, and politics inform notions of religious authenticity and reactions to particular religious identities in the public square. She also demonstrates how compensatory responses to these external pressures drive internal religious change. In her exploration of the boundaries of Islamic identity and practice in the Maldives, La Toya Waha centers her inquiry on tensions between historically normative religious forms and state-sponsored religious influences within and beyond the borders of the nation state. Waha's exploration of political Islam in the Maldives wrestles with questions of compatibility between democratic and Islamic ways of life. In line with Waha's investigation, Ahmet Kuru revisits the topic of freedom of religious dissent in Muslim majority countries. His paper offers a fresh interpretation in a long-standing discussion regarding the religion-state nexus in both Islam and Christianity and challenges entrenched assumptions of an essential connection between Islam and the State.

Nil Mutluer's analysis of ethnographic data gathered from a number of Muslim German Turkish communities illuminates processes of identity negotiation, religio-political alliances, and dissent among transnational communities. Her methodology centers reflexivity and feminist-critical discourse analysis, according to which Mutluer tracks shifts in perceptions and enactments of religious dissent at various scales of social engagement. Questions of internal tension and external influence are also taken up by Jed Forman, who offers a diachronic exploration of Buddhist spiritual epistemologies and dissenting opinions regarding access to religious knowledge. Continuing in a related epistemological vein, Nerida Bullock surveys the overlapping landscapes of emic/etic and authorised/ unauthorised religious narratives related to practices and prohibitions of polygamy within The Church of Jesus Christ of Latter-Day Saints. The issue concludes with Hayim Katsman's essay, which presents diachronic processes of religious change in the State of Israel while discussing the contours of religious dissent in contexts of Israeli internal migration. In doing so, he offers insight on the ways modern-Orthodox communities settling in the northern Negev are reformulating understandings of rabbinic authority.

It is with a spirit of gratitude for each author's contribution that we present their work to readers. Our hope is that this robust conversation on dissent will be the first of many as IJOR looks to the future.

On behalf of the IJOR Editorial Board,

Eric M. Trinka, PhD

Assistant Editor

International Journal of Religion
ISSN: 2633-352X (Print) | ISSN: 2633-3538 (Online)
journals.tplondon.com/ijor

TRANSNATIONAL PRESS®
LONDON

International Journal of Religion
November 2020
Volume: 1 | Number 1 | pp. 9 – 22
ISSN: 2633-352X (Print) | ISSN: 2633-3538 (Online)
journals.tplondon.com/ijor

TRANSNATIONAL PRESS®
LONDON

First Submitted: 4 May 2020 Accepted: 31 October 2020
DOI: https://doi.org/10.33182/ijor.v1i1.980

Dissent among Mormons in the 1980 Senatorial Election in Idaho

Ronald Hatzenbuehler[1]

Abstract

The ecclesiastical organization of the Church of Jesus Christ of Latter-day Saints (Mormons; or LDS; or Saints) is rigidly hierarchical, extending downward from the President. An important exception to the Church's top-down approach lies in the area of partisan politics, where the Church as an organization dons the mantle of political neutrality. This official stance notwithstanding, politics does intrude itself into Church affairs, especially in hotly contested elections. The 1980 senatorial election in Idaho severely tested the Church's commitment to political non-involvement. Church leaders extended accolades to incumbent Democratic Senator Frank Church for his support of causes favorable to the organization, but polling data and documentary evidence indicate that rank-and-file members dissented from their leaders' positive attitudes, culminating in an important realignment in electoral behavior in the state.

Keywords: *Church of Jesus Christ of Latter-day Saints; Mormons; Frank Church; Idaho politics; "morality issues".*

Introduction

The ecclesiastical organization of the Church of Jesus Christ of Latter-day Saints (Mormons; or LDS; or Saints) is rigidly hierarchical, extending downward from the President, who cloaks himself in the mantle of "prophet, seer, and revelator" to the faithful, as did the Church's founder, Joseph Smith. The First Presidency (the President and his First and Second Counselors) along with the Quorum of the Twelve bear witness in the name of Jesus Christ and lead the Church in all matters, spiritual and temporal (Church of Jesus Christ of Latter-day Saints, n. d.). To guide the beliefs and behavior of church members, LDS leaders frequently take stands on hot-button societal issues, such as LGBTQ recognition, initiatives favoring alcohol or gambling, state-funded abortions, or similar ballot initiatives. For example, polling results indicate that LDS leaders' support for a 2004 constitutional amendment to the Utah Constitution defining marriage as between a man and a woman did affect the voting behavior of Mormons (Monson, et al., 2005).

An important exception to this top-down approach in temporal affairs lies in the area of partisan politics, where the Church's leaders forswear allegiance to organized political parties, and the Church as an organization preaches political neutrality. This official stance notwithstanding, politics does intrude itself into Church affairs and severely tests Church leaders' commitment to political non-involvement. A case in point centers on the 1980 senatorial election in Idaho that pitted incumbent Democratic Senator Frank Church against US Representative Steve Symms. In late 1978, LDS President Spencer W. Kimball and other members of the Church's leadership greeted Senator Church at LDS headquarters in Salt Lake City and praised him for his support of causes favorable to the body. Polling data of voters' attitudes and documentary evidence, however, indicate that rank-and-file members in Idaho dissented from their leaders' favorable attitudes. This essay probes the depths

---

[1] Ronald L. Hatzenbuehler, Professor Emeritus, Idaho State University, United States. E-mail: hatzrona@isu.edu

of this dissent and suggests that a dramatic shift in support for Senator Church among Mormon voters beginning in 1968 led to an important realignment in electoral behavior in the state and provided a signpost to more recent elections. Because voting behavior among Mormons has been less studied than that of other religious groups (Fox, 2006; Shafer and Spady, 2014), this study also has relevance for scholars who study the interplay between religion and politics.

I

In the fall of 1978, Idaho Senator Frank Church accepted an invitation initiated by a student group at Brigham Young University (BYU) to speak at the Provo, Utah, campus on the subject of foreign relations. As chair of the Senate Foreign Relations Committee, Church was eminently qualified to address the topic, and he chose as his title of the address, "The Yen to Make a Mark with the Dollar: A Franc Look at Our International Economic Policy". An itinerary for the day indicates that following the talk the senator and his wife Bethine attended a luncheon with BYU officials, selected faculty, and guests; met with students and friends from Idaho; and had dinner with BYU President and Mrs. Dallin H. Oaks and guests (Church Papers, Ser. 8.2, Box 18, Folder 14; hereafter, Church Papers, 8.2, 18:14).[2]

Before returning to Idaho the next day, the Churches had breakfast with the First Presidency and other ranking officials in Salt Lake City. At the meeting, President Spencer W. Kimball presented the senator with a two-volume personal genealogy and thanked him for his work on two specific pieces of legislation—one to designate the Mormon Trail a National Historic Trail, the other to repeal portions of an 1862 law that limited the amount of land which churches could hold in US territories. The latter legislation was especially important to Church leaders because of their plans to build a Temple in American Samoa. In a letter of gratitude regarding the senator's actions in behalf of both pieces of legislation in October 1978, President Kimball praised Church for his "high minded action. You have risen to a position of considerable influence in the United States Senate and we compliment you for your proper using of your influence in this matter. We have appreciated your friendship over the years and commend you for your integrity". In reply, Church wrote, "Religious discrimination for whatever reason or causes, is abhorrent to a free people. That this law was allowed to remain on the statute books of the federal government for a century is an affront to every person who cherishes freedom of religion. I count it an honor to have had a hand in its repeal" (Church Papers, 8.2, 18:14; Kimball, Scrapbook Collection).

The invitation to meet with the First Presidency in the Church's offices in Salt Lake City witnessed to the importance Church leaders accorded Idaho's senior senator. The publisher of the *Deseret News*—the Salt Lake City newspaper owned by the Church—wrote to Church: "Your remarks touched us deeply. I think you know of the great affection and esteem that the leadership of the Church holds for you". Another member of the Church Presidency echoed these sentiments: "You made a sincere impression upon the Presidency. We know you are a friend to our people". In a handwritten note to President Kimball from the senator, Church expressed gratitude "for our breakfast together [;] I shall always remember and appreciate it as a highlight in my public career. Bethine joins me in thanking you for the generosity of your friendship, and for all the good work you do in God's service". According to Peter Fenn in an interview with the author (Fenn organized Church's trip to BYU and later became the senator's Chief of Staff), the senator was pleased with the Utah visit and

---

[2] Dallin H. Oaks is currently the First Counselor in the Church hierarchy. Oaks (Oaks, 1991) later praised Senator Church for his role in lobbying Chinese officials in early 1979 to allow a BYU variety show to go to China: "Idaho Senator Frank Church, then chairman of the Senate Foreign Relations Committee, wrote Chinese officials on our behalf. His enthusiastic endorsement of BYU was extremely helpful."

"thought maybe it was a breakthrough" in cementing support from Church officials (Church Papers, 8.2, 18:14). At the same time that Senator Church was receiving and returning accolades from the LDS President and his top advisors, however, polling data that the senator's staff was viewing painted a far different picture.

The first public opinion poll that appears in the senator's files occurred in 1960. At that time, Louis Harris and Associates asked various questions of respondents, including their religious affiliation, which the poll divided into "Catholic and Protestant." Mormon Church affiliation was added to the religious spectrum in 1962.

Table 1. "Polling Results: US Senate Race, 1962" (Church Papers, 5.3, 8:16)

	Church %	Hawley %
Statewide	62	38
By Area:		
CD #1	58	42
CD #2	66	34
By Religion:		
Protestant	54	46
Catholic	71	29
Latter Day Saints	76	24

A couple of important conclusions may be drawn from Table 1. First, overall support for Senator Church was higher in 1962 in the predominately Mormon counties in Idaho's second congressional district than in the first (66 to 58 percent).[3] Second, although a majority of the respondents to the poll who self-identified as Protestant, Catholic, or Mormon indicated support for the senator against his Republican opponent, important differences existed in the level of support, with Mormons and Catholics indicating a higher level of support than Protestants (76, 71, and 54 percent, respectively). The text accompanying this report highlighted the fact that Church's support was highest among self-identified Mormons, but it also noted that this group demonstrated a "heav[y] concentration of undecided voters". This fact notwithstanding, the report observed, "It is abundantly clear…that the swing vote in this election are the members of the Church of Latter Day [sic] Saints. This was the group that broke heavily for Church six years ago…. It is a group that provides him with his comfortable edge today" (Church Papers: 5.3, 6:18).

In preparation for his 1968 contest with second congressional district US Representative George Hansen (who was a Mormon), the Church campaign contracted with John F. Kraft pollsters to conduct "A Study of Attitudes of Voters in Idaho," and Mormon voters figured prominently in the analysis of the March 1968 poll. In a letter from the senator to Kraft early in the year, Church stressed, "I presume the classification questions you have included on the last page of your questionnaire are meant to enable you to break down, by area, occupation, income, religion, etc…. This is vital information, and…I draw your attention to the fact that the three important religious divisions in Idaho, listed in order of their respective importance, are: Mormon, Protestant, and Catholic. Your

---

[3] Please see Figure 1. Southeastern Idaho counties in the second congressional district are adjacent to Utah (Interstate 15 runs from Butte, MT, through Salt Lake City, and Las Vegas, NV, to Los Angeles, CA. In contrast, Interstate 90 in northern Idaho runs from Seattle, WA, to Boston. A quip in line with the state's regionalism posits that Idaho has three capitals: Boise, ID; Spokane, WA; and Salt Lake City, UT).

'key groups' should include these three groups in the religious category" (Church Papers, 5.3, 6:17).[4] As a control on the popularity of Congressman Hansen with voters, Kraft's pollsters also asked respondents for whom they would vote in a Hansen-Church race and a James McClure-Church race (McClure at that time was the congressman in Idaho's first congressional district).

Figure 1. "Map of Idaho's Major Cities, Congressional Districts, and Counties"

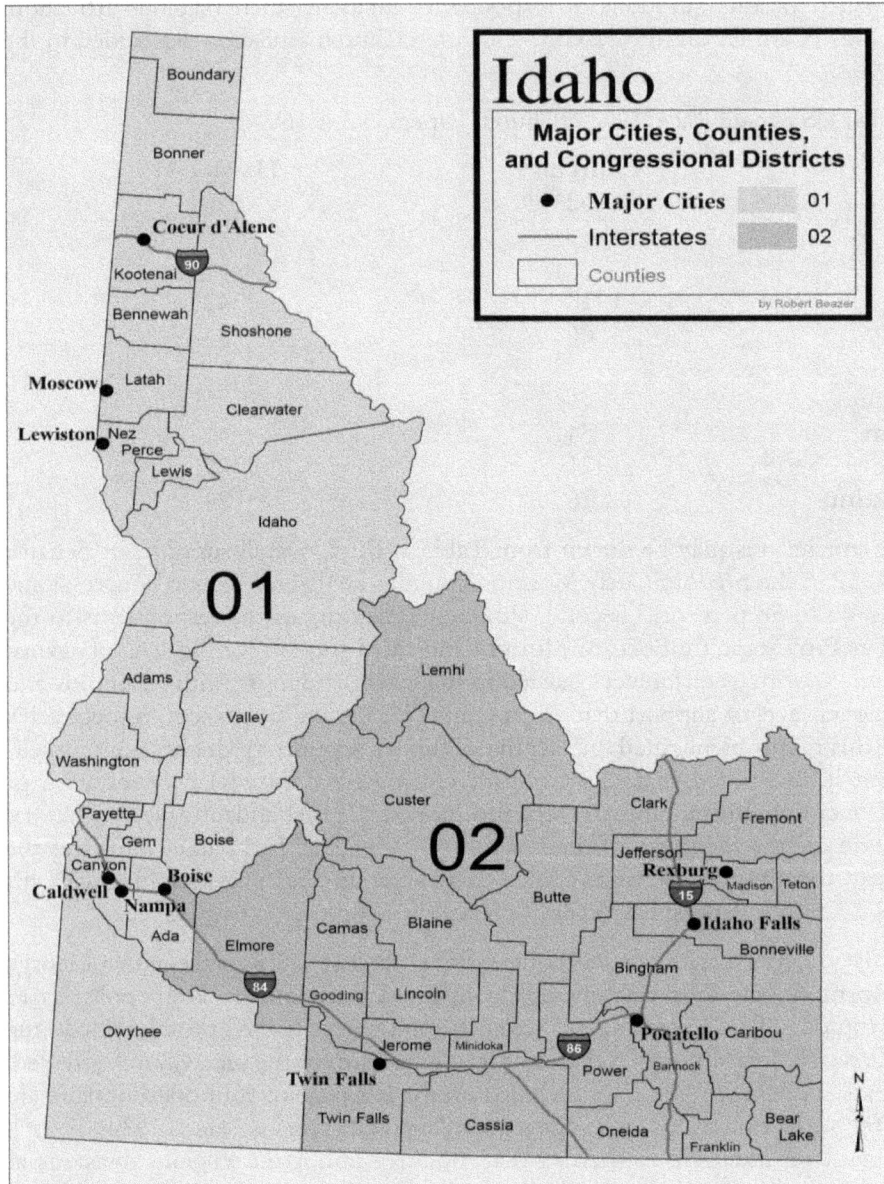

Source: (Beazer, 2010:75)

---

[4] A Peter D. Hart Research Associates, Inc., poll in July 1979 assessed the strength of the groups in the electorate: Protestants, 50 percent; Catholics, 12 percent; and Mormons, 27 percent (Church Papers, 5.7, 1:8).

Table 2. "A Study of Attitudes of Voters in Idaho, March 1968" (Church Papers, 5.3, 6:18)

	% Hansen	% Church	% Not Sure	% McClure	% Church	% Not Sure
By Area						
C. D. #1	39	54	7	39	54	7
C. D. #2	38	50	12	12	67	21
By Religion						
Protestant	34	58	8	39	54	7
Mormon	41	44	15	12	65	23
Catholic	21	70	9	15	70	15

The results of the polling reveal both continuity and change in attitudes toward Senator Church since 1962. In a hypothetical race against Congressman McClure, support for Church was again higher in the second than the first congressional district (67 to 54 percent), but in a race versus Congressman Hansen, Church's support was projected as stronger in the first than the second district (54 to 50 percent). Among respondents who volunteered their religious affiliation, Church's support was highest among Catholics in both districts (70 percent in both), with Mormon support trailing in both (65 percent in District 1, but only 44 percent in District 2). The Kraft group concluded from its poll, "Mormons are apparently aware of Hansen's religion and somewhat torn about voting for one of their own over a Senator with whom they are well pleased" (Church Papers, 5.3, 6:18).

Subsequent polls of political attitudes among Mormon voters reflect the persistence of these changes in attitudes revealed in the 1968 vote. An October 1973 poll conducted by Peter D. Hart Research Associates asked respondents to assess their degree of support for Senator Church along a spectrum from "Totally [Support]" to "Only Slight[ly] Support." In comparison to the 1962 poll where Protestant voters were the group least likely to support Church (54 percent), by October 1973, the figure (without reservations) had climbed to 77 percent, and Mormon numbers during the same time period decreased from 76 to 64 percent. This trend continued, as reflected in a July 1974 poll conducted by the same Hart group, which showed that 63 percent of Protestants gave Church an "excellent" or "good" rating compared to 58 percent of Mormons (Church Papers, 5.7, 1:2).[5]

Beginning in July 1979 and continuing for the subsequent fourteen months, the Hart group conducted four polls of voters' attitudes toward the senator and his likely opponent in the 1980 election, first district congressman Steve Symms. In the July 1979 poll, Catholic respondents favored Senator Church over the other groupings, but not by much (Catholics, 55 percent; Protestants, 52 percent; and Mormons 50 percent—these numbers combine "strong" and "weak" support for Church (Church Papers, 5.7, 1:8). By February 1980, however, important changes had occurred in both Protestant and Mormon respondents.

In February 1980, Mormons supported Church substantially less than either Protestants or Catholics, and the level of support among this group continued to plummet until by September 1980 only 29 percent supported Church, a decline of 11 percent since February 1980; 21 percent since July 1979; 31 percent since July 1974; and 47 percent since 1962.

---

[5] A companion question, however, showed no difference between Protestants and Mormons who were "strong" Church supporters (49 percent Protestant; 48 percent Mormon; 54 percent Catholic).

Table 3. "Percent Support for Church and Symms by Religious Affiliation, 1980" (Church Papers, 5.7, 1:10)

	Church Voters, Feb. 1980	Church Voters, June 1980	Church Voters, Sept. 1980	Symms Voters, Feb. 1980	Symms Voters, June 1980	Symms Voters, Sept. 1980	Undecided Voters, Sept. 1980
All Voters	46	48	42	46	44	49	9
Religion							
Protestant	47	50	45	47	44	48	7
Catholic	55	66	46	37	23	43	11
Mormon	40	35	29	52	57	64	7

II

Documentary evidence from the 1980 election supports the polling data. Throughout the second congressional district, a brisk warfare developed in "Letters to the Editor" in small, rural newspapers concerning the Church-Symms election. These texts fall predominately into three groups: 1) writers who openly identified as members of the LDS Church; 2) authors who quoted from the *Book of Mormon* or high Church officials; and 3) individuals who charged that Senator Church's stands on issues were not in line with LDS beliefs. The subjects of the letters cover many topics, but the so-called "morality issues" of the 1980 campaign—especially abortion—loom largest in eastern Idaho, compared to Senator Church's role in shepherding the 1977 Panama Canal Treaty through the Senate and other topics statewide.[6] Space permits only a small sampling from each type.

An example of the first type of letter may be found in a June 17, 1980 edition of the Rexburg (Madison County; see Figure 2) *Standard* by a self-identified church member who charged, "[Church] honors the LDS Church with headline-making rhetoric, but his heart and his voting record are far from the mainstream of Mormon thought both politically and philosophically". Asserting that Church "gives US MORMONS lip-service in his speeches," but his voting record supported funding for "government programs which will destroy the MORAL FIBER of OUR youth, undermine OUR families, and subject schools like BYU and RICKS [the LDS junior college in Rexburg, now BYU-Idaho] to government regulation". In early September, the same newspaper published a letter refuting charges that Symms was a "womanizer" and "beer-drinker". Claiming to know Symms personally, the writer said he had never seen Symms take a drink of alcohol—even in private—whereas Church went to all the Washington cocktail parties. The "womanizer" label was also false according to this "friend" of Symms, because Symms told him that he was as strongly committed to family life "as those who are members of the LDS Church".[7]

---

[6] See, for example, letters to the editor from September through the election in the Lewiston (Nez Perce County) *Tribune*. Church knew that his sponsorship of the treaty was unpopular and issued radio and newspaper ads speaking to the necessity of the agreement, largely due to the fact that the largest ships could no longer pass through the canal (Church Papers, 5.6, 7:6).

[7] Church's supporters were divided over whether to attack Symms on aspects of his personal life that Mormons might find objectionable. Specifically, it might have been pointed out that Symms' family owned the St. Chapelle winery in southwest Idaho, and there were various

Also in the fall (Oct. 23, 1980), the Preston (Franklin County) *Citizen* printed a letter signed by seven men who said they were writing "not in any official LDS Church capacity, but as individual citizens who are disturbed by some of the things that are going on in the Church-Symms campaign as it relates to members of our church". The men indicated that they appreciated Symms' approach in the campaign, of not "being deliberately patronizing of any particular religious group," whereas Senator Church had "directly embarked on a campaign to court the Mormon vote by utilizing Mormon surrogates who use their official stationary [sic] to imply broad LDS support for Senator Church and by presenting half-truths as to his position on vital issues".

A second type of letter used Mormon Church authorities and scripture to lend support to the Symms campaign. The Montpelier (Bear Lake County) *News-Examiner* printed a letter in early October (October 9) where the author quoted from a respected Mormon leader to support his contention that people "in our lack of concern and desire, are letting government gain more and more control in our daily lives…. We need an individual who has personal restraint and integrity to follow the desires of his constituents. Steve Symms is such a man. Steve Symns [sic] is Idaho's only <u>TRUE</u> friend".[8] Following the election (November 6), a writer to the Preston (Franklin County) *Citizen* quoted from the *Book of Mormon* in order to show how voters had rejected Church because he had "made fun of the people who came to hear him and did not stand up with his followers". Instead, the people had chosen Steve Symms who believed "our [C]onstitution is inspired of God, and America did not just happen, it was a divine plan".

The final type of letter continued the theme of the last letter, but more subtly. As political scientist Jeffrey C. Fox (2006:169-70) notes, abstractions like "freedom" and "free will" are ubiquitous in Mormon theology, [9] and these terms—frequently juxtaposed with "socialism," "Communism," "liberalism," or all three in combination—were prominent fixtures in many letters. Most notably, a person wrote to the *Citizen* (October 23) that Church deserved no support in that area of the state (bordering on Utah) because "[he] supports socialism, or as we call it liberalism. Do not trade your future freedom from Communism for seniority". Another letter in the Soda Springs (Caribou County) *Caribou County Sun* (October 16) that purported to have been written by a girl in Rexburg (Madison County) stated: "I'm very concerned about the trend our government has been taking this past 25 years. I'm 19 and my future children are depending on me for a free society. Do I want to vote for Frank Church and continue wallowing in the present situation? No, no! I'm voting for Steve Symms. He and I are for America".[10]

In addition to printing these letters, some editors directly involved themselves in the partisan warfare by officially endorsing Symms and by using the editorial page to support his candidacy. The editor of the Rigby (Jefferson County) *Jefferson County Star*, for example, made direct appeals to Mormon voters

---

news reports of the congressman's "colorful" life in Washington. Independent of the official campaign, some Church supporters did print bumper stickers that read, "Wine, Women, and Symms"—a reference to Symms' remark after a trip to Libya that there was "no chance to drink or chase women" in the Arab nation during a brief visit that he made there (*Wall Street Journal*, 1980). Peter Fenn, Church's Chief of Staff in 1980, later told the author that he was one of those who wanted "to go after Symms hard…. If we had known then what we know now, we should have gone harder". Mormon voters later became disappointed with Symms and his family's ownership of the winery (Margolis, 1986).

[8] The last line of this message turns upside down a Frank Church campaign button that read, "Idaho Never Had a Better Friend".

[9] John Harrington (1980), a reporter for The Nation, opined that a political action committee that called itself "The Freemen Institute" had LDS connections.

[10] It should be noted that the authors of some of these anti-Church letters may have been non-Mormons who masqueraded as one of the faithful for the purpose of political manipulation, but the decision to print the letters rested with editors, who perhaps believed that their readers would approve of the stated position or who were themselves avowedly pro-Symms (i.e., the Rigby [Jefferson County] *Jefferson County Star*).

to oust Church from the Senate. On September 17, the editor urged readers to honor "Constitution Day". Quoting from "a modern patriot, Ezra Taft Benson" (more on Benson later), the newspaper asked that the people of Jefferson County "study the Constitution in a meaningful way. Look for the principles of government that make America the first nation on earth to be truly free". On the same page, there were four letters to the editor, two for Symms, one for Church, and one lamenting how immoral the city of Rigby was becoming.

In the final two weeks of the campaign, this editor devoted his columns to the candidates' positions on "the two most important issues in the campaign—ERA [the Equal Rights Amendment] and abortion." In an October 30 editorial entitled, "Candidates differ sharply on ERA, abortion issues," the editor juxtaposed the positions of the two men, arguing that Church favored, and Symms opposed, ERA. The abortion issue was more complicated as Church claimed to hold "the same views as that of the LDS Church. To clarify that, I called the church offices, and—yes, they do permit abortion in cases of danger to the life of the mother, rape and incest. However, added to that is—after much fasting, and prayer and counseling with your Bishop…. Federally funded abortions will never parallel the guidelines of the LDS Church or most other churches I'm sure".

On October 30, the editor of the *Star* encouraged his readers "not to lose sight of the importance of the freedom we enjoy that allows us to participate. We are each free to support and work for any party or candidate we choose". Countless other editors across the US undoubtedly used similar language to encourage citizen participation in the 1980 election, but these words sounded a special call to Mormon readers. The faithful were being asked to reaffirm the most basic, core beliefs of their lives and witness to their faith in their religion, their nation, and themselves. "Tuesday is the day that we each have the privilege to show what this country is all about".

III

Congressman Symms won the 1980 senatorial election with a plurality of 4,262 votes out of over 440,000 cast (approximately 2,200 more ballots, it should be noted, than in the presidential election, which marked a first in Idaho political history).[11] Tellingly, Church carried Idaho's most populous county (Ada, where the capital Boise is located) and the first congressional district as a whole. Simply put, the outcome of the election hinged on voters in the second congressional district, as witnessed by the fact that of the twenty-four counties where support for Senator Church changed the most in 1980 from prior elections (and five of the top six), fifteen (62.5 percent) were in southern and eastern Idaho. Interest in the election among these predominately Mormon counties was also unusually high. Of the twenty-eight counties where turnout exceeded the statewide average, twenty (71.4 percent) were in the second congressional district, including the county with the highest turnout (Oneida), with 93.1 percent of eligible voters voting (Hatzenbuehler and Marley, 1987).[12]

---

[11] Voters cast 33,000 more votes for either Church or Symms than for President Jimmy Carter or challenger Ronald Reagan

[12] The Hatzenbuehler-Marley article (1987) investigates—and downplays—the importance of three other possible explanations for Church's defeat: the involvement of national conservative political action committees in the election; the "Reagan landslide" in 1980; and President Jimmy Carter's early concession of defeat when polling places were still open in Idaho's ten northern counties in the Pacific Time Zone.

Table 4 uses linear multiple regression analysis to compare the decline in support for Church from previous elections among Mormon voters with other possible factors—including economic and other demographic variables—that may have influenced voters' behavior.[13]

Table 4. "Decline in Support for Senator Church, 1956-1980: Linear Multiple Regression Analysis"

Variable	R	Multiple R	Multiple R²	Beta
FIRST CONGRESSIONAL DISTRICT				
Average Acres/Farm, 1979	-.57	.57	.32	-.57**
Number Catholics/Registered Voter	-.47			-.34
Percentage Unemployment, 1979	-.40			-.29
Average Value Farm/Acre	.41			-.07
Percent Population Change, 1970-1980	.29			.19
Number Mormons/Reg. Voter	.29			.21
Per Capita Income, 1979	.16			.08
Percent Private Land, 1979	.17			.01
Percent Federal Land, 1979	-.20			-.03
Percent Rural, 1980	-.39			-.23
Totals		.95	.89	
SECOND CONGRESSIONAL DISTRICT				
Number Mormons/Reg. Voter	-.54	.54	.29	-.54***
Percent Population Change, 1970-1980	.19	.65	.42	.37*
Average Value Farm/Acre	.22			.27
Percent Rural, 1980	.13			.4
Percent Federal Land, 1979	.12			-.32
Number Catholics/Registered Voter	.26			.09
Average Acres/Farm, 1979	.05			-.12
Percent Private Land, 1979	-.12			.32
Per Capita Income, 1979	.38			.03
Percentage Unemployment, 1979	.08			-.13
Totals		.81	.66	

(* = $p<.05$; ** = $p<.01$; *** = $p<.005$)

The correlations of two variables with Church's decline in the second congressional district were statistically significant—the numbers of Mormons per registered voter ($p<.005$) and the percent of population change between 1970 and 1980 ($p<.05$). The directions of these associations are also important. The Mormon variable correlated negatively with Church's decline, meaning that the higher

---

[13] Simply put, multiple linear regression analysis models the linear relationship between two or more (in this case, 10) explanatory, or independent, variables and a single response, or dependent, variable (average decline in support for Church from prior elections). The Office of the LDS Church Historian supplied the numbers of Mormons per county in 1980; numbers of Catholics per county, 1980, supplied by the Roman Catholic Diocese of Boise.

the concentration of Mormons (+), the greater was the extent of Church's decline (-). Concerning population change, however, the positive correlation coefficient indicates that the largest decline in Church's support came in counties where population change was the least. Interpretively, these explanations are persuasive since the highest concentrations of Mormons per county lie in the predominately rural counties in the second congressional district that did not experience substantial population changes between 1970 and 1980. Together, the two variables account for approximately 42 percent of the variance in the model, and the remaining eight variables—predominately economic in nature—that were not statistically significant added little to the overall fit of the regression, as the ten variables together accounted for about 66 percent ($r^2 = .66$) of the variance.

Interestingly, when the same variables are applied to Church's decline in the first congressional district, a different fit occurs. Although farms are larger on the average in the second district, the average size of farms per acre correlated most strongly with Church's decline in the first district, and in a negative direction. In other words, Church's decline was the highest in those counties with the largest farms.[14] Also, the ten variables taken together fit the nature of Church's decline better for the first district than for the second ($r^2 = .89$), indicating that economic variables better explain Church's decline there. Of note from the perspective of religious affiliation, Catholics are the predominant religious group in the first congressional district, and their stands on ERA, birth control, abortion, and other similar issues conform in many respects to those of Mormons. In the regression analysis, however, the Catholic variable (similarly in the negative direction) only *approached significance* ($p < .09$).[15] While it is true that both the Catholic and LDS Churches oppose abortion, it is not at all clear that the abortion issue played out similarly in both groups in 1980. For example, one Idaho Catholic wrote a letter to the editor in the *Idaho [Catholic] Register* stating that Symms' stated views favoring a constitutional amendment banning abortion were closer to the Catholic Church's than Senator Church's, but "the position that all morality is in one corner or the other is not understandable. The Catholic Church of Idaho is in very real danger of being used by those who want to paint Senator Church as an evil man because he is opposed to the Constitutional amendment. We cannot allow the Catholic Church to be misused in that way. Nor can it be used by the other side" (Church Papers, 5.6, 2:10).[16]

Psychologists and political scientists tell us that many people guard their political opinions for fear of introducing unwanted conflict into their lives (Dunham, 1991, Ch. 2). In 1980, however, the desire of voters to weigh in on the two candidates in the Idaho senatorial election comprises the most interesting aspect of this election. For especially Mormon voters, the timing of the 1980 election appears to have been significant in this regard. A steady erosion in support for Senator Frank Church beginning in 1968, but accelerating beginning in July 1979, and the "morality issues" of the 1980 election invited Mormon voters to project their attitudes and values onto the senatorial election (Bennett, 1980a, 1980b; Greenfield, 1982; Westen, 2007). It is also possible that Mormon voters were attending to important changes that were occurring in the late-1970s among non-LDS believers.

---

[14] The average size of farms in 1980 was 721 acres, with a standard deviation of 437 acres, in the first congressional district compared to 907 acres, with a standard deviation of 879 acres, in the second.

[15] Political scientist Fox (2006) notes that in addition to holding similar views on many social issues the hierarchical nature of the Catholic and Mormon Churches lead members of these denominations to "seek spiritual guidance to dealing with the complexities of the political world. If religion teaches eternal truths, the religious doctrine should offer cues for understanding earthly events and provide a framework of values and principles that one can apply to the social and political spheres. Messages spoken from the pulpit by church leaders are especially important in reconciling the two worlds" (p. 37).

[16] Historian James T. Patterson (2005) notes that by 1980 "[m]ost American Catholics…made it clear that they did not subscribe to church teachings concerning birth control, abortion, and divorce" (p. 140).

According to historian James T. Patterson (Patterson, 2005:139-40), Jerry Falwell's creation of his "Moral Majority" and other evangelicals' endorsement of direct involvement in political affairs "encouraged a surge of grass-roots religious activity that boosted socially conservative Christian ideas after 1979 and…ultimately propelled cultural issues into the center of public debate in the United States".

Subsequent presidential elections have reinforced this voting realignment among Idaho's Mormons, as the same southeastern Idaho counties that demonstrated the greatest decline in voting for Senator Church have recorded the highest support for Republican presidential candidates since 1980 (Hatzenbuehler and Swanson, 1988; Beazer, 2010).[17] An interesting exception to this consistent trend, however, occurred in the presidential election of 2016. When former CIA operations officer Evan McMullin (a BYU graduate, Utah resident, and self-professed Mormon) declared as an independent candidate for president in August 2016, he injected turmoil into the presidential election in Idaho. Not only did McMullin outpoll Democratic candidate Hillary Clinton in five of the predominately Mormon counties in southeastern Idaho but also he dramatically weakened support for Republican candidate Donald Trump. Of the top quartile of counties supporting Trump in the election, nine were in Idaho's first congressional district compared to seven in the second (in the top two quartiles, the split was 50-50).

McMullin's disruption of Mormons' support for Trump was equally significant in Utah. In the 2012 election, Republican presidential candidate (and self-professed Mormon) Mitt Romney garnered 73 percent of the vote in Utah, whereas candidate Trump received only 45 percent in 2016 (McMullin's share was 21 percent; Hillary Clinton's, 27 percent). As BYU Political Science Professor Quin Monson opined (Roche, 2018), "[Mormons are] happy with some of [Trump's] policies but unhappy with his style—very unhappy in some cases. With a normal Republican president, I would expect his approval among Mormons to be in the high 70s". Monson—who also is a pollster—criticized the Gallop Poll in 2016 for having a single category that lumped all Protestant denominations together (including Mormons). "What I say with a lot of confidence," Monson said, "is the percentage of Mormons who voted for Donald Trump in 2016 was much lower than the percentage of white evangelicals".[18]

IV

One final note. As noted earlier, considerable angst existed among Senator Church's campaign staff in his 1968 matchup with second district Congressman George Hansen. Not only was Hansen Mormon but also he touted his membership in the John Birch Society (an anti-Communist society founded in the 1950s), which had a strong following in eastern Idaho. In February 1967, John Rousselot (the Birch Society's national public relations director) came to Idaho Falls (Bonneville County) and told a reporter for the local *Post-Register* that there were "about 25 chapters in East Idaho" with approximately 500 members "because people here have strong constitutional beliefs [and] strong religious convictions…. Most of our goals are educational in nature, and we like situations in which people can articulate and understand the conservative point of view" (Church Papers, 5.3, 6:9).

---

[17] Historian Thomas G. Alexander's study (1995) of gubernatorial and legislative elections in Utah from 1970-1992 reveals a similar shift in Mormon voters to the Republican Party beginning in the 1960s. Alexander also notes that the Republican Party's political culture of social conservativism attracted Mormon voters, but he attributes Mormons' voting alignment more to economic than social factors (esp. p. 260).

[18] Recent polls (Guarnieri, 2018; Burr, 2018; Schwadel and Smith, 2019) indicate that current support for Trump among Mormons is even higher than among evangelicals.

A contemporaneous visit by Ezra Taft Benson—former Secretary of Agriculture under Dwight Eisenhower, member of the Birch Society, and later President of the LDS Church (Fox, 2006:1-2)—to Pocatello (Bannock County) led Church's staff to fear that LDS leadership might be throwing its support behind Congressman Hansen. Speaking at a Religious Emphasis Week program at Idaho State University (ISU), Benson castigated the US Supreme Court for "leading the nation down the road to atheism and Communism by one tragic decision after another. The Communists have held victory rallies to honor the Supreme Court and its decisions. The Book of Mormon tells us what corrupt judges can do to freedom" (Church Papers, 5.3, 6:9). Finally, an often-Xeroxed letter in the Church Papers from a member of the LDS First Presidency in March 1967 to a bishop of the Church in Thornton, Idaho (Madison County) further documents the danger that Senator Church felt in this regard. The letter informed the bishop that the First Presidency had issued a statement "disclaiming any contact with or sympathy with the Birchites" and advised "our people everywhere to do their duty to the Church and keep out of this kind of entanglement", but it also acknowledged "that the Birchites are still trying to make it appear that the President of the Church and the Church itself favors their society…. You are at liberty to say to your people that the Church, as such, does not endorse the Birch Society nor does the President of the Church, although he allows all members to exercise their free agency. But when they attempt to invoke the Church in their policies they are out of line and our people should remain true to the truth and not be upset by these obvious efforts to divert their interests and activities" (Church Papers, 5.3, 6:9).

As described above, Church's level of support fell in 1968 in the second congressional district from prior elections and sensitized the senator to the importance of reaching out to Mormon voters. Following a June 23 speech at the LDS Institute of Religion at ISU, he received a letter from the acting chair of the Department of Government at ISU who attended the event and expressed concern to the senator that

> there were small things that kept some people from accepting you wholeheartedly. One such thing to a Mormon…may be the fact that you are non-Mormon and Hansen is L.D.S. Although I don't believe that the Mormon people as a whole are highly biased against non-Mormon candidates…the fact that Hansen is a Mormon in good standing and espouses many "principles" being articulated by Ezra Taft Benson—who appears to be highly respected in this area—may cause some members to feel a tinge of disquiet over abandoning one of the "brothers in the faith".

To counter this situation, the author of the letter suggested that Church use "key phrases in your comments…to establish a stronger identity with L.D.S. audiences…. I am persuaded that political decisions are influenced by nuances and seemingly inconsequential behavior that voters notice and rely upon in making judgements. These small points may help to strengthen the impression that you leave with Mormon audiences. At least, it may help you to overcome any initial advantage that Congressman Hansen may have with this significant group in Eastern Idaho" (Church Papers, 5.3, 6:17). In response to the author, Church thanked him for "the list of phrases taken from the L.D.S. literature and dialogue, which will be most helpful" (Church Papers, 5.3, 6:17). And helpful they were. From 1969 onward, Church's speeches on important Mormon holidays increasingly used direct quotations from Mormon scripture, Mormon settlers' diaries, and prominent Church leaders. In 1978 Pioneer Day remarks, for example, Church relied on the Mormon precept, "The glory of God is intelligence," and in sponsoring legislation the same year to mark the Mormon Pioneer Trail from Nauvoo, Illinois, to Salt Lake City, Utah, he quoted from LDS prophet Brigham Young, histories of the Mormon trek westward, and a prominent Mormon hymn during the course of his remarks (Church Papers, 8.1, 6:13; 8.1, 12:9; and 8.1, 10:96 and 97).

In light of fears in the 1968 election that the political opinions of LDS leaders might sway Mormon voters to support his opponent, it is possible that Senator Church relied on a false sense of confidence that the respect accorded him by LDS Church hierarchy in December 1978 would positively influence the voting behavior of Idaho's rank-and-file Mormons. Unfortunately for him, however, LDS voters in Idaho were moving in opposite directions from the Church's leaders. Senator Church's relationship with the Church's principals may have been at its zenith in late 1978, but this position of respect did not carry over to the 1980 election, which brought to culmination a quarter century of change in political attitudes among Mormon voters.

Acknowledgements

A version of this paper was presented at the Political History Conference, Lebanon Valley [PA] College, in May 2019. The author is grateful to Robert Beezer for permission to reprint Figure 1.

References

Alexander, T.G. (1995). "The Emergence of a Republican Majority in Utah, 1970-1992". In R. Lowitt (ed.) *Politics in the Postwar American West*, Norman, OK: University of Oklahoma Press.

Beazer, R. (2010). Idaho's Varied Political Landscape: Elections and Realignment in Idaho, 1920 to 2008. Unpublished MA thesis, Idaho State University, Pocatello, ID.

Bennett, W. L. (1980a). *Public Opinion in American Politics*. New York: Harcourt.

Bennett, W.L. (1980b). "Myth, ritual and political control", *Journal of Communication*, XXX: 166-179.

Burr, T. (2018). "In national poll 61 percent of Mormons approve of President Donald Trump, the highest of any religious group", *Salt Lake Tribune* (1/12): https://www.sltrib.com/news/politics/2018/01/12/national-poll-61-percent-of-mormons-approve-of-president-donald-trump-highest-of-any-religious-group/.

Church of Jesus Christ of Latter-day Saints (n.d.). "Leadership and organization": https://newsroom.churchof jesuschrist.org/leadership-and-organization/ (accessed 3/31/2020).

Dunham, P. (1991). *Electoral Behavior in the United States*. Englewood Cliffs, NJ: Prentice-Hall.

Fox, J. C. (2006). *Latter-Day Political Views*. Lanham, MD: Lexington Books.

Frank Church Papers, Boise State University Special Collections and Archives, Boise, ID.

Greenfield, J. (1982). *The Real Campaign: How the Media Missed the Story of the 1980 Election*. New York: Summit Books.

Guarnieri, G. (2018). "Mormon approval of Trump's job performance was more than any other religious group in 2017". *Newsweek* (1/14): http://www.newsweek.com/mormons-donald-trump-approval-religion-781134.

Harrington, J. (1980). "The Freemen Institute: A Mormon PAC"? *The Nation* (Aug. 16-23): 153.

Hatzenbuehler, R.L. and B.W. Marley (1987). "Why Church Lost: A preliminary study of the Church-Symms election of 1980". *Pacific Historical Review*, LVI: 99-112.

Hatzenbuehler, R.L. and M.W. Swanson (1988). "Has Idaho ever had a realigning election"? In C.B. Short (ed.) *Democratic Demise, Republican Ascendency? Politics in the intermountain west*, Pocatello, ID: Idaho State University Press.

Kimball, S. C. Scrapbook Collection. History Library, Church of Jesus Christ of Latter-day Saints, Salt Lake City, UT.

Margolis, J. (1986). "Idaho Mormons learn Symms isn't what they thought", *Chicago Tribune*, (Oct. 1): https://www.chicagotribune.com/news/ct-xpm-1986-10-01-8603140416-story.html.

Monson, J.Q. (et al.) (2005). Dominant Cue Givers and Voting on Ballot Propositions. Paper Presented at the Annual Meeting of the American Political Science Association, Washington, DC.

Oaks, D.H. (1991). Getting to Know China. Speech at Brigham Young University, (Mar. 12): https://speeches.byu.edu/talks/dallin-h-oaks/getting-know-china/.

Patterson, J. T. (2005). *Restless Giant: The United States from Watergate to Bush v. Gore*. New York: Oxford University Press.

Roche, L.R. (2018). "Mormons give Trump highest support of any religious group in poll", Deseret News (1/12): https://www.deseretnews.com/article/900007499/mormons-give-trump-highest-support-of-any-religious-group-in-poll.html.

Schwadel, P. and G.A. Smith (2019). "Evangelical approval of Trump remains high, but other religious groups are less supportive", Pew Research Center (Mar. 18) https://www.pewresearch.org/fact-tank/2019/03/18/evangelical-approval-of-trump-remains-high-but-other-religious-groups-are-less-supportive/.

Shafer, B.E. and R.H. Spady (2014). "The Catholics and the Others: The denominational backdrop to modern American politics", *The Forum*, 11 (4): 531-59.

Wall Street Journal (1980). "Personal attacks spread in this year's congressional races", Oct. 31:1.

Westen, D. (2007), *The Political Brain: The Role of Emotion in Deciding the Fate of the Nation*. New York: Public Affairs.

International Journal of Religion
November 2020
Volume: 1 | Number 1 | pp. 23 – 43
ISSN: 2633-352X (Print) | ISSN: 2633-3538 (Online)
journals.tplondon.com/ijor

TRANSNATIONAL PRESS®
LONDON

First Submitted: 2 July 2020 Accepted: 1 November 2020
DOI: https://doi.org/10.33182/ijor.v1i1.1073

Creating the Internal Enemy: Opportunities and Threats in Pro and Anti-LGBT Activism within South Korean Protestantism

Hendrik Johannemann[1]

Abstract

In recent years, South Korea has experienced significant mobilization against LGBT rights, mainly emanating from conservative Protestant forces. This anti-LGBT mobilization has been attributed to the need to create an "external enemy" as a means for covering up internal scandals. This study examines how the Protestant anti-LGBT movement creates an "internal enemy", too, by fighting against pro-LGBT activism and attitudes within its faith. Applying the contentious politics and movement-countermovement frameworks to the study of religious conflict, the article uncovers the mechanisms at work in the complex interactions among anti-LGBT, moderate, and LGBT-affirmative actors. The analysis of five cases – heresy trials against a pro-LGBT pastor, conflicts at Christian universities, vilifications of a progressive Christian online newspaper and a church association, and the controversy around a moderate junior pastor – shows that perceived and deliberately created threats play a productive, opportunity-like role in religious contention over LGBT issues. Longstanding religiopolitical cleavages come to the fore, too, involving conflictual relations with state actors external to Korean Protestantism.

Keywords: *pro and anti-LGBT activism; South Korean Protestantism; opportunities and threats; contentious politics; movement-countermovement dynamics*

Introduction: Contention over LGBT issues in Korean Protestantism and beyond

In South Korea (henceforth: Korea), conservative Protestant groups have been fighting against various political initiatives in favor of lesbian, gay, bisexual, and transgender (LGBT) rights since the early 2000s. Anti-LGBT campaigns, many of which were successful, included campaigns against anti-discrimination bills, against human rights ordinances, against gay men in the Korean military, and against school textbooks disseminating information on homosexuality. Recent scholarship considers several explanatory avenues for the emergence of anti-LGBT activism in South Korea, arguing, for example, that while the Christian doctrine may play an important role in the fight against homosexuality, the decisive reason is to be found in the crisis of Korean Protestantism. By focusing on the opposition against LGBT issues, church leaders and professionalized anti-LGBT groups try to deflect attention away from declining church memberships and scandals like embezzlement and sexual harassment (Shiwoo, 2018: 36-46). In Han's view, conservative Protestant church leaders use anti-gay rhetoric to create an "external enemy" or threat to help increase their political leverage and at the same time lessen the divisions among notoriously fragmented denominations (Han, 2017: 180-181).

Existing social scientific research on conservative Christian opponents of LGBT rights mainly investigates how Christian forces strive to prevent or undo pro-LGBT legislation in the arenas of

---

[1] Hendrik Johannemann, Freie Universität Berlin, Germany. E-mail: hendrik.johannemann@fu-berlin.de

politics and law (Kim, 2016 on Korea; Hark & Villa, 2015 on Germany; Béraud & Portier, 2015 on France; Stone, 2016; Dorf & Tarrow, 2014; Fejes, 2008; Fetner, 2008; Green, 2000; Herman, 1997 on the United States). Taking the example of Korea, this study examines how anti-LGBT activists create an "internal enemy" by fighting and vilifying LGBT-affirmative tendencies within Protestantism – going beyond theological and attitudinal (Moon, 2014; Rich, 2016; Choi, 2014) as well as exclusively political disputes. This perspective on the dynamics between Christian pro and anti-LGBT groups complements similar studies, for example on LGBT groups at Christian universities in the United States (Coley, 2018, 2017, 2014) by taking into consideration a broader range of forms and arenas of contention.[2] Korea is a worthwhile case study for at least three reasons: it features a rather strong anti-LGBT movement based in conservative Protestantism.[3] Korean Protestantism in general is characterized by a high degree of factionalization and internal conflicts (Clark, 2008: 220). Finally, Korea can serve as an example of how religious contention over LGBT issues works in a non-western context.

Protestant anti-LGBT activists and LGBT-affirmative actors enter into various forms of struggles, which are analyzed by adapting the contentious politics framework (Tilly & Tarrow, 2015; Tarrow, 2011; McAdam et al., 2001) and movement-countermovement dynamics (Meyer & Staggenborg, 1996) for the study of religious conflict. These approaches emphasize the importance of interaction between collective actors and their opponents. They focus on the interplay of "members" and "challengers", i.e., between actors with power or access to powerful parts of a certain community and actors who challenge the former's position or worldview. This conceptual lens helps understand what a crucial role perceived or deliberately constructed threats and opportunities play in this interaction. By concentrating on relational, cognitive, and constructivist aspects, this investigation identifies the mechanisms at work as well as the action repertoires used in the contentious relations among anti-LGBT, moderate, and LGBT-affirmative actors within Korean Protestantism.

I argue that the attacks against pro-LGBT stances within Protestantism are crucial to understand the motivations, strategy, and the complex actor constellations of Protestant anti-LGBT activism in Korea. Many major Protestant denominations and their anti-LGBT factions aim at creating an image of Korean Protestantism standing united against homosexuality and related, allegedly anti-Christian "ills". This unity, however, shows distinct cracks. Dissent does not only arise between an uncompromising anti-LGBT camp and other conservative, yet more moderate voices. Explicitly affirmative attitudes have also become visible in recent years.

This study has two main findings. First, through being framed as a threat, LGBT-affirmative activism within Protestantism can be strategically utilized as an additional incentive to fight LGBT issues. The anti-LGBT movement can stress the urgency to eliminate this threat, thus trying to mobilize fellow believers for the struggle against an "internal enemy". Second, despite these efforts of anti-LGBT factions, practicing Christian LGBT individuals and their allies have become more active and gained greater visibility owing to the very oppression originating from their bellicose Christian "fellows".

---

[2] This study goes beyond perspectives that focus on one party or aspect of the conflict only, like the Korean LGBT movement (Kwon Kim & Cho, 2011; Bong, 2009; Park-Kim et al., 2006), benevolent Christian congregations in Seoul (Yi et al., 2017), ex-gay activism within the Christian anti-LGBT movement (Pak, 2018), the latter's transnational connections (Yi et al., 2017), anti-LGBT "scientific" argumentative strategies (Baek, 2018), and the human rights discourse on the proposed anti-discrimination bills in Korea (Kim, 2019).

[3] Protestant Christianity makes up about 21% of the Korean population, Catholicism 7%, Buddhism 24% (Baker, 2016: 46). For general perspectives on the history and the development of Korean Protestantism, especially its phenomenal growth during Korean industrialization from the 1960s onwards, see Baker (2016), Buswell and Lee (2006). For more detailed studies on Korean Protestantism's theological conservatism and fundamentalism, see Hwang (2008) and Kang (2004).

The study builds on a qualitative content analysis[4] of articles from the conservative Christian daily newspaper Kukmin Daily (*kungmin ilbo*).[5] I consciously chose this newspaper for its frequent and negatively biased reporting on LGBT issues, presuming it covers more instances of LGBT-related contention than other major newspapers.[6] For a larger research project,[7] I singled out all the Kukmin Daily articles including the search term "*tongsŏngae*" ("homosexuality") for the period of January 1990 till April 2020 and subsequently selected the pieces covering instances of anti-LGBT activism in Korea. I then used this database to identify cases of protracted strife over LGBT issues inside Korean Protestantism, which constitute the specific sub-cases to be analyzed here. Other newspaper articles and press statements from relevant organizations will also be included to complement the datasets of the identified cases and to remedy Kukmin Daily's anti-LGBT bias. I found that concrete internal struggles over LGBT issues only emerged and soon substantially expanded from 2015 onwards.

The article will proceed as follows: after presenting the analytical framework, I offer an overview of the contentious interactions over LGBT issues within Korean Protestantism and beyond. The main body of the study consists of an analysis of five case studies, namely heresy trials against a pro-LGBT pastor, conflicts at Christian universities, the vilification of the progressive National Council of Churches in Korea and the Christian newspaper Newsnjoy, and the controversy around an arguably moderate junior pastor of a Protestant congregation. The conclusion summarizes and further contextualizes the results of my analysis.

Contentious politics and movement-countermovement dynamics in the religious context

Religious movements have been analyzed from various angles, including cultural or ideological and organizational approaches (Kniss & Burns, 2004: 696). Further areas of research encompass the intersection of genuinely political movements with religious ones, their respective collective identities, and strategies pursued in relation to the state or society at large (Snow & Beyerlein, 2019: 576-580). This study deals with two specific subsets of research on religious movements and adds a third aspect: social movements within religious organizations, religion as a resource or facilitator for the emergence of movements and their actions (Kniss & Burns, 2004: 695), and religious conflict. While conflict between religious groups is not unusual and has been the subject of extensive scientific investigation, a systematic analysis of such an actor constellation – especially concerning contention over LGBT

---

[4] Qualitative content analysis as applied in this study is a systematic, rule-based and thus replicable technique to analyze different types of communication (Mayring, 2015: 468). I followed Kuckartz' (2014) approach, building categories both deductively (based on the contentious politics and movement-countermovement framework) and inductively (to guarantee openness for new findings and theorization) and have coded the dataset accordingly, using the MAXQDA software. This approach is an explicitly qualitative one, since it does not quantify textual units, but rather aims at focusing on the concrete content of the original text while at the same time taking into consideration its communicational context (Mayring, 2015: 469).

[5] Korean terms and organization names are transliterated using the McCune-Reischauer romanization system. Should different transliterations be common, these will be used, followed by the italicized McCune-Reischauer version in brackets the first time the term appears in the text. Korean names are presented in the Korean order (surname – name), unless indicated differently by the persons cited themselves. All direct and indirect quotes from original Korean texts are my own translations.

[6] Kukmin Daily was established in 1988 by Cho Yonggi, founder of the Yoido Full Gospel Church, one of the largest Christian congregations worldwide. Kukmin Daily praises itself as "the only national Christian general-interest daily newspaper in the world" (Kang 2013). In comparison to other conservative daily newspapers with a wider circulation than Kukmin Daily (Chosun Daily, Dong-a Daily, and JoongAng Daily), Kukmin Daily covers Christian issues preferentially, also including a specifically Christian section called "Mission Life". Kukmin Daily was selected for analysis also because it is more widely known and has, presumably, a larger readership than other conservative Christian media like the online-only Christian Today (*k'ŭrisŭch'ŏn t'udei*).

[7] i.e., the author's PhD thesis on the contentious politics of the Korean anti-LGBT movement in general, which is work in progress.

issues in religious contexts – is still lacking. This study will fill this lacuna by applying and adapting two approaches commonly used for the study of conflict in social movement studies: *movement-countermovement dynamics* and the *contentious politics* framework.

Protestant anti-LGBT and pro-LGBT actors in Korea enter into diverse conflicts with each other, one reacting to the other's actions and vice-versa. Social movement scholars speak of "movement-countermovement dynamics" (Meyer & Staggenborg, 1996) or "opposing movements" (Dugan, 2004) when referring to such actor constellations. While this article is not so much concerned with the circumstances around the emergence of countermovements, it will still show that the opportunity structures identified in Meyer and Staggenborg's seminal article (1996: 1635-1643) play an important role in the dynamic interactions between religious pro and anti-LGBT actors. These opportunity structures include the following aspects: the opposing movement shows signs of success, it poses a threat to vested interests or values of dissenting groups, and it receives support from elite allies.

Concerning the role of threats and elite actors, the contentious politics approach (Tilly & Tarrow, 2015; Tarrow, 2011; McAdam et al., 2001) is a helpful complement to the analytical framework of this study. The approach transcends the traditional social movements approach by taking into consideration a less restricted set of actors,[8] and it highlights the environmental, relational, and cognitive mechanisms at work in contentious interactions.[9] McAdam et al. (2001: 5) define contentious politics as "episodic, public, collective interaction among makers of claims and their objects when (a) at least one government is a claimant, an object of claims, or a party to the claims and (b) the claims would, if realized, affect the interests of at least one of the claimants." The "political" bias of this definition may pose problems to the analysis of religious contexts. McAdam and Tarrow (2011: 5) themselves acknowledge that such a state-centeredness excludes many phenomena worthy of study. I contend that by reconceptualizing the government from the definition above as a powerful, authoritative religious body, this bias can be remedied for the purpose of this study. Authoritative religious bodies are important because they wield power over subordinate religious organizations and individual believers. Moreover, they define what kind of attitudes and actions are legitimate from a perspective of religious doctrine and ethics. Influential religious actors possess capacities similar to those of (authoritarian) states. For example, they have a repressive potential, repression being defined as "efforts to suppress either contentious acts or groups and organizations responsible for them" (McAdam et al., 2001: 69, originally italicized).[10] Certification and decertification represent important mechanisms for (de)mobilization in this context: "Certification entails the validation of actors, their performances, and their claims by external authorities. Decertification is the withdrawal of such validation by certifying agents" (McAdam et al.,

---

[8] Tarrow defines social movements as "collective challenges, based on common purposes and social solidarities, in sustained interaction with elites, opponents, and authorities" (Tarrow, 2011: 9, originally italicized). I argue that the general properties of this definition apply to the Korean anti-LGBT movement within Protestantism, but less so to LGBT-affirmative activism inside Korean Protestantism. As we shall see, pro-LGBT activities often take place on an ad-hoc basis and are rather uncoordinated, at least when excluding the services offered by certain churches or groups like "Rainbow Jesus" (*mujigae yesu*) that explicitly cater LGBT Christians. For perspectives on religious movements and their particularities see Snow and Beyerlein (2019) and Kniss and Burns (2004).

[9] McAdam et al. (2001: 24) define mechanisms as "a delimited class of events that alter relations among specified sets of elements in identical or closely similar ways over a variety of situations." Mechanism-based social scientific research represents an alternative to variable-based, quantitative methods and seeks to explain causality in procedural terms (Hedström & Ylikoski, 2010; Tilly, 2001).

[10] Repression can take abstract forms as well. If, for example, a certain religious doctrine presenting homosexuality as morally bad is continuously communicated and thus well known, this can already exert a suppressive effect both on the individuals affected and on their potential allies.

2001: 121). This corresponds to the support of influential allies in the movement-countermovement approach seen above.

Authoritative religious bodies can, as shall be demonstrated in the context of this article, consist of denominational leaders, general assemblies of specific denominations, church associations, or the leaderships of Christian universities. Such religious bodies can function as claim makers themselves, or they can assist the members, i.e., constituted actors with privileged or routine access to these bodies, in their fight against their challengers (cf. McAdam et al., 2001: 12). The focus on religious actors does not preclude the possibility that either members or challengers may receive or seek support from authorities external to the religious arena. In fact, it is rather common that actors attempt to appropriate existing organizations or communities to gain benefits and mobilize more effectively (McAdam et al., 2001: 44).

I argue that unlike contention in democratic regimes, many religions or their religious subsets – especially fundamentalist factions – do not allow for open deliberation over certain doctrinal and moral aspects of religion, thus impeding the emergence and actions of what one may call a civil society within religion (cf. Tilly & Tarrow, 2015: 56-58; Tarrow, 2011: 179). Therefore, it can be expected that challengers will resort to *transgressive forms of contention*. Transgressive contention involves challengers employing innovative collective action, often out of necessity, since *contained contention,* i.e., using established forms of claim making within existing institutions, may not be available to them (McAdam et al., 2001: 7-8).

Repression may threaten challengers, while transgressive counteraction can in turn represent threats to members. The contentious politics framework calls attention to the fact that such threats – as well as opportunities – only become relevant as soon as they are perceived, and in some cases constructed. As McAdam et al. (2001: 43) argue, "[r]ather than look upon 'opportunities and threats' as objective structural factors, we see them as subject to attribution". The necessity of *attribution* accentuates the deliberate, strategic construction of opportunities and threats as opposed to the traditional, rather static opportunity structures agenda of social movement studies (McAdam et al., 2001: 14-15). Meyer and Staggenborg also refer to such cognitive and dispositional mechanisms, claiming that the parties to a conflict react dynamically to the actions of the respective opponent and, if the conflict is prolonged, continuously create constraints and opportunities for each other. Consequently, "[t]he opposing movement is a critical component in the structure of political opportunity the other side faces" (Meyer & Staggenborg, 1996: 1633). While *opportunities* consist of "the [perceived] probability that social protest actions will lead to success in achieving a desired outcome" (Goldstone & Tilly, 2001: 182, cited in Tarrow, 2011: 160), *threats* are commonly perceived ex negativo as "the risks and costs of action or inaction" (Tarrow, 2011: 160). This study emphasizes the productive, opportunity-like potential of threats. In comparison to opportunities and mere grievances,[11] threats involve a greater sense of urgency and intensity (Almeida, 2019: 44). Tilly (1978: 134–135) argues that "a given amount of threat tends to generate more collective action than the 'same' amount of opportunity." The attribution or creation of threats, I argue, thus represents an attractive tactical choice for the actors involved in contention.

---

[11] Grievances being defined as "troublesome matters or conditions, and the feelings associated with them – such as dissatisfaction, fear, indignation, resentment, and moral shock" (Snow and Soule, 2010: 23).

The complex interactions of pro and anti-LGBT actors in Korean Protestantism and beyond

Regarding the specific constellation of religious actors under investigation in this study, the assumption of a clear-cut picture seems tempting: the actors enforcing anti-LGBT stances within Korean Protestantism can be regarded as the original movement to which LGBT-affirmative counteractors react. However, when taking into consideration non-religious actors as well, the picture becomes more complicated. The Korean anti-LGBT movement can be regarded as a countermovement to begin with, which then engendered opposition from newly forming actors. As Zald and Useem (1987: 249) note, sometimes "a countermovement may in turn generate a counter-countermovement that is different from the original movement." Figure 1 illustrates the complex web of contentious interaction in which both pro and anti-LGBT activism within Korean Protestantism are embedded.

Figure 1. Actor constellation and actor overlaps (Venn diagrams) of Protestant and non-religious pro and anti-LGBT actors interrelating with each other and with the state. Source: author's figure.

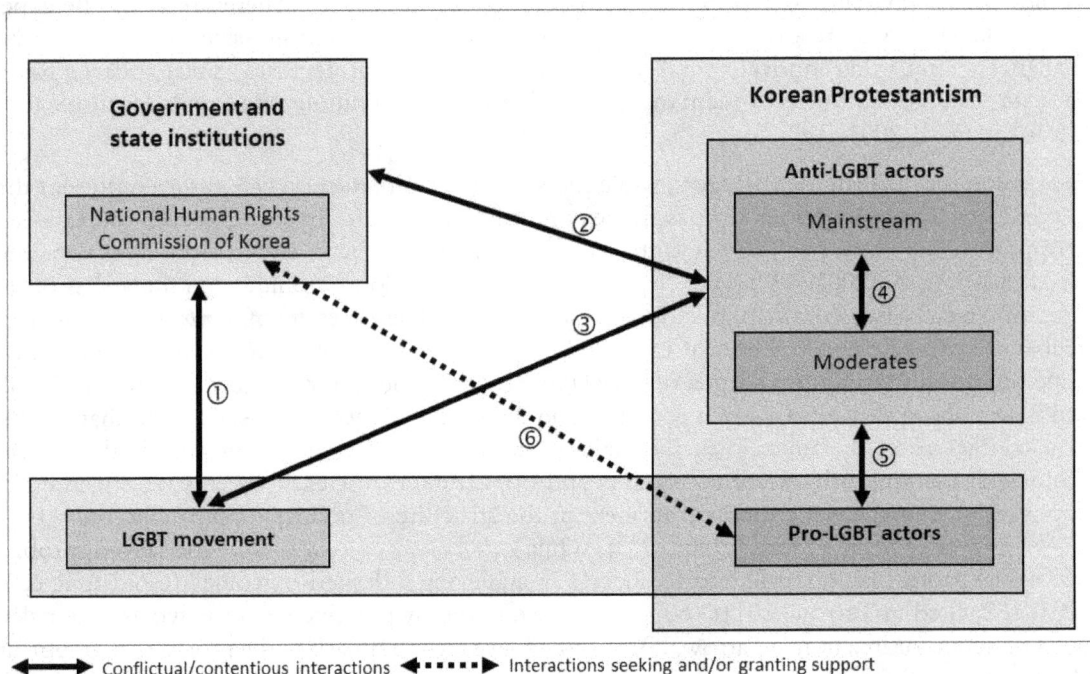

The counter-countermovement, consisting of pro-LGBT activities within Protestantism, emerged only at a later stage in the process of contentious interaction around LGBT issues in Korea (depicted as solid double arrows in Figure 1). While the respective forms of interaction shall be the cornerstone of this analysis, a linear or procedural perspective can illuminate the specific relations among actors and may help identify potential circular interactions. For the sake of clarity, some actor overlaps such as those between governmental actors and the Protestant anti-LGBT camp have been excluded.[12]

---

[12] There have been, for example, ministers and ex-ministers, as well as members of parliament from several political parties, supporting the anti-LGBT movement.

Figure 1 thus represents a simple, ideal-typical depiction of the actor constellation at hand, with a focus on the actors and interactions relevant to this study.

The Korean LGBT movement represented the initial spark. It emerged in the mid-early 1990s after the democratization of South Korea and started lobbying for LGBT rights (arrow ① in Figure 1). In response, from the early 2000s onwards, a subset of actors within conservative Korean Protestantism started problematizing LGBT issues. The Christian Council of Korea (CCK), an umbrella organization of conservative Protestant churches, was an early central actor in this respect (Cho, 2011: 303-304), and numerous other Protestant groups and organizations joined this fight. Several groups and coalitions were even newly created, with the main or sole purpose of opposing LGBT rights.[13] Moreover, several Protestant denominations have included clauses into their church laws condemning and excluding homosexuals in recent years (Paek, 2016). These groups and activists engage in contentious relations both with the LGBT movement and with state actors, which they perceive to excessively promote LGBT rights, purportedly to the detriment of religious freedom of Korean Christians (②, ③).[14]

I argue that for large portions of institutional Protestantism in Korea, anti-LGBT stances have become a dominant feature of their faith, which is why I call this group the "mainstream". I use this term also to differentiate these actors from those who hold less vociferous, less exclusionary attitudes towards lesbian, gay, bisexual and trans people. As I will show in the next section, such "moderate" positions – despite being rather unimportant in terms of quantity – face strong opposition from mainstream anti-LGBT forces (④). Finally, there is conflictual interaction between pro-LGBT and anti-LGBT forces within Protestantism (⑤). These last two types of interrelation will constitute the main focus of the five case studies below. However, actors external to Korean Protestantism also get entangled, at times in a circular manner. As already mentioned, certain state institutions come under fire for their defense of LGBT rights. When Christian pro-LGBT actors then approach these state institutions to seek support against their anti-LGBT opponents (⑥), the anti-LGBT camp resumes its attacks against the state institution in an even more vigorous manner.

Case studies of contention over LGBT issues within Korean Protestantism

The cases identified as involving protracted contention over LGBT issues cover a broad range of actors and interactions. Both individual and collective actors become targets of anti-LGBT activism, including the attacks against Pastor Lim Borah and two instances of punishments for pro-LGBT students at Christian universities. Two cases comprise more institutionalized actors, the progressive Christian online newspaper Newsnjoy and the progressive church association NCCK, which are criticized for their LGBT-affirmative stances. Finally, the case of Bundang Woori Church proves relevant as it demonstrates how even slightly dissenting voices can be perceived as a threat. As we

---

[13] Some of the newly established groups have a specialized focus, like the "Korean Association of Family and Health" (*han'guk kajok pogŏn hyŏphoe*) dealing with the danger of HIV/AIDS allegedly emanating from LGBT individuals and the "Just Military Human Rights Institute" (*parŭn kunin'gwŏn yŏn'guso*) fighting against lenient attitudes towards gay men serving in the army. Others like the "Coalition for Moral Sexuality" (*parŭn sŏngmunhwa rŭl wihan kungmin yŏnhap*) have a broader anti-LGBT focus. Yet others concentrate on the production of online content like the blog "God Man Woman Union" (*GMW yŏnhap*).

[14] Interestingly, one could argue that the LGBT groups' perception is the exact opposite. From their perspective, state actors are often unwilling, or fail to enact human rights protection for sexual minorities (which, of course, may be due to the powerful anti-LGBT activism of certain Protestant groups). To be clear, I do not argue that the anti-LGBT movement emerged because of or in opposition to the LGBT movement and state actors only. It might also be, e.g., a reaction to more general changes in society (cf. Mottl, 1980).

shall see, these conflicts reflect broader religious and socio-political cleavages in Korean Protestantism and society at large.

(De)certification and scale shift: the heresy trials against Pastor Lim Borah

Openly LGBT-inclusive congregations are scarce in Korea, but they do exist (Yi et al., 2017). There is even an association of (pro-)LGBT Christians called "Rainbow Jesus", with members from many Protestant denominations and from Catholic Church. Sumdol Hyanglin Church (*sŏmdol hyangnin kyohoe*) is perhaps the most famous of the LGBT-affirmative congregations, with its founding pastor Lim Borah (*Im Po-ra*) being one of the first in Korean Protestantism to speak out against hatred and discrimination against LGBT people (Schumacher 2016). Sumdol Hyanglin Church belongs to the theologically progressive *Kijang* denomination (Presbyterian Church in the Republic of Korea, PROK) and is the only Presbyterian congregation in Korea explicitly welcoming sexual minorities (Yi et al., 2017: 1462; Rode, 2018).

Pastor Lim became active in supporting LGBT rights when Protestant anti-LGBT forces began fighting against the inclusion of homosexuality into anti-discrimination bills from 2007 onwards.[15] She organized discussion events bringing together different Christian views on homosexuality, arguing herself that homosexuals are not objects to be healed or pitied, but that they are part of God's good creation (Yi, T., 2008). Along with other LGBT-affirmative pastors from Rainbow Jesus, Pastor Lim has been a regular attendant of the annual Seoul Queer Culture Festival (SQCF), running a booth and participating in the pride parade (Kang, 2014). The involvement of Christian groups in the SQCF is a recurrent subject of scandal with conservative Christian media (Yi, T., 2018; Ch'oe, 2016). Pastor Lim consistently reaffirmed her strong pro-LGBT attitude and demanded changes in Korean Christianity: "Homosexuality is not a matter of pro or contra, it is about whether we embrace the dignity of a life or not" (as cited in Pak & Chin, 2014). Pastor Lim also points to the opportunities a welcoming attitude towards LGBT believers could have for her own denomination.

> The Presbyterian Church in the Republic of Korea (PROK) is afraid to take the lead role in advocating for human rights of sexual minorities because they worry about additional loss of members, even though they usually like to see themselves as pioneers. I think taking on this matter and openly advocating for the rights of sexual minorities would enrich the profile of PROK. It might even bring new members. Many LGBT Christians are hurt and deeply disappointed by the church and they are longing for a congregation that welcomes them as they are. (as cited in Schumacher, 2016)

Conservative Protestant denominations did not only refuse to follow Pastor Lim's recommendations, but accused her of heresy, that is, beliefs or opinions against the established doctrinal principles of a religion (cf. Tutino, 2012). At the General Assembly of Presbyterian Churches in September 2017, the heresy task forces (*idan taech'aek wiwŏnhoe*) of eight major Protestant denominations[16] demanded that Pastor Lim be declared guilty of heresy. These task forces claimed that her advocacy for homosexuals and her participation in translating the Queer Bible Commentary were unacceptable and that her interpretation of the Bible constituted an "irrevocable error" as well as a threat to Korean

---

[15] Anti-discrimination bills were proposed to the Nation Assembly in 2007, 2010, and 2013, but all failed due to strong opposition, mainly emanating from Protestant anti-LGBT groups. The passing of an anti-discrimination law including the categories of sexual orientation and gender identity remains a contentious topic in South Korean socio-political debates to this day.

[16] These denominations included the Presbyterian Church of Korea (PCK, *T'onghap*), the General Assembly of Presbyterian Church in Korea (GAPCK, *Hapdong*), the Presbyterian Church of Korea (*Daesin*), the Kosin Presbyterian Church in Korea (*Kosin*), the Korean Presbyterian Church (*Hapsin*), the Korean Methodist Church, the Korea Evangelical Holiness Church, and the Korea Baptist Convention.

Protestantism (Paek, 2017d). In this investigative process, Pastor Lim Borah was not given any opportunity to defend herself directly (Kang, 2019). Here, the repressive power of churches and their leadership structures becomes evident. The demand to declare Pastor Lim a heretic is a clear example of decertification: powerful actors external to her own denomination tried to delegitimize her.

At the same time, the controversy around this pro-LGBT reverend provided an opportunity to extend the conflict by expanding the number of actors involved. The group "Anti-Homosexuality Christian Solidarity" (AHCS, *pandongsŏngae kidok simin yŏndae*), for example, joined the chorus of opposition against Pastor Lim by criticizing her mother denomination PROK for allowing such a heretical behavior (AHCS, 2017). This process constitutes a case of *scale shift*, "a change in the number and level of coordinated contentious actions leading to broader contention involving a wider range of actors and bridging their claims and identities" (McAdam et al., 2001: 311). While the coordinated quality of the contention at hand may be questionable, the extension of the conflict is not. In fact, not only did professionalized anti-LGBT groups join the fight; progressive Christian organizations intervened as well, showing their solidarity with Pastor Lim and by so doing, at least to a certain extent, (re)certifying her. Already when Lim Borah was still under investigation for heresy, the Women's Committee (*yŏsŏng wiwŏnhoe*) of NCCK issued a supportive statement (Kim, 2017), as did the United Church of Canada, demonstrating international support (Yi, Ŭ., 2017b). The "PROK Life Mission Solidarity" (*saengmyŏng sŏn'gyo yŏndae*) also issued a statement criticizing both the hypocritical behavior of the denominations prosecuting Pastor Lim in light of their own scandals and wrongdoings, and the negative attitude of PROK's general assembly president towards sexual minorities. At a meeting with other denominations' presidents, he had supported a statement against homosexuality and same-sex marriage, thus further isolating PROK's Pastor Lim (Yi, Ŭ., 2017a). These instances of supportive statements for Pastor Lim on the one hand, and dismissive ones on the other, hint at broader underlying conflicts within Korean Protestantism. Moreover, the latter statement by PROK's Life Mission Solidarity evidences that contention over LGBT issues exists even within this progressive denomination. A year later, when the Presbyterian denominations *T'onghap* and *Daesin Paeksŏk* actually declared Pastor Lim heretical, PROK displayed a firmer stance, demanding the withdrawal of these decisions and urging the two denominations to apologize to Pastor Lim (Kim, 2018a).

Repressive measures and their implications: punishing LGBT activism at Christian universities

Contention over LGBT issues can be encountered at Christian universities in Korea as well. In February 2016, theology and missionary students at the Methodist Theological University (*kamsin daehakkyo*) protested against the Korean Methodist Church's decision to include an official ban on homosexuality into its church constitution. The protesters were all wearing masks hiding their faces, fearing potential consequences following their activism against discrimination (Paek, 2016). However, most LGBT-related activism at Christian universities consists of publicly declaring one's aversion to homosexuality, which has been done by whole universities (e.g. Handong University, Yu, 2017), by groups of Christian professors (Paek, 2017b; Paek, 2017e) and by students (Paek, 2017a).

I will focus on two cases of extended contention over LGBT issues at Christian universities, more specifically conflicts that involved a broader range of actors in protracted interactions. In late 2017, the feminist students club "Wildflower" (*tŭlkkot*) of Handong University, a private Christian university located in the city of Pohang in south-western Korea, planned to hold a lecture event on prostitution. The university administration forbade this event, but the club proceeded with the event regardless, inviting feminist scholars who also talked about polyamory and homosexuality. As a result, Handong University considered taking disciplinary measures against three members of Wildflower, two participants, as well as against a professor who indirectly supported the lecture (Yu, 2018). One student was eventually expelled.[17]

The student club Wildflower challenged the repressive measures taken by their university and filed a complaint with the National Human Rights Commission of Korea (NHRCK). In this action, the students sought help from an institution outside their Christian university and indeed received support (interaction ⑥ in Figure 1 above). The NHRCK recommended that Handong University withdraw the disciplinary measure as it constituted an act of discrimination of sexual minorities and thus a violation of human rights. Yet, Handong University did not accept this decision (NHRCK, 2019).[18] In February 2020, a court ruled that while the disciplinary measure taken by Handong University was severe, it was rightful since the lecture event violated the founding philosophy of the school (Chang, 2020).

The NHRCK was established in 2001 as an independent state agency to protect and advocate human rights in Korea. As soon as the NHRCK started an investigation of the Wildflower incident, contention became more heated and shifted towards the NHRCK as the main target. Christian parents' groups staged several protests in front of the NHRCK building in Seoul, gathering up to 300 participants (Paek, 2019b). Press statements reprimanding the NHRCK for infringing on the religious and academic freedom of Christian universities were also issued by various Christian organizations.[19] The Korean Association of Church Communication *(han'guk kyohoe ŏllonhoe,* KACC), mouthpiece of the conservative parts of Korean Protestantism such as the CCK, even demanded that the NHRCK be dismantled: "[..] the National Human Rights Commission of Korea […] should be dissolved to properly stop the destruction of human dignity and values, and to stop it putting undue pressure on schools that practice correct teaching" (KACC, 2019a). It is remarkable that although the lecture event organized by the student club Wildflower was predominantly about issues other than homosexuality, most of the statements overemphasize this aspect, accusing the NHRCK of taking a biased stance, overly favoring LGBT rights as against the freedom of religion (Paek, 2019a; Yu, 2019; Paek, 2018).

Similar repressive measures against pro-LGBT activism were taken by Changshin University, another private Christian university in south-western Korea, located in the city of Changwon. Commemorating the international day against homophobia on May 17, 2018, eight students of the student club "Am-ha'aretz" dressed in rainbow-colored clothes and entered the altar area holding a rainbow flag after a church service at Changshin University. The group shared pictures of this rainbow performance on social media. The university leadership did not approve of this action and immediately started an investigation of the students involved, asserting that they violated the regulations of the school and of the *T'onghap* denomination Changshin University belongs to. In a press statement, the students expressed their disappointment with the university's actions, claiming

---

[17] A related case concerns the lecturer Kim Tae-ok who was dismissed from Handong University for not meeting the requirements for reappointment. Kukmin Daily reported that reasons for his dismissal could be found in his lack of opposition against homosexuality and his support for the student club Wildflower (Ku, 2018). Kim Tae-ok was subsequently found guilty of heresy in a decision "to protect the Korean church" taken by the general assembly of the Presbyterian *Paeksŏk* denomination in September 2019. "Pastor Kim Tae-ok interprets the Bible arbitrarily, teaches greatly wrong ideas in core doctrines, and advocates Islam and homosexuality" (cited in Yi, Ŭ., 2019c).

[18] The NHRCK issued a similar recommendation to protect the human rights of sexual minorities in a case that occurred at Soongsil University, a private Christian University in Seoul. The university had prohibited the screening of a movie as the university deemed the film to show a beautifying image of homosexuality (NHRCK, 2019).

[19] Press statements were issued by, among others, the "Handong University Parents' Prayer Association" *(handong taehakkyo hakpumo kidohoe)*, the "Christian Voters Union" *(han'guk kidokkyo yugwŏnja yŏnhap)*, and the "National Union of Professors against the Legalization of Homosexuality and Same-Sex Marriage" *(tongsŏngae tongsŏnghon hapbŏphwa pandae chŏn'guk kyosu yŏnhap)* (Paek, 2018; Paek, 2019a; Yu, 2019).

that their rights of freedom of expression and freedom of conscience were infringed (Yi, Y., 2018).[20] Nonetheless, in July 2018 four students were suspended from attending Changshin University. With the support from "Hope and Law" (*hŭimang ŭl mandŭnŭn pŏp*), a lawyers' association advocating human rights, the penalized students successfully appealed against their university's verdict. As opposed to the Wildflower case, a court decided in July 2019 that their suspensions were invalid, albeit only due to procedural flaws (Yi, Ŭ., 2019b). In a press statement, the KACC condemned this decision and accused the court of showing disrespect for Christianity. The KACC (2019b) also demanded Changshin University to take disciplinary measures against the students yet again – this time legally – in order to protect the church and society at large from an unwanted influx of homosexuality. The KACC statement reveals the ideological and political implications of Protestant anti-LGBT activism by further elaborating on the alleged dangers of homosexuality:

> Homosexuality cannot simply be regarded as encompassing sexual minorities or the weak, but it is a ruse conceived by Satan, which aims to destroy the church through 'Cultural Marxism'. Homosexuality is not just a matter of sex, it is sex politics, it is sex ideology, it is sex revolution. What they seek to do is destroying Christian values, families, society, and the church as a whole. (KACC 2019b)

While disparaging homosexuality is a common feature of KACC press releases, it is striking that a relatively minor rainbow performance provokes such a strong response. Indeed, any activism in favor of homosexuality – no matter how innocuous – is met with dramatic allegations such as an intent of church destruction, social decay, and communist conspiracy.[21] In such a discursive environment, engaging in LGBT-affirmative activism entails high risks for the people involved. When Protestant denominations, universities, and specialized anti-LGBT organizations dominate the discourse and institutionalize anti-LGBT stances, established ways of deliberation, e.g. at denominational general assemblies, are no longer available. Pro-LGBT actors have to resort to other means, consistently risking shaming, disciplinary measures, and exclusion. Under such circumstances, even seemingly small acts of dissent represent transgressive and potentially threatening actions.

The repressive measures against students who are (perceived to be) fighting for LGBT rights on campus are already noteworthy phenomena in themselves. Even more remarkable, though, is the fact that a broader range of Protestant anti-LGBT actors only mobilized as soon as these "incidents" created a stir also outside the Christian arena – another example of scale shift. When the NHRCK got involved in the Wildflower case at Handong University, other Protestant anti-LGBT forces started mobilizing, staging protests and issuing press statements. Similar furor emerged when a court rendered a verdict in favor of the rainbow performance students. This extended contention brings to light even more fundamental conflicts that have been shaping Korean Protestantism. The liberal political and judicial elites (or those libeled as such) in general and governmental institutions like the

---

[20] In the press statement, "Am-ha'aretz" also claim that they are not affected by the church regulation since it only mentions staff members of universities and not students. The church constitution of the Presbyterian Church of Korea *T'onghap* states in article 26-12: "Those who support and advocate homosexuals and homosexuality are against the teachings of the Bible, and those who support and advocate homosexuals and homosexuality shall not be members of the Church and professors and faculty members of the Theological University." Moreover, the students argued that the university regulations did not mention homosexuality at all (Yi, Y., 2018).

[21] South Korea's geo-political and historical background is the reason for a general favoring of argumentative strategies building on anti-communism (Kim et al., 2015). Furthermore, in recent years, the Korean anti-LGBT movement and other right-wing political actors worldwide have been increasingly using the narrative of "cultural Marxism", a conspiracy theory claiming that basically anything far-right actors deem evil, such as political correctness, multiculturalism, "big government", LGBT rights, and feminism, derives from the neo-Marxist teachings and strategies of the Frankfurt School theorists Adorno, Horkheimer, and Marcuse (Mirrless, 2018).

NHRCK in particular have been longstanding targets of attacks by conservative Protestants.[22] This church-state antagonism enables, and contributes to counteraction. If this cleavage emerges in conflicts internal to Protestantism as well, the purported threat becomes greater and counteraction more urgent. Furthermore, if this is the case, anti-LGBT actors can resort to well-established arguments and action repertoires more easily.

Reproducing the progressive/conservative divide: the cases of Newsnjoy and NCCK

Institutional Protestant actors like the progressive Christian online newspaper Newsnjoy and the theologically liberal church association NCCK (National Council of Churches in Korea) have been under attack for their support of LGBT issues as well. Anti-LGBT groups take issue, for example, with Newsnjoy's positive reporting on LGBT topics. In December 2018, a pastor of the Anti-Homosexual Christian Solidarity started organizing several rallies against Newsnjoy. The protesters decried this "anti-Christian press" as a "destructive force that infiltrated the church" and as a supporter of communism, demanding that churches supporting Newsnjoy financially halt their funding (Kim, 2018b; cf. also Chang, 2019). Subsequently, the "National Association of Professors against the Legalization of Homosexuality and Same-Sex-Marriage"[23] issued a statement condemning Newsnjoy's critical articles on Christian anti-LGBT activists in particular. Newsnjoy "is the newspaper most supportive of homosexuality among domestic media, it has a strong hostility toward anti-homosexual activism and is releasing all kinds of malicious articles" (Kang, 2019). Newsnjoy features a section in which it conducts fact checks of "fake news" produced by representatives of the anti-LGBT movement. Viewing this kind of reporting as acts of defamation, several anti-LGBT activists sued Newsnjoy. In January 2020, a court ruled that Newsnjoy had to pay compensations for reporting "beyond the scope of legitimate media activities of monitoring, critique, and checking" and demanded that the articles in question be deleted (Paek, 2020a).[24] In March 2020, the gay mens' organization "Chingusai" announced that Newsnjoy would receive the 14th rainbow human rights award for being the only media within the Korean Christian community to actively fight against hatred and discrimination against minorities (Paek, 2020b).

As an association including liberal Protestant denominations, the NCCK[25] is also a frequent target of conservative Protestant critique. Like Newsnjoy, the NCCK has the potential of reaching many church members – threatening the image agitated for by the anti-LGBT camp of the Korean churches standing united against homosexual "evils". Theologically positive perspectives on homosexuality and related subjects directly call into question the conservatives' worldview and fundamentalist interpretation of the Bible. Therefore, the NCCK was met with fierce and partly violent protests when, for example, it published a translated theological book on homosexuality (Pak, 2015). The

---

[22] The NHRCK is mainly criticized for the inclusion of "sexual orientation" in its anti-discrimination mandate (article 2 of the NHRCK act). Courts have been targets of conservative Protestant protest on many occasions, too. For example, Protestant groups tried to exert influence on trials of the Supreme Court, fighting successfully against the lift of the ban on homosexuality in the Korean military, but unsuccessfully against the elimination of a strict prohibition of abortions.

[23] Although the name of this professors' group suggests differently, homosexuality has never been officially criminalized on the state level in Korea. Only the military penal law of South Korea includes a provision (article 92-6) punishing sex between men. Historically, however, this provision has not been implemented until recently.

[24] As of October 14, 2020, the fact checking articles of Newsnjoy were still accessible in full online, suggesting that Newsnjoy appealed the court ruling.

[25] NCCK's member denominations include, for example, the Presbyterian Church in the Republic of Korea (PROK, *Kijang*), the Anglican Church of Korea, the Lutheran Church in Korea, but also more conservative ones like the Korean Orthodox Church, the Assemblies of God of Korea, and the Presbyterian Church of Korea (PCK, *T'onghap*) (NCCK 2020).

NCCK was also criticized when it invited a gay film director who advocates same-sex marriage for a lecture event on anti-discrimination (Sin and Paek, 2016), and when it demanded that the political parties in the newly elected National Assembly quickly pass an anti-discrimination law (KACC, 2020). The latter controversy on NCCK's advocacy for the anti-discrimination law illustrates the broader socio-political and religious cleavages underlying the contention over LGBT issues. The "Christian Liberty Unification Party" (*kidok chayu t'ongildang*), a minor right-wing Christian political party, for example, in a press statement denounced NCCK as a left-wing religious political force:

> They [the NCCK] claim they are active for the weak who are faced with discrimination and want to realize justice, but in fact, they habitually shout the political slogans of the Democratic Party [Korea's ruling party] on fake equity and fake peace like parrots, thereby advocating the anti-discrimination law which would legalize actions to promote homosexuality and to destroy the church and normal social culture. (cited in Yu, 2020)

Rivalry does not only exist in the area of political inclinations, but also among Korean Protestant associations. The leader of the conservative Christian Council of Korea (CCK), for instance, joined a rally against the NCCK, decrying its support for the anti-discrimination law (Chi 2020). There are also calls for the NCCK, the CCK and other conservative church associations[26] to reunite in order to strengthen Korean Protestantism, but the NCCK's promotion of homosexuality and its alleged support of North Korea are presented as making such an endeavor impossible. Therefore, the KACC argues, it would be better to no longer recognize NCCK as a church association (KACC, 2016).

Contention over LGBT issues renders visible the rifts that run deeper than simple disagreements over the theological or ethical assessment of homosexuality. Longstanding conflicts between ideologically, theologically, and politically opposing parts of Korean Protestantism come to the fore here. Anti-LGBT forces strategically use well-established arguments to disavow their internal enemies, such as anti-communism and nationalism, when maintaining that by advocating progressive issues, the NCCK, Newsnjoy, and others willfully damage not only the church, but also families and the country as a whole. The fault lines, however, do not run merely between progressive and conservative Protestant forces. They are also observable within conservative Protestantism itself, as the next case exemplifies.

Critique, backlash, and strategic accommodation: the case of Bundang Woori Church

On June 5, 2019, a junior pastor of Bundang Woori Church (*pundang uri kyohoe*), a missional church located in the city of Seongnam south of Seoul, committed an act he would come to regret afterwards. In a sermon that was televised online but later deleted, he claimed that the obstinate and uncompromising focus on homosexuality shed a negative light on Korean Protestantism. In his view, people engaging in activism against homosexuality lost track of societal trends and could thus be regarded as *"kkondae"*, a derogatory appellation for people with outdated values which they try to impose on others in a more or less aggressive way. Although the junior pastor also voiced his view that from a Biblical perspective homosexuality was a sin, his sermon was met with immediate and fierce backlash from within the church. Protestant anti-LGBT activists denounced him and the senior pastor of Bundang Woori Church as advocates of leftist and anti-Christian ideas, resulting in several official apologies and reaffirmations of the two pastors' strong anti-gay stance. The junior pastor

---

[26] Conflicts exist within organized conservative Korean Protestantism, too. For example, 20 denominations split from the CCK in 2012 due to disagreement over the election of a new leadership, forming the Communion of Churches in Korea (CCIK, *han'guk kyohoe yŏnhap*) (Paek, 2017c).

promised he would not preach for the duration of one year after this incident, and the senior pastor announced he would establish a Christian research institute on the topic of homosexuality (Yi, Ŭ., 2019a).

This episode illustrates how even moderate attitudes towards LGBT issues are met with fierce resistance from anti-LGBT forces within South Korean Protestantism. Anti-LGBT groups have not only presented the actions of the Bundang Woori Church junior pastor as a threat for the Korean church. Other prominent church actors have also been criticized if they or their entourage are not in alignment with the hegemonic anti-LGBT discourse. For instance, the anti-LGBT group AHCS demanded an apology from the chairman of the South Kyŏngsang Province Christian Council (*kyŏngnam kidokkyo ch'ongyŏnhaphoe*) as a reaction to his son's promotion of queer theology via social media (AHCS, 2018). Another peculiar example concerns the leadership of Chongshin University, a private Christian university in Seoul belonging to the conservative *Hapdong* denomination, which came under fire from anti-LGBT groups for dismissing a homophobic professor. Students had taken issue with the professor teaching in a bioethics lecture that homosexual acts were against the creation order and harmful to health (Im, 2020).

The fierce verbal attacks against Bundang Woori Church are surprising, since its senior pastor had actively preached the sinfulness of homosexuality in the past (The Bible-smith Project, 2016). It seems as though the junior pastor's sermon did not come under attack so much for his relatively moderate stance on homosexuality. Rather, the reason for being faced with an immense backlash is the fact that the junior pastor – very much like Newsnjoy – openly attacked the anti-LGBT factions of Korean Protestantism. The act of pointing out critical aspects of anti-LGBT activism from within conservative Protestantism poses a particular threat to the intended image of a united church. Therefore, the Protestant anti-LGBT movement immediately and forcefully responded to the junior pastor's announcements. Their response proved effective: with the announcement to create a Christian research institute in order to deal with the problem of homosexuality, the senior pastor publicly demonstrated his willingness to atone for the "mistakes" committed. In a sense, Bundang Woori Church appears keen to become an overachiever as a means to convincingly prove its firm anti-LGBT attitude. Such a behavior can be called *strategic accommodation*, a kind of "dramatic ingratiation" to (re)gain the favor of certain actors by "fostering the impression that values, aims, and/or conduct are in conformity with, or at least not incongruent with, certain values, traditions, and normative standards within the ambient society" (Snow, 1979: 30, cited in Snow & Beyerlein, 2019: 579).

The threat posed by the junior pastor's sermon is productively used by the anti-LGBT movement. The anti-LGBT actors achieved their goal of forcing Bundang Woori Church to "realign" with the anti-LGBT mainstream. They set another warning example for all those who may hold similar affirmative or just moderate opinions and are pondering whether to act upon them. So Kang-sŏk, a senior pastor of New Eden Church (*sae eden kyohoe*), a mega-church located in the city of Yongin south of Seoul, is both an active member of the Protestant anti-LGBT movement and a frequent contributor to the Kukmin Daily. In a column, he analyzes the "exhausting controversy" around Bundang Woori Church and put forward an interesting comparison:

> The historian Toynbee said that if a civilization succeeded in responding to an external challenge, such as a harsh natural environment or external invasion, that civilization could continue and develop. If it fails, the civilization disappears behind the stage of history. Interestingly, civilizations that have not been challenged have gone a path of collapse. [...] In this sense, the attack of anti-Christian forces on the Korean church is a good challenge

for us. If the Korean church does not accept this challenge but makes compromises, it will surely go extinct. Recently, there was an exhausting controversy over the issue of homosexuality in the Korean church. However, by resisting the opinion that homosexuality is only a mayfly and that this trend has already ended, Korean churches have succeeded in becoming one again. (So, 2019)

This passage allows for an insight into the logics underlying the opposition against pro-LGBT tendencies within Protestantism. While LGBT-affirmative actions and attitudes are perceived and/or presented as acute threats to the church, families, and to the society as a whole, they also constitute opportunities – opportunities to reiterate anti-LGBT arguments, to reinvigorate and thus mobilize church members, and to recreate an image of a church standing united against inimical groups. The internal enemy thus becomes a productive force for anti-LGBT activism.

Whether such opportunities "pay off" for the anti-LGBT forces in the long run remains questionable, though. As I have shown, pro-LGBT actors are increasingly visible and assertive within Korean Protestantism. The continuous and relentless activities of the Protestant anti-LGBT forces certainly played its part in propelling counteractors into existence. To some extent, the threat emanating from anti-LGBT activism creates opportunities for pro-LGBT actors, too, and increases the urgency for resistance. Admittedly, counteraction has been minor and scattered so far, certainly when compared to the excessive anti-LGBT reactions that ensued. There are also many who are intimidated by the ferocious anti-LGBT forces and the effects they yield, such as the reproduction and reinforcement of homophobic attitudes in Christian families. But others refuse to endure the ubiquitous repression, discrimination, and hatred in their churches any longer. They stage rainbow performances, they openly participate in queer events and seek support from external institutions if necessary, making the existence of Christian LGBTs and their allies a visible reality in South Korean Protestantism.

Conclusion

This article has explored the contention between anti and pro-LGBT actors within Korean Protestantism, focusing on the relational, cognitive, and constructivist aspects at work in such interactions. I have suggested that the perception and attribution of threat play important roles in opposing LGBT-affirmative tendencies. The greater the threat, the more active anti-LGBT activism gets. Anti-LGBT actors themselves strategically increase the threat by engaging in extreme allegations such as church destruction, communist collaboration, and imperilment of the nation. Anti-LGBT counteraction is particularly strong when external opponents such as the NHRCK enter the conflict in defense of LGBT rights. In such cases, the anti-LGBT movement often resorts to established narratives and action repertoires. The enlarged threat thus opens up greater opportunities to attack the opposing forces. In other words, if the "internal enemy", i.e., the pro-LGBT activists within Korean Protestantism, is joined by the "external enemy" (Han, 2017), ferocious counteraction is considered even more urgent.

Socio-political and church-internal cleavages are deeply rooted in the history of Korean Protestantism. These denominational and ideological rifts break open in the contention over LGBT issues as well. Anti-LGBT actors try to win over whole church communities, thereby creating a religious "regime" that often acts repressively against LGBT individuals and LGBT-affirmative attitudes. Alongside other action repertoires such as protests and issuing press statements, concrete repressive measures represent a common action form in this context, consisting of punishing pro-LGBT students and declaring pastors heretical. These attempts at delegitimization do not go unchallenged, though. Pro-LGBT actors also receive support from within and outside the church, encouraging them to remain steadfast against endeavors to exclude and denigrate them. Others, however, when faced with fierce backlash, quickly refrain from their moderate attitudes and engage in even more diligent anti-LGBT activities as a result, as the case of Bundang Woori Church reveals.

This study demonstrated that several mechanisms like scale shift, certification and decertification, and the attribution of threat can be observed in the contentious interactions of pro and anti-LGBT actors within Korean Protestantism. Applying the contentious politics and movement-countermovement frameworks to the study of religious conflict thus proved fruitful, in particular as it allowed for a new take on the actors involved such as state-like, repressive authoritative religious bodies. Future research could continue on this avenue and apply this approach to other cases of contention involving religious actors, both in Korea and beyond. This way, one could test if similar mechanisms and action repertoires are observable in further instances of LGBT-related struggles. One should also consider comparing the mechanisms uncovered in this study with those at work in the broader socio-political contention over LGBT issues in Korea. The interactions between anti-LGBT forces and secular state actors in particular, which this investigation revealed to be of great significance for anti-LGBT mobilization, should become an object of detailed examination, including a thorough analysis of its ideological background (anti-communism and nationalism), which this study could only cursorily cover.

References

Almeida, P. D. (2019). "The Role of Threat in Collective Action". In: D. A. Snow, S. A. Soule, H. Kriesi, & H. J. McCammon (eds.) The Wiley Blackwell Companion to Social Movements, Hoboken: Blackwell.

Anti-Homosexual Christian Solidarity (2017, September 4). Pandongyŏn sŏngmyŏng_kijang kyodan Im Po-ra moksa rŭl myŏnjiksik'yŏra [Press statement of the Anti-Homosexuality Christian Solidarity_Kijang denomination, dismiss pastor Lim Borah]. http://www.antihomo.net/~info01/view?p=6&article_id=201

Anti-Homosexual Christian Solidarity (2018, July 17). Kyŏngnam kich'ong hoejang xxx moksa nŭn adŭl xxx chŏndosa ŭi idan k'wiŏ sinhak ongho e taehae ch'aegim chigo sagwahara! [Pastor xxx, chairman of the South Kyŏngsang Province Christian Council, you have to take responsibility and apologize for your son XXX's promotion of the heretical queer theology!]. http://www.antihomo.net/~statement/view?p=3&article_id=506

Baek, J. (2018). Han'guk posu kaesinkyo sŏngsosuja hyŏmo tamnon ŭi hyŏngsŏng kwa chŏngae yangsang: 'sŏnggwahak' chisik ŭl t'onghan hyŏmo chaegusŏng [Anti-Sexual Minorities Discourses Constructed by Korean Conservative Protestant Churches: Politics of Disgust in the Name of Scientific Knowledge]. Master's thesis.

Baker, D. L. (2016). "The impact of Christianity on modern Korea: an overview". Acta Koreana, 19 (1): 45-67. https://doi.org/10.18399/acta.2016.19.1.002

Béraud, C., & Portier, P. (2015). "'Mariage pour tous': The Same-Sex Marriage Controversy in France". In: K. Dobbelaere & A. Pérez-Agoto (eds.) The Intimate. Polity and the Catholic Church: Laws about Life, Death and the Family in the So-Called Catholic Countries, Leuven: Leuven University Press.

Bong, Y. D. (2009). "The Gay Rights Movement in Democratizing Korea". Korean Studies, 32: 86-103. https://doi.org/10.1353/ks.0.0013

Buswell, R. E. Jr., & Lee, T. S. (eds.) (2006). Christianity in Korea. Honolulu: University of Hawai'i Press.

Chang, C. (2020, February 21). Pŏbwŏn "handongdae, tajasŏnggae kang'yŏn chuch'oehan haksaeng chinggye nŭn chŏngdang" [Court: "The punishment for a student who hosted lecture on polyamory is proper]. Kukmin Daily. http://news.kmib.co.kr/article/view.asp?arcid=0924124105

Chang, M. (2019, January 8). 'Nyusŭaenjoi' pinan e koppi p'ullin pandongsŏngae chinyŏng [Anti-homosexual camp gets unbridled, faced with critique from Newsnjoy]. Newsnjoy. http://www.newsnjoy.or.kr/ news/articleView.html?idxno=221967

Chi, Y. (2020, April 22). Posu kaesinkyo tanch'e, 'NCCK' kyut'an kisŭp siwi... kŭ iyu nŭn? [Conservative Protestant groups hold surprise protest condemning NCCK... Why?]. OhmyNews. http://www.ohmynews.com/ NWS_Web/View/at_pg.aspx?CNTN_CD=A0002635349&CMPT_CD=P0010&utm_source=naver&utm_medium=newsearch&utm_campaign=naver_news

Cho, M. (2011). "The Other Side of their Zeal: Evangelical Nationalism and Anticommunism in the Korean Christian Fundamentalist Antigay Movement since the 1990s". Theology & Sexuality, 17 (3): 297-318. https://doi.org/10.1179/tas.17.3.xx56t21243207121

Ch'oe, Y. (2016, August 18). "Ch'ongsindae enŭn tongsŏngaeja tongari ŏpda"... k'wiŏ ch'ukche ch'amgaja ch'ongsindae myŏng ŭi toyong ["There is no homosexual club at Chongshin University"... A participant of the queer festival stole its name]. Kukmin Daily. http://news.kmib.co.kr/article/view.asp?arcid=0010867878

Choi, E. (2014). "Religion, Religiosity, and Socio-Political Attitudes in South Korea". Korea Observer, 45 (2): 321–346.

Clark, D. N. (2008). "Protestant Christianity and the state: religious organizations as an example of civil society in South Korea". In: S. Pares (ed.) The Past and the Present (2 volumes): Selected Papers from the British Association for Korean Studies Baks Papers Series, 1991-2005, n.p.: Global Oriental.

Coley, J. S. (2018). Gay on God's Campus: Mobilizing for LGBT Equality at Christian Colleges and Universities. Chapel Hill: University of North Carolina Press.

Coley, J. S. (2017). "Reconciling Religion and LGBT Rights: Christian Universities, Theological Orientations, and LGBT Inclusion". Social Currents, 4 (1): 87-106. https://doi.org/10.1177/2329496516651639

Coley, J. S. (2014). "Social Movements and Bridge Building: Religious and Sexual Identity Conflicts". Research in Social Movements, Conflicts, and Change, 37 (1): 125-151. https://doi.org/10.1108/S0163-786X20140000037005

Dorf, M. C., & Tarrow, S. (2014): "Strange Bedfellows: How an Anticipatory Countermovement Brought Same-Sex Marriage into the Public Arena". Law & Social Inquiry, 39 (2): 449-473. https://doi.org/10.1111/lsi.12069

Dugan, K. B. (2004). "Strategy and 'Spin': Opposing Movement Frames in an Anti-Gay Voter Initiative". Sociological Focus, 37 (3): 213-233. https://doi.org/10.1080/00380237.2004.10571243

Fejes, F. (2008). Gay Rights and Moral Panic: The Origins of America's Debate on Homosexuality. New York: Palgrave Macmillan.

Fetner, T. (2008). How the Religious Right Shaped Lesbian and Gay Activism. Minneapolis: University of Minnesota Press.

Goldstone, J. A.; & Tilly, C. (2001). "Threat (and Opportunity): Popular Action and State Response in the Dynamics of Contentious Action". In: R. R. Amnizade et al. (eds.) Silence and Voice in the Study of Contentious Politics, New York: Cambridge University Press.

Green, J. C. (2000): "Antigay: Varieties of Opposition to Gay Rights". In: C. A. Rimmerman, K.D. Wald, & C. Wilcox (eds.) The Politics of Gay Rights, Chicago and London: The University of Chicago Press.

Han, C. (2017). Wae han'guk kaesinkyo nŭn 'tongsŏngae hyŏmo' rŭl p'iryoro hanŭnga? [Why does the South Korean Protestant church need 'hatred against homosexuality'?]. In: Chŏng, H. (ed.): Yangsŏng p'yŏngdŭng e pandaehanda [Opposing gender equality], n.p.: Gyoyangin.

Hark, S., & Villa, P. I. (eds.) (2015). Anti-Genderismus: Sexualität und Geschlecht als Schauplätze aktueller politischer Auseinandersetzungen. Bielefeld: Transcript Verlag.

Hedström, P., & Ylikoski, P. (2010). "Causal Mechanisms in the Social Sciences". Annual Review of Sociology, 36: 49-67. https://doi.org/10.1146/annurev.soc.012809.102632

Herman, D. (1997). The Antigay Agenda: Orthodox Vision and the Christian Right. Chicago: The University of Chicago Press.

Hwang, J. (2008). "A Study of the Fundamentalist Tendency in Korean Protestantism: With Special reference to the Korean Presbyterian Church". Acta Koreana, 11 (3): 113-142.

Im, P. (2020, January 28). Tongbanyŏn, Yi Sang-wŏn kyosu e ch'uga chinggyesim ŭi hanŭn ch'ongsindae chaedan isahoe kyut'an [Tongpanyŏn condemns Chongshin University Foundation board of directors for considering additional disciplinary measure]. Kukim Daily. http://news.kmib.co.kr/article/view.asp?arcid=0014174447

Kang, I. (2004). "Protestant Church and Wolnamin: An Explanation of Protestant Conservatism in South Korea". Korea Journal, 44 (4): 157-190.

Kang, J. (2013, October 28). The Kukmin Daily: The world's only Christian general-interest paper. Kukmin Daily. http://www.kukmindaily.co.kr/article/view.asp?page=&gCode=7111&arcid=0007695884&code=71111101

Kang, J. (2014, June 6). Yesunim ŭn tongsŏngae rŭl ŏttŏke taehasilkka [How would Jesus treat homosexuality?]. Kukmin Daily. http://news.kmib.co.kr/article/view.asp?arcid=0008394549

Kang, T. (2019, January 25). Pandongsŏngae kwangp'ung gwa 20 nyŏn hu han'guk kyohoe [Anti-homosexuality craze and Korean Church 20 years later]. Newsnjoy. http://www.newsnjoy.or.kr/news/articleView. html?idxno=222194

Kim, D., Pohlmann, C., & Szèll, G. (eds.) (2015). Pangong ŭi sidae: han'guk kwa tog'il, naengjŏn ŭi chŏngch'i [The age of anti-communism: Korea and Germany, cold war politics]. Seoul: Tolbaegae.

Kim, N. (2016). The Gendered Politics of the Korean Protestant Right. Palgrave Macmillan.

Kim, J. (2017, August 10). NCCK "Im Po-ra moksa idan sibi e ch'amdam [NCCK declares "The dispute around pastor Lim Borah is a tragedy"]. Christian Today. https://www.christiantoday.co.kr/news/303047

Kim, J. (2018a, September 13). Kijang "Im Po-ra moksa e taehan idanmori kwangp'ung mŏmch'wŏra [PROK demands that "the heresy with hunt against pastor Lim Borah has to stop"]. Christian Today. https://www.christiantoday.co.kr/news/316011

Kim, J. (2018b, December 18). "Kyohoe p'agoe seryŏk nyusŭaenjoi, chŏngch'e rŭl palk'yŏra!" [Destructive force for the church, Newsnjoy, reveal your identity!"]. Christian Today. https://www.christiantoday.co.kr/news/318534

Kim, J. (2019). Han'guk ŭi in'gwŏn tamnon kwa chŏngch'aek – p'ogwaljŏk ch'abyŏlgŭmjibŏp ippŏb ŭi chedojŏk kyŏngno wa tamnon ŭi yŏkhal [Human Rights Discourse and Policy in Korea – The Institutional Path of Anti-Discrimination Act and Role of the Discourse on Human Rights]. Yonsei University, PhD thesis.

Kniss, F., & Burns, G. (2004). Religious Movements. In: D. A. Snow, S. A. Soule, & H. Kriesi (eds.): The Blackwell Companion to Social Movements, Malden: Blackwell.

Korean Association of Church Communication (2016, May 18). Kyŏkpyŏnhanŭn sahoe, han'guk kyohoe kyodan yŏnhap kigwandŭl hana doeŏya [In a rapidly changing society, Korean church associations have to become one]. http://168.126.51.180/board/?r=home&m=bbs&bid=commentarypds&iframe=Y&p=10&uid=977

Korean Association of Church Communication (2019a, January 10). Kukka in'gwŏnwi ka 'makchang dŭrama' taebon ŭl ssŭnŭnga? [Is the National Human Rights Commission of Korea writing a 'soap opera' screenplay?]. http://168.126.51.180/board/?r=home&m=bbs&bid=commentarypds&p=2&uid=1224

Korean Association of Church Communication (2019b, July 23). Pŏbwŏn ŭi tongsŏngae mujigae sagŏn, haksaeng chinggye muhyo kyŏljŏng [Decision of court that punishment of students involved in the homosexuality rainbow incident is invalid]. http://chprorg.dlinkddns.com/board/?r=home&m=bbs&bid=commentarypds& iframe=Y&uid=1279

Korean Association of Church Communication (2020, April 23). NCCK, chŏngsin ch'ari sipsio! [NCCK, please come to your senses!]. http://chprorg.dlinkddns.com/board/?r=home&m=bbs&bid=commentary pds&iframe=Y&uid=1344

Ku, C. (2018, January 3). Handongdae, tongsŏngae pandaehaji annŭndanŭn iyu ro kyojikkwŏn haeim nollan [Handong University, controversy over dismissal of faculty members for not opposing homosexuality]. Kukmin Daily. http://news.kmib.co.kr/article/view.asp?arcid=0012024051

Kuckartz, U. (2014). Qualitative Inhaltsanalyse. Methoden, Praxis, Computerunterstützung. Weinheim: Beltz Juventa.

Kwon Kim, H., & Cho, J. (2011). "The Korean gay and lesbian movement 1993-2008". In: G. Shin, & P. Y. Chang (eds.) South Korean Social Movements. From democracy to civil society, London: Routledge.

Mayring, P. (2015). „Qualitative Inhaltsanalyse". In: U. Flick, E. Kardoff, & I. Steinke (eds.) Qualitative Forschung. Ein Handbuch, Reinbek bei Hamburg: Rowohlt Taschenbuch Verlag.

McAdam, D., & Tarrow, S. (2011). "Introduction: Dynamics of Contention Ten Years On". Mobilization: An International Quarterly, 16 (1): 1-10. https://doi.org/10.17813/maiq.16.1.61m83k7n14813365

McAdam, D., Tarrow, S., & Tilly, C. (2001). Dynamics of Contention. Cambridge: Cambridge University Press.

Meyer, D. S., & Staggenborg, S. (1996). "Movements, Countermovements, and the Structure of Political Opportunity". American Journal of Sociology, 101 (6): 1628-1660. https://www.jstor.org/stable/2782114

Mirrless, T. (2018). "The Alt-Right's Discourse of 'Cultural Marxism': A Political Instrument of Intersectional Hate". Atlantis Journal, 39 (1): 49-69.

Moon, D. (2014). "Beyond the Dichotomy: Six Religious Views of Homosexuality". Journal of Homosexuality, 61 (9): 1215-1241. https://doi.org/10.1080/00918369.2014.926762

Mottl, T. L. (1980). "The Analysis of Countermovements". Social Problems, 27 (5): 620-635. https://doi.org/10.2307/800200

National Council of Churches in Korea (2020). Hoewŏn, yugwan kigwan [Members and related institutions]. http://www.kncc.or.kr/eventView/member

National Human Rights Commission of Korea (2019, May 7). Sŏngsosuja in'gwŏn ch'imhae mit ch'abyŏl kwŏngo haedang taehaktŭl pulsuyong [Recommendation on human rights violations and discrimination against sexual minorities unacceptable to universities concerned]. https://www.humanrights.go.kr/site/program/board/basicboard/view?&boardtypeid=24&menuid=001004002001&pagesize=10&boardid=7604082

Paek, S. (2016, February 21). Sinhaktae kkaji pŏnjin 'tongsŏngae ongho'… daehak mada ongho moim hwaldong uryŏ ['Support of homosexuality' even at theological universities… Concern that each university has such support groups and activities]. Kukmin Daily. http://news.kmib.co.kr/article/view.asp?arcid=0923435710

Paek, S. (2017a, August 8). 43 kae daehaksaengdŭl "tongsŏngae tongsŏnghon hŏyong hŏnbŏp kaejŏng pandae" [Students of 43 universities "oppose the permission of homosexuality and same-sex marriage through constitutional amendment"]. Kukmin Daily. 2020 http://news.kmib.co.kr/article/view.asp?arcid=0923795354

Paek, S. (2017b, August 11). Taehaksaengdŭl iŏ kyosu 2204 myŏng "tongsŏngae happŏhwa kaehŏnan pandae" [2204 professors follow university students in declaring "opposition against the legalization of homosexuality and against the constitutional amendment"]. Kukmin Daily. http://news.kmib.co.kr/article/view.asp?arcid=0923797135

Paek, S. (2017c, August 27). Hankiyŏn, hankich'ong, NCCK… yŏnhap kigwan ŭl asinayo [Do you now the church associations Hankiyŏn, CCK, and NCCK?]. Kukmin Daily. http://news.kmib.co.kr/article/view.asp?arcid=00117 07548

Paek, S. (2017d, September 4). 8 kae kyodan "Im Po-ra, idanjŏk kyŏnghyang"… Im moksa "ponmaljŏndo pulk'wae" [Eight denominations declare "Lim Borah has heretical tendency"… Pastor Lim says "mistaking the means for the end is unpleasant]. Kukmin Daily. http://news.kmib.co.kr/article/view.asp?arcid= 0923809885 &code=23111113 &cp=nv

Paek, S. (2017e, September 26). Ch'imsindae kyosudŭl "tongsŏng kyŏlhon happŏphwa pandae" sŏngmyŏngsŏ [Professors of Korea Baptist University issue statement "opposing the legalization of same-sex marriage]. Kukmin Daily. http://news.kmib.co.kr/article/view.asp?arcid=0011785560

Paek, S. (2018, April 4). Handongdae hakpumodŭl "In'gwŏnwi, kidokkyo sŏllip chŏngsin ch'imhae malla" [Parents of Handong University: "National Human Rights Commission, don't violate the foundational spirit of Christianity"]. Kukmin Daily. http://news.kmib.co.kr/article/view.asp?arcid=0012251276

Paek, S. (2019a, January 8). Tongbangyoyŏn "tajasŏngae maech'un ŭl in'gwŏn ŭro p'ojanghan in'gwŏnwi kyut'an" [National Union of Professors against the Legalization of Homosexuality and Same-Sex Marriage: "We condemn the NHRCK for presenting polyamory and prostitution as human rights"]. Kukmin Daily. http://news.kmib.co.kr/article/view.asp?arcid=0012973831

Paek, S. (2019b, January 23). "Kajja in'gwŏn ŭro kidokkyo malsal" handongdae hakpumodŭl siwi [Christianity will be annihilated by fake human rights", protest of Handong University parents]. Kukmin Daily. http://news.kmib.co.kr/article/view.asp?arcid=0924058177

Paek, S. (2020a, January 20). "Nyusŭaenjoi, tongsŏngae silch'ae allin kangsa, maech'e e ch'ong 3000 man wŏn paesanghara" ["Newsnjoy has to pay 30 million Won as compensation to a lecturer and to media outlets that inform about the truth on homosexuality]. Kukmin Daily. http://news.kmib.co.kr/article/ view.asp?arcid=0924118872

Paek (2020, March 27). Kungnae ch'oedae ŭi gei tanch'e ka nyusŭaenjoi e sang ŭl chundago? [The biggest gay group in Korea gives an award to Newsnjoy?]. Kukmin Daily. http://news.kmib.co.kr/article/ view.asp?arcid=0014415229

Pak, C. (2015, December 17). NCCK "tongsŏngae kongnon ŭi chang e naenok'o taehwahae pwaya" [NCCK: "Let's have a public conversation on homosexuality]. Kukmin Daily. http://news.kmib.co.kr/article/ view.asp?arcid=092 3362204

Pak, C., Chin S. (2014, October 19). Kat'ollik ch'oejong pogosŏ 'tongsŏngae' ŏngŭp sakche… kyogye panŭng ['Homosexuality' deleted from Catholic final declaration… Reactions of churches]. Kukmin Daily. http://news.kmib.co.kr/article/view.asp?arcid=0008776455

Pak, P. (2018). 'T'aldongsŏngae undong' ŭi kanjŭng sŏsa wa kŭ chŏllyak: yut'yubŭ ŭi t'aldongsŏngaeja kusul yŏngsang (2013-2017) punsŏk [The ex-gay movement's testimony narration and strategy: analysis of YouTube videos with oral statements of ex-gays (2013-2017)]. Master's thesis.

Park-Kim, S., Lee-Kim, S., & Kwon-Lee, E. (2006). "The Lesbian Rights Movement and Feminism in South Korea". Journal of Lesbian Studies, 10 (3/4): 161-190. https://doi.org/10.1300/J155v10n03_11

Rich, T. S. (2016). "Religion and Public Perceptions of Gays and Lesbians in South Korea". Journal of Homosexuality, 64 (5): 606-621. https://doi.org/10.1080/00918369.2016.1194122

Rode, E. (2018, April 25). Amid anti-gay sentiment, LGBT-affirming churches provide fellowship and advocacy. The Groundtruth Project. https://thegroundtruthproject.org/amid-anti-gay-sentiment-small-community-lgbt-affirming-churches-provide-fellowship-advocacy/

Schumacher, K. (2016, November 22). From hurt to welcome: an interview with Rev. Bora Lim, South Korea. Affirm United. https://affirmunited.ause.ca/from-hurt-to-welcome-an-interview-with-rev-bora-lim-south-korea/

Shiwoo (2018). K'wiŏ ap'ok'allipsŭ: sarang kwa hyŏmo ŭi chŏngch'ihak [Queer Apocalypse: The Politics of Love and Hatred]. Seoul: Hyunsilbook.

Sin, S., & Paek, S. (2016, April 29). NCCK in'gwŏn sent'ŏ, "ch'abyŏl omnŭn sesang ŭl kkumkkunŭn iyagi madang e taehan p'ongnyŏkchŏk panghae nŭn pulbŏb haengwi" [NCCK Human Rights Center: "Disturbing the talk dreaming of a world without discrimination in violent ways is an illegal activity"]. Kukmin Daily. http://news.kmib.co.kr/article/view.asp?arcid=0010576140

Snow, D. A. (1979). "A Dramaturgical Analysis of Movement Accommodation: Building Idiosyncrasy Credit as a Movement Mobilization Strategy". Symbolic Interaction 2: 23-44. https://doi.org/10.1525/si.1979.2.2.23

Snow, D. A., & Beyerlein, K. (2019). "Bringing the Study of Religion and Social Movements Together: Toward an Analytically Productive Intersection". In: D. A. Snow, S. A. Soule, H. Kriesi; & H. J. McCammon (eds.) The Wiley Blackwell Companion to Social Movements, Hoboken: Blackwell.

Snow, D. A., & Soule, S. A. (2010). A Primer on Social Movements. New York: W.W. Norton.

So, K. (2019, August 27). Sion ŭi sori: tojŏn ŭn kŭkpogiji t'ahyŏb i anida [The voice of Zion: the challenge is to overcome, not to compromise]. Kukmin Daily. http://news.kmib.co.kr/article/view.asp?arcid=0924094861

Stone, A. L. (2016). "The Impact of the Anti-Gay Politics on the LGBTQ Movement". Sociology Compass, 10 (6), 459-467. https://doi.org/10.1111/soc4.12373

Tarrow, S. (2011). Power in Movement. Social Movements and Contentious Politics (revised and updated 3rd ed.). New York: Cambridge University Press.

The Bible-smith Project (2016, May 12). Pundang uri kyohoe chuil yebae tongsŏngae nŭn choe da(1) by Yi Ch'an-su moksanim 20160501 [Bundang Woori Church Sunday service: homosexuality is sin (1), by pastor Yi Ch'an-su 20160501] [video file]. https://www.youtube.com/watch?v=jqZ2bvGZuNQ

Tilly, C. (2001). "Mechanisms in Social Processes". Annual Review of Political Science, 4: 21-41. https://doi.org/10.1146/annurev.polisci.4.1.21

Tilly, C. (1978). From Mobilization to Revolution. Reading, MA: Addison-Wesley.

Tilly, C., & Tarrow, S. (2015). Contentious Politics (2nd ed.). Oxford: Oxford University Press.

Tutino, S. (2012). "Heresy". In: M. Juergensmeyer, & W. D. Roof (eds.) Encyclopedia of Global Religion, Los Angeles: Sage.

Yi, J., Jung, G., & Phillips, J. (2017). "Evangelical Christian Discourse in South Korea on the LGBT: the Politics of Cross-Border Learning". Society, 54 (1): 29-33. https://doi.org/10.1007/s12115-016-0096-3

Yi, J., Jung, G., Segura, S. S., Phillips, J., & Park, J. Z. (2017). "Gay Seouls: Expanding Religious Spaces for Non-Heterosexuals in South Korea". Journal of Homosexuality, 65 (11): 1457-1483. https://doi.org/10.1080/00918369.2017.1377492

Yi, T. (2008, January 30). 'Sŏnggyŏng ŭn hanande…' Tongsŏngae kyŏnhae kŭk kwa kŭk ['The Bible is one…' Extremely different opinions on homosexuality]. Christian Today. https://www.christiantoday.co.kr/news/190216

Yi, T. (2018, July 16). Chae 17 hoe k'wiŏ chukche sok 'kidokkyo'? ['Christianity' at the 17th Queer Festival?]. Christian Today. https://www.christiantoday.co.kr/news/314371

Yi, Ŭ. (2017a, August 5). "Im Po-ra moksa koripsik'in ch'onghoejang sagwahara" ["President of the general assembly who isolated pastor Lim Borah, apologize to her!"]. Newsnjoy. http://www.newsnjoy.or.kr/news/articleView.html?idxno=212447

Yi, Ŭ. (2017b, August 17). K'aenada yŏnhap kyohoe "Im Po-ra moksa wa yŏndaehanda" [The United Church of Canada "shows solidarity with pastor Lim Borah"]. Newsnjoy. http://www.newsnjoy.or.kr/news/articleView.html?idxno=212609

Yi, Ŭ. (2019a, June 11). 'Tongsŏngae ishyu ro sikkŭrŏun bundang uri kyohoe: pandongsŏngae chinyŏng, sŏlgyo ilbu hwaktae haesŏkhae pumoksa maengbinan… pumoksa, nollan ilja tu ch'arye sagwa [Bundang Woori Church noisy with 'homosexual issue': the anti-homosexual camp overinterprets part of a sermon and harshly condemns junior pastor… the junior pastor apologizes two times for this controversy]. Newsnjoy. http://www.newsnjoy.or.kr/news/articleView.html?idxno=223954

Yi, Ŭ. (2019b, July 18). Pŏbwŏn 'mujigae p'ŏp'omŏnsŭ' changsindae haksaengdŭl chinggye 'muhyo' [Court: punishment against students of Changshin University who did a 'rainbow performance' was 'invalid']. Newsnjoy. http://www.newsnjoy.or.kr/news/articleView.html?idxno=224488

Yi, Ŭ. (2019c, September 20). Yejang paeksŏk, handongdae chŏn kyomok Kim Dae-ok moksa 'idan' chŏngjoe [Pastor Kim Dae-ok, a former school chaplain at Handong University, is guilty of 'heresy']. Newsnjoy. http://www.newsnjoy.or.kr/news/articleView.html?idxno=225190

Yi, Y. (2018, May 21). Changsindae, sŏngsosuja wihae 'mujigae' kitpal tŭn haksaengdŭl chosa [Changshin University investigates students who held up a rainbow flag for sexual minorities]. Newsnjoy. http://www.newsnjoy.or.kr/news/articleView.html?idxno=217778

Yu, S. (2018, January 8). P'aeminijŭm kangyŏn chunbihaettago haksaengdŭl chingye nasŏn handongdae [After declaring they wanted to organize a feminist lecture Handong University takes action and punishes students]. Kyŏnghyang Sinmun. http://news.khan.co.kr/kh_news/khan_art_view.html?art_id=201801080600045

Yu, Y. (2017, May 26). Handongdae, kungnae daehal ch'oech'o-ro tongsŏngae tongsŏng kyŏlhon pandae ch'ŏnmyŏng [Handong University becomes the first university in Korea to declare its opposition against homosexuality and same-sex marriage]. Kukmin Daily. http://news.kmib.co.kr/article/ view.asp?arcid=0011495868

Yu, Y. (2019, February 2). Han'guk kidokkyo yugwŏnja yŏnhap sŏngmyŏng "kukka in'gwŏnwi nŭn tongsŏngae ongho chŭkkak chungdanhara" [Korean Christian Voters Union: "NHRCK has to stop advocating homosexuality immediately]. Kukmin Daily. http://news.kmib.co.kr/article/view.asp?arcid=0013038077

Yu, Y. (2020, April 22). Kidok chayu t'ong'ildang "tongsŏngae ongho ch'abyŏl kŭmjibŏp chejŏng NCCK kyut'an" [Christian Liberty Unification Party: "We condemn NCCK for supporting the passing of the anti-discrimination law which would promote homosexuality]. Kukmin Daily. http://news.kmib.co.kr/article/view. asp?arcid=001450
3940&code=61221111&cp=nv

Zald, M. N., & Useem, B. (1987). "Movement and Countermovement Interaction: Mobilization, Tactics, and State Involvement". In: M. N. Zald, & J. D. McCarthy (eds.) Social Movements in an Organizational Society, New Brunswick: Transaction.

International Journal of Religion

ISSN: 2633-352X (Print) | ISSN: 2633-3538 (Online)

journals.tplondon.com/ijor

TRANSNATIONAL PRESS®
LONDON

International Journal of Religion
November 2020
Volume: 1 | Number 1 | pp. 45 – 59
ISSN: 2633-352X (Print) | ISSN: 2633-3538 (Online)
journals.tplondon.com/ijor

TRANSNATIONAL PRESS®
LONDON

First Submitted: 15 July 2020 Accepted: 1 November 2020
DOI: https://doi.org/10.33182/ijor.v1i1.1089

Is Right-wing Populism a Phenomenon of Religious Dissent? The Cases of the Lega and the Rassemblement National

Luca Ozzano[1] and Fabio Bolzonar[2]

Abstract

The current global political landscape is increasingly marked by the growth of right-wing populist parties. Although this party family has been the subject of a bourgeoning scholarship, the role played by religion in shaping its ideology is still an under-researched topic. Drawing on the qualitative context analysis of a large database of newspaper articles, electoral manifestos, and parties' documents, this article studies the influence of religion on the political platforms of the Lega Nord (LN – recently rebranded just Lega) in Italy and the Front National (recently renamed Rassemblement National – RN) in France since the early 1980s. Our aim is twofold. Firstly, we would like to describe the role of religious values in the different political phases of the life of these parties. Secondly, we wish to assess whether and to which extent the appropriation of religion by these parties can be considered a phenomenon of religious dissent. Our analysis focuses on LGBT+ rights, a policy field that tends to bear the imprint of religion norms. Past studies have noted that right-wing populist parties support not only a nativist idea of citizenship, which prompts anti-immigrants and anti-Islamic stances, but also conservative interpretations of Christian values in terms of family issues and gender roles. In the last three decades, European right-wing populist parties have partly revised their positions on these issues. While some of them, like the Lega, have strengthened or made only marginal changes to their religiously-inspired moral conservatism, others, like the RN, have shown new openings on gender equality and LGBT+ rights.

Keywords: *Right-wing populism; religious dissent; Catholicism; LGBT+ rights; France; Italy.*

Introduction: Populism, Religion and LGBT+ issues

In the twenty-first century, the political landscape of several countries has undergone a remarkable transformation as a consequence of the rise of populist parties. Although populism has become an increasingly popular concept in contemporary politics, it is a contested and elusive term that has been often used to describe political phenomena that may appear mutually exclusive (Müller 2016, 7). Heads of the state like Donald Trump and Hugo Chavez, political parties like SYRIZA in Greece and Law and Justice in Poland, and anti-establishment movements that are difficult to locate on the right-left scale, like the Five Star Movement in Italy, all have been considered populist. In this article, we adopt an ideational approach to populism, according to which populism is a set of ideas with a limited programmatic scope that depicts societies as divided between the "pure people" and the "corrupted elites". Starting from this Manichean and moralistic distinction, populist leaders present themselves as the better defenders of the general will and claim 'that politics is about respecting popular sovereignty at any cost' (Mudde and Rovira Kaltwasser 2018, 1669). The anti-elite side of populism, however, is only its 'vertical' dimension, which is shared by right-wing, left-wing and officially non-partisan populist movements and parties. What specifically singles out right-wing

---

[1] Prof. Luca Ozzano, University of Turin, Italy. E-mail: luca.ozzano@unito.it

[2] Dr Fabio Bolzonar, Université Libre de Bruxelles, Belgium. E-mail: fabio.bolzonar@cantab.net

populism is its 'horizontal' dimension, that is, the opposition to others who are perceived – or at least portrayed – as threatening towards the local/national community, its values, and its wellbeing.

Besides a clearer operationalization of their concepts, scholars who have been studying populism would foster a better accumulation of knowledge if they cross-fertilize their studies with other fields to explore new avenues of research (Mudde and Rovira Kaltwasser 2018, 1686). Some recent works on the religious side of populism, arguably one of the most understudied areas in the bourgeoning scholarship on populism (DeHanas and Shterin 2018) seem to go in this direction (Haynes 2019; Ozzano 2019; Arato and Cohen 2017; Brubaker 2017; Marzouki and McDonnell 2016). Arato and Cohen have pointed out how the politicization of religion by right-wing populist movements undermines the open, pluralistic, and inclusive principles that characterize the civil society in democratic countries. In other words, populists use religion to further their political agenda (Arato and Cohen 2017, 283), which systematically aims to suppress civil society (Müller 2016, 4). Populist parties' invocation of religion is often linked with the central tenets of the thin-centred ideology of these parties (Mudde, 2004) notably the "pure people" and the "corrupted elites". Marzouki, McDonnell, and Roy have claimed that right-wing populist parties hijack religion to define the people, conceived in nativist and exclusionary terms, and to distinguish the people from the others, particularly Muslim migrants, considered a threat for the national community (Marzouki et al. 2016). In doing that, for far-right populist movements, religion is nothing more than an identity marker rather than a matter of belief, in the context of a battle against 'two groups of "enemies of the people": the elites who disregard the importance of the people's religious heritage, and the "others" who seek to impose their religious values and laws upon the native population' (Marzouki and McDonnell 2016: 2). The appropriation of religion by right-wing populist parties varies in different national contexts. The state-religion arrangements, the prevailing idea of nationalism in a given country, and the ideological roots of the various populist movements influence the populist religiosity (Scrinzi 2017) that ranges from 'Christianist secularism', where a republican idea of citizenship prevails, to civilizational discourses, to political claims deeply imbued of devotional religiosity (Haynes 2019; Ozzano 2019; Arato and Cohen 2017; Brubaker 2017; Marzouki and McDonnell 2016). However, the public display of religious tropes by populist leaders to sustain their political agenda have created strains with religious authorities, particularly with the Vatican: Pope Francis, for example, has expressed strong condemnation of the forms of sovereignism of populism.[3] In his latest encyclical titled Fratelli Tutti (All Brothers) issued in October 2020, the Pope has even stigmatized 'those who appear to feel encouraged or at least permitted by their faith to support varieties of narrow and violent nationalism, xenophobia and contempt, and even the mistreatment of those who are different.' (Francis 2020, Paragraph 86). However, the positions of Francis are not unanimously shared by the Catholic hierarchy and the community of believers. The internal pluralism that has always characterized Catholicism along all its history has also come out about populism. Some senior prelates, like Cardinal Raymond Leo Burke and Cardinal Carlo Maria Viganó, who are close to the Trump administration, have raised strong criticisms against the Pope. This mounting opposition within the Church has also triggered growing polarization among the community of believers itself. In this case, the main cleavage is often between practising believers, who recognize religious leaders as the ultimate source of authority, and occasionally practicing and non-practising believers, who prioritize political ideologies and an identity-driven idea of Catholicism (Ozzano 2019, 2016).

---

[3] La Stampa, August 9, 2019.

The complex and multi-faceted questions that loom large in the relationship between right-wing populism and religion would suggest giving a closer look to them to study whether and to what extent the populists' appropriation of religion can be considered a case of religious dissent, thereby populist leaders re-elaborate and re-interpret religious tenets to provide an alternative understanding of religion in contrast with the official positions of religious authorities.

A promising perspective that allows highlighting the religious side of populism, and particularly the phenomena of religious dissent it can be linked to, is provided by gender and sexuality, which offer the most challenging dimensions in a consideration of the contemporary relevance of religion. (Vaggione 2005, 233) and the object of an ongoing revision of the political platforms of several right-wing populist parties (Brubaker 2017; Scrinzi 2017; De Lange and Mügge 2015). Right-wing populism has traditionally rejected gender diversity policies (Verloo 2018). This attitude is often linked to traditionalist religious doctrines sustained by conservative Catholic groups and the Catholic Church (Kuhar and Paternotte 2017). However, gender and sexuality issues are difficult subjects for populists that consider them as peripheral concepts that have to be adapted in accordance with the prevailing cultural values in a given society (Mudde and Rovira Kaltwasser 2015). Accordingly, when we put religion in relation to gender issues, the positions of right-wing populist movements reveal a great diversity that varies from an exclusionary vision of society based on conservative religious values rejecting gender equality, to platforms seemingly open to 'philosemitism, gender equality, and support for gay rights', although mainly in anti-Islamic perspective (Brubaker 2017).

This paper casts light on the relations between populism and religion, through a study of the role of religious values and tropes in sustaining the positions of the Lega Nord (Northern League – LN, later renamed just Lega) in Italy and the Front National (FN, recently rebranded Rassemblement National – RN) in France on LGBT+ rights.[4] We chose these two parties, which belong to the European right-wing populist party family (Ignazi 2006), because their ideological developments on religion and LGBT+ issues have followed paradigmatically different trajectories in the last three decades. While the Lega has maintained or only marginally changed its moral conservatism that it justified on the ground of a traditionalist understanding of Catholic anthropological values, the RN has left aside its early religious conservatism to adopt more permissive positions on LGBT+ issues.

Drawing on qualitative context analysis of political discourses, electoral manifestos, policy papers, and a large database of newspaper articles, we first argue that the different positions among Italian and French right-wing populists about LGBT+ issues are partly a consequence of different traditions of religion/politics arrangements, nationalism, and citizenship in the two countries. Moreover, in accordance with the main theme of the special issue of which this paper is part, we conclude that the appropriation of religion by the League and the RN is not primarily a phenomenon of religious dissent, and mostly pertains to the sphere of symbolic and electoral politics, and to the identification of the Church hierarchies as part of the "elite" opposed to the "pure people", although it is also the expression of cultural roots ill at ease with a multicultural understanding of the world, and, more specifically, with post-conciliary Catholicism. As described below, in the early years of both parties this orientation made their leaders to sympathize with anti-conciliary movements such as Msg. Lefebvre's (and, in the case of the LN, also with neo-Paganism). In recent years, with a leadership change in both parties, the FN/RN has experienced a secularist turn, with a downplay of religious identity in favour of a secular (although identity-driven) nationalism; on the other hand, Salvini's

---

[4] Although the paper is the result of a common effort of the authors, the analysis of the Italian case has been elaborated and written by Luca Ozzano, and that of the French case by Fabio Bolzonar.

Lega seems instead to have opted for an ostentatiously devotional and identity-based Catholicism, openly at odds with pope Francis's view of the Church. It is too soon to say if this development – started with the campaign for the 2018 elections – will develop into a fully-fledged phenomenon of religious dissent. However, the controversies it is creating within the Catholic community itself seems to show that it caters on real cleavages at work within the Church and the community of believers.

This paper proceeds as follows: following this introduction, the next two empirical sections explore the evolution of the positions of the Lega and the RN on LGBT+ issues, to understand which kind of religion or religiosity they can be inscribed to. The concluding remarks compare our two cases, and try to answer our research questions, relating our conclusions to the wider literature on right-wing populism, religion and gender in contemporary Europe, and religious dissent.

The Case of the Lega in Italy

Introduction

Although LGBT+ organizations, and outspoken homosexual intellectuals – such as Pierpaolo Pasolini – had been active in Italy since the early 1970s, homosexuality has for a long time been a taboo in the Italian public discourse. This was a consequence of several factors: particularly, the predominantly Catholic culture of the country, and the hegemony of the Democrazia Cristiana party in the Italian governments until the early 1990s (Garelli, Guizzardi, and Pace 2003; Diotallevi 2002); and the predominance of a tradition of partial tolerance of homosexual behaviours only insofar they remained purely private, without any public display: a feature of Fascism which the DC party had later mostly upheld (Rossi Barilli 1999). It was only in the 2000s that the issue really came to the fore in the national media, both thanks to an increased visibility of the LGBT+ movements, and to the election of LGBT+ activists as MPs. All this made possible the inclusion of the legalization of same-sex unions in the platform of the centre-left coalition for the 2006 and the 2013 elections.[5] In both cases, the very narrow victory of the coalition, and the fact that it included centrist Catholics strongly influenced by the Church (Moscati 2010) did not make possible the approval of a law (Ozzano and Giorgi 2016). Same-sex unions were finally legalized only in 2016, also thanks to the lower profile adopted on this issue by the Catholic Church (Ozzano 2020). However, other LGBT+-related pieces of legislation, such as a law specifically punishing homo- and trans-phobia, haven't been approved yet, mainly because of Catholic opposition (Garbagnoli and Prearo 2017; Ozzano and Giorgi 2016).[6]

The Lega (Nord) Party, Religion, and LGBT+ Issues

The Lega Nord party (insofar LN) was created in 1991 as the federation of several regionalist parties based in northern Italy. At the time it was mainly focused on the centre vs. periphery cleavage, with a strong opposition against both Rome's elites and immigration from Southern Italy. At the time, the party did not refrain to rely on neo-Pagan rituals and anticlerical speeches to try to build a distinctive northern Italian identity and to mark its distance from Rome. Notwithstanding, a very committed conservative Catholic faction, the 'Catholic Padans' already existed within the party, and the party did not refrain even from showing sympathy for pre-conciliary Catholic traditionalism and the Lefebvrian congregation. These orientations occasionally came to the fore, for example in the debate about the inauguration of the 'Great mosque' of Rome in 1995 (McDonnell 2016; Guolo

---

[5] In the other Italian elections of the 21st century, including 2018, LGBT+ issues have not played a significant role in the campaign.

[6] At the time of finalizing this article, in October 2020, a new draft bill on the subject, proposed by Alessandro Zan (Democratic Party), is being discussed by the Parliament.

2011). This event prefigured some LN positions of the 2000s and 2010s, when the party seemed at times ill at ease with the post-Council Catholic Church (mainly in terms of support of multiculturalism and religious dialogue), especially after the rise of Pope Francis to the Holy See.

The first great emergence of LGBT+ issues in the Italian public debate happened as a consequence of the World Pride parade held in Rome in July 2000. It is not by chance, therefore, that we can find the first clear LN's reference to LGBT+ issues in a September 2000 discourse of the party leader, Umberto Bossi:

> The strong powers support the homosexual family. They can't have children, so values are dismantled. And the left, the red Nazis, they don't like the traditional family. Allied to the bankers and the strong powers, they dream of a utopia. Of a single moral code, a single race, a single size, the artificial uterus.[7]

Bossi also explicitly defined the Pride event as "a wakeup call", while reiterating the idea that, although he invited people to oppose the "homosexual lobbies", homosexual behaviour had not to be condemned insofar it remained "under the blankets" (a position which someway recalled the attitude of the Fascist regime and the DC party throughout most of the 20th century) (Rossi Barilli 1999). As a consequence, Bossi defined marriage equality as "a laughable issue".[8] This statement is striking because it not only sketched very clearly the positions adopted by the party on LGBT+ issues in the following years; but it also prefigured other right-wing populist tropes, such as the defence of the "traditional family", and the opposition to the leftist elites, Europeanization, and economic globalization.

This attitude, which combined the rejection of the idea that the LGBT+ community deserved any right – and, indeed, any acknowledgement outside the idea of "homosexual lobby" – and the use of deliberately politically incorrect language and puns, was very evident in the following years. For example, during the debate about the legalization of same-sex marriage in Spain, La Padania, the official newspaper of the party, used titles such as "La favola di finocchio" (The fable of faggot).[9] It is therefore not a surprise that, when the Italian parliament, after the centre-left victory in the 2006 elections, started to discuss projects of legalization of same-sex partnerships (first according to the model of the French 'PACS', and later, as a consequence of the Catholic opposition, according to the model of the German 'registered partnerships') the LN representatives aligned with the Catholic world and were indeed among the staunchest opponents of any draft bill on marriage equality. In the same way, the party opposed several draft bills on the punishment of homophobic crimes and sexual discrimination against LGBT+ people that were put forward by LGBT+ activists elected as MPs in the centre-left parties. This opposition to LGBT+ rights was often explicitly framed in religious terms by the party representatives: Calderoli, for example, justified his position by saying that "the good God made us with different qualities: man and woman".[10] Most LN statements on the issue seemed indeed linked to a patriarchal and machismo-inspired worldview of the mainly male party leadership, rather than to theological concerns and religious dissent. Nevertheless, the LN representatives did not refrain from harshly criticizing the positions of the Catholic Church and its

---

[7] La Repubblica, September 18, 2000.

[8] Ibid.

[9] La Padania, April 25, 2005.

[10] La Repubblica, 4, September 2005.

representatives, whenever they clashed with the party's platform, especially in relation to immigration, multiculturalism, religious pluralism, and relations with Islam (Ozzano 2016; Ozzano and Giorgi 2016; Guolo 2011).

These policy and discursive choices were part of a larger strategy of the party that, after displaying ambiguous attitudes towards religion and the Catholic Church until the 1990s, now poised as the defender of 'traditional values' and the 'traditional family'. As a consequence, the LN engaged not only against LGBT+ rights, but also against medically assisted procreation and stem cell research, in favor of the crucifix in public classrooms, and in support of the inclusion of a reference to 'the Christian roots' of Europe in the preamble to the draft EU constitution (Ozzano and Giorgi 2016). Its main focus, however, became the struggle against Islamic immigration, and the public signs of its presence in Europe, particularly in terms of places of worship and dress code: a target which however in the LN discourse was not rarely merged with LGBT+ issues (as already shown in the above quoted Bossi speech) and even abortion rights to polemicize against EU and national elites (allegedly willing to lower the birth rate in European countries and to favour Muslim immigration, in order to deconstruct the family-based 'traditional society') (Ozzano 2016).

This kind of discourse became more explicit in the 2010s, when many opponents of the recognition of LGBT+ rights, also in the centrist Catholic field, started to frame this opposition in the context of an alleged 'gender conspiracy' – promoted by the left, the supranational elites and the 'homosexual lobbies' – in order to mainstream the idea that gender was not a biological fact, but a free choice of the individual. This idea also inspired the mobilization of the sentinelle in piedi (standing sentinels), a grassroots movement composed mainly by conservative Catholic and right-wing people who silently stood in city squares reading a book to signify their opposition to the 'gender ideology' (Garbagnoli 2017; Garbagnoli and Prearo 2017).

The main target of the anti-gender mobilization in the mid-2010s was once again the idea of legalizing same-sex unions, since the centre-left coalition had included in its programme for the 2013 election a law on the issue. This time, the coalition also included a party, Left, Ecology and Freedom (Sinistra Ecologia e Libertà – SEL) which was led by an outspoken homosexual and pro-LGBT+ rights activist, Nichi Vendola, who during the campaign did not refrain from stressing the issue, also at the personal level, in reference to his desire to marry his partner.[11] Moreover, Pope Francis's Vatican seemed much less focused on sexuality and morality issues than it was in the previous decade, and the Church representatives now often signified their opposition in terms of priorities and opportunities in times of economic crisis, rather than 'natural law' and 'common good' as they had done in the 2000s (Ozzano and Giorgi 2016; Ozzano 2015). This paved the way for an even harsher divide between the positions of the party and the Vatican, which however mostly centered around immigration and multiculturalism-related issues.

In the meantime, the LN had undergone a major change, with the rise to power within the party – after a period of electoral crisis and scandals – of a new leader, Matteo Salvini. This latter completed the transformation of the LN (hereby referred to simply as 'Lega') from a regionalist into a fully-fledged right-wing nationalist and populist party with a main focus on immigration (not necessarily framed in religious terms) and security (Ozzano 2019; Passarelli and Tuorto 2018): a change also shown by the choice to drop the word 'nord' (north) from the LN symbol. This new political phase also brought a new approach style in relation to LGBT+ issues. On the one hand, the Lega stood

---

[11] Il Fatto Quotidiano and Pubblico, 5 September 2012.

out as the staunchest opponent of the draft bill on same-sex unions: a point well shown not only by the parliamentary and public debate, but also by the fact that, at the moment of the final discussion in the Senate, about 5,000 of the 6,000 total amendments to the text on the parliamentary floor had been proposed by Lega representatives.[12] Moreover, the party strongly supported a Family Day event that had been organized – with the purpose to show the alleged opposition of the civil society to the bill – by conservative sectors of Catholic associationism and right-wing groups (while the Vatican and the main Catholic movements had mainly avoided to officially endorsing the event, although in some cases commending it) (Prearo 2017): which was another demonstration that a growing divide between populist-inspired and centrist/progressive positions was also developing at the civil society, not only political, level, and among the Italian Catholic community itself.

On the other hand, in terms of principles, Salvini aligned with the new dominant discourse of relative openness towards the recognition of some basic LGBT+ rights (in the 2010s even some high-level representatives of the Catholic Church expressed their approval for the recognition of some individual rights for homosexual people). In May 2015 (still far away from the moment of the actual discussion of the law in parliament) he signalled thus a limited openness towards the recognition of some LGBT+ rights, provided the peculiarity of marriage between man and woman was defended.[13] This evolution went hand-in-hand with a new linguistic approach, which refrained from adopting an exaggerated politically incorrect language, as happened in the 2000s. Indeed, while carrying on the battle in parliament, the Lega representatives did not stand out for their interventions in the public debate, mostly limiting themselves to references to the defence of the family, traditional marriage, and children (in relation to the possibility of adoption for same-sex couples).

This duality also emerged in the following years, when, after the 2018 elections, the party managed to form a coalition government with the Five Star Movement and Salvini became Vice-Prime Minister and Minister of the Interior. In this case, the Lega was crucial for the decision to create a Ministry of Family and Disability and to appoint for that task Lorenzo Fontana. This latter, a former LN Vice-Secretary and European Parliament MP, had never hidden his ultra-conservative Catholic and right-wing identity, and defined himself "a crusader", as an opponent of abortion, euthanasia, LGBT+ rights and the 'gender ideology': issues which, in his view, cooperated with mass immigration in promoting the "erasure of our community and our traditions […] the erasure of our people" (Oggiano 2018).

The LN also expressed its support for the defence of the 'traditional family' by bestowing the government's endorsement to the very controversial World Congress of Families, held in Verona (home of Fontana) in March 2019. Three Lega ministers (Salvini, Fontana and the Minister of Education Bussetti) also officially participated and spoke at the event. During electoral rallies and political debates, Salvini also started to openly use religious symbols, such as the Gospel and the crucifix, and to use religious references and tones (a behaviour stigmatized not only by other politicians, but also by the Vatican itself). At the same time, however, since the creation of the government, Salvini made very clear – when a major discussion erupted on the national media about Fontana's positions – that he did not want to put into question the laws on abortion and same-sex unions, since these issues were not in the government platform.[14]

---

[12] La Repubblica, 22 January, 2016; Il Manifesto, 23 January, 2016.

[13] La Repubblica, 23 May, 2015; Il Giornale, 23 May, 2015.

[14] Giornale, June 3, 2018.

To sum up, the party has started in the 1980s and 1990s from a political ideology marked by patriarchalism and a familiarity with a pre-conciliar traditionalist vision of Christianity which did not disdain criticism towards the Vatican, not rarely portrayed as part of the elites. In the 21st century, with the party's transformation into a nationalist right-wing populist party, this orientation has translated into positions strongly hostile towards LGBT+ rights and other planks of the progressive agenda (although with the use of more politically correct tones and words in the 2010s). While these positions were often in line with the Vatican's own stances, the disagreements with this latter have not stopped (mainly because of their antithetic positions about immigration and the idea of a pluralist society), while a cleavage between different and scarcely compatible conceptions of militant Christianity has become more evident also at the civil society level.

The Case of the Rassemblement National in France

Introduction

The strict separation between the state and the Church, the principle of the laïcité (secularism) of the Republic enshrined in the first article of the Constitution, and the assertive secularism of state authorities (Kuru 2007, 571) may lead to assume that religious values have a limited role in the public sphere of contemporary France. However, the reinterpretations of the principle of the laïcité have opened the way to an accommodation of the place of religion in the French public sphere (Baubérot 2015) and Catholic values have continued to shape social and political behaviours, despite Catholicism as a metaphysical faith has shown declining appeal among French people (Le Bras and Todd 2013, 72). The mass public demonstrations against gay marriage in the streets of Paris in 2013 have also highlighted how Catholicism can still have an enduring capacity of mobilization in France (Béraud and Portier 2015). While past studies have acknowledged the influence of Catholicism on mainstream French right-wing parties (Haegel 2012; Rémond 2007), little focused debate has been devoted to exploring the interactions between religion and politics French right-wing populism.

The Front National/Rassemblement National, Religion, and LGBT+ Issues

Jean-Marie Le Pen established the FN in 1972 by aggregating several fringe radical right movements. In the 1980s, this new party was focused on immigration, security, and the promotion of neoliberal economic reforms. Although religion had a marginal role in the FN's political documents, Jean-Marie Le Pen was used to emphasize the importance of Catholic morality in his political action (Winock 2017, 1082–1085) and enrich his speeches with tropes taken from the Catholic repertoire (Alduy and Wahnich 2015, 57). The linkages between the FN and French Catholic traditionalist circles were promoted by Bernard Antony, a European deputy for the FN and one of the founders of the Committees Chrétien-Solidarité, an association that organized the pilgrimages to the cathedral of Chartres and the FN's marches for celebrating Jeanne d'Arc on 1st May. Despite the opinions expressed by Bernard Anthony and the Committees Chrétien-Solidarité were close to the positions of Msg. Lefebvre, the schismatic bishop who rejected the aggiornamento of Vatican II, they were not part of the Catholic dissent spearheaded by Lefebvre's movement (Durand 1996, 150). Bernard Antony, and Jean-Marie Le Pen alike, did not show much interest in the pastoral and theological disputes that inspired Lefebvre's movement, and they only hijacked Catholic tropes to strengthen the FN's nationalistic message and attract the votes of conservative Catholic electors.

Despite the early FN did not elaborate any distinct religious politics, its family policies bore the imprint of Catholic moralism (Invaldi 2012, 104). In the book-manifesto issued in 1985, Jean-Marie Le Pen defined the family as the place for the transmission of genetic, cultural, and spiritual heritage

(Le Pen 1985, 131), blamed 'the so-called feminist lobbies' for being responsible for the devaluation of the role of housewives (Le Pen 1985, 128), and criticized the evolution of moral values that led French governments to promote a kind of 'pro-cohabitation legislation' and support access to abortion (Le Pen 1985, 127–128).

A conflation of sexist nationalism (Crépon 2015) with Catholic moralism also characterized one of the few statements on LGBT+ issues made by Jean Marie Le Pen in the 1980s. During an interview released some weeks ahead of the 1984 European elections, the FN's President said that homosexuality was not a question to be debated, but only 'a biological and social anomaly' whose activities were a threat to civilization.[15] According to Le Pen, homosexuality was a dangerous 'other', and the biological infertility of homosexual couples made them a threat to the survival of French civilization. However, as noted by the enquiries carried out by Nicolas Lebourg and Joseph Beauregard (2012), this firm rejection of homosexuality was accompanied by more tolerant attitudes toward homosexual militants, whose presence in the FN was well-known and accepted,[16] as long as they did not politicize their sexual identity. This positioning thus led the FN to tolerate homosexual people but to strongly reject any extension of LGBT+ rights, like the bill on civil partnership (Pacte Civil de Solidarité – PACS) introduced in 1999, that the FN defined a law that imposed a 'deviant behaviour as a normative social model' (FN 2002, 42). Here, we can note some similarities between the FN's stances on LGBT+ questions and the positions of the Catholic Church that since Vatican II asked to accept homosexual people, but was against the legal recognition of homosexual unions, that the Congregation for the Doctrine of the Faith considered the approval of deviant behaviour (Congregation for the Doctrine of the Faith 2003, Conclusion). Notwithstanding the FN's claims on gender and LGBT+ questions shared several common aspects, French bishops were deeply distrustful toward Jean-Marie Le Pen and his party. Without mentioning it, in 1992, Msg. Duval, the President of the Bishops' Conference of France, wrote that Christians should not be seduced by a party that sustains certain Catholic values, but whose ideological roots are not consistent with the teaching of the Gospel.[17]

The FN's discourse on LGBT+ issues started to change in the early 2000s, and this evolution went hand-in-hand with a declining salience of Catholicism in the FN's official statements. The early 2000s were also characterized by the rise of Marine Le Pen, Jean-Marie's daughter, who intended to convey a more moderate image of the party. This strategy, popularly called de-demonization (dédiabolisation), implied a normalization of the FN's discourse that was evicted from some of its most radical claims. This development also implied a revision of the FN's positions on religion and LGBT+ issues. While in the 2002 presidential elections manifesto the PACS was defined as an example on the 'regressive social models' that will make French people disappear (FN 2002, 6), in an interview in December 2006, Jean-Marie Le Pen declared that 'I do not see much interest in this formula [PACS], but basically, if it allows some people to testify reciprocally their material interests, I do not see any inconvenience'.[18] However, the FN's founder had never completely left aside his homophobic attitudes, which he expressed in several public events.

---

[15] Antenne 2, February 13, 1984.

[16] 'We [the FN] do not practice the fly policing.' (Jean-Marie Le Pen quoted in Le Point, 14 February, 2013).

[17] www.la-croix.fr, 2020.

[18] Liberation, December 22, 2006.

The 'dédiabolisation' promoted by Marine Le Pen needed a change in the party leadership. This opportunity was provided by the national congress held in Tours in January 2011 in which the delegates were asked to choose the successor of Jean-Marie Le Pen. Two candidates contended for the party presidency: Bruno Gollnisch and Marine Le Pen. While Gollnisch, who was a long-lasting member of the FN and had close relationships with Catholic traditional circles (Delwit 2012, 33), did not intend to introduce any major change in the politics of the FN, Marine Le Pen, who was supported by the party apparatus and a generation of young militants, wanted to further the process of 'dédiabolisation' of the FN. This latter position prevailed, and Marine Le Pen obtained a landslide victory against Gollnisch.[19]

Marine Le Pen impressed several ideological readjustments to the FN's ideology (Dezé 2017), also on religion, gender, and LGBT+ issues (Crépon 2015). She left out the references to Catholicism that characterized her father's speeches, to champion the secularism of the French Republic, that, according to her, was violated by some 'Muslim political-religious groups, which seek to impose religious laws at the expense of the laws of the Republic'.[20] This 'falsified secularism' (Baubérot 2013), a misleading interpretation of it to stigmatize Muslim communities, was accompanied by the inclusion of homosexual persons among the people that the FN intended to defend. In a speech given in Lyon in 2010, Marine Le Pen declared:

> I hear more and more testimonies about the fact that in some neighbourhoods it is not good to be a woman, neither homosexual, nor Jewish, nor even French nor white. [21]

The neighbourhoods Marine Le Pen was speaking about were those suburban areas, mostly inhabited by Muslim people, that she blamed for their allegedly sexist, homophobic, anti-Semitic, and racist attitudes. The new President of the FN thus abandoned the homophobic and religious rhetoric of her father only to support a nativist and anti-Muslim politics that relied on a biased interpretation of the principle of the laïcité. This ideological revision of the FN's stances on LGBT+ and religious issues was further emphasized by the decision of Marine Le Pen to appoint homosexual people in senior party positions and avoid to take part in the social protests against gay marriage in 2012–2013, organized by an umbrella organization called Manif pour Tous, which was principally composed of Catholic traditionalist groups (Béraud and Portier 2015).

Against this background, the FN's President was not well-placed to present herself as a reference for traditionalist Catholic organizations, whose positions were supported within the FN by Marion Maréchal-Le Pen, the niece of Marine Le Pen, a Catholic militant who acquired media visibility for her participation in the Parisian marches against gay marriage. However, Marion Maréchal-Le Pen did not promote any aggregation of conservative and traditional Catholic groups around the FN. Similarly to Jean-Marie Le Pen, she defended Catholic traditionalist positions on family, bioethical, and LGBT+ issues principally to build her public image as a Catholic-friendly politician and to strengthen a nationalist identity politics, not to uphold a distinct conception of Catholicism. In any case, her retirement from political life in May 2017 deprived the conservative Catholic wing of the FN of one of the most senior figures that could contest the leadership of Marine Le Pen and possibly

---

[19] Le Figaro, January 16, 2011.

[20] L'Express, April 3, 2011.

[21] Marine Le Pen quoted in Le Figaro, December 11, 2010.

become a magnet to attract the more intransigent groups of French Catholic traditionalism within the orbit of the FN.

The more tolerant attitude of Marine Le Pen toward homosexual persons did not imply a remarkable change of the party programmatic platform on gender issues and LGBT+ rights. A kind of political genderphobia (Henning 2018), and an ideologically-grounded defence of 'natural' gender roles continued to characterize the FN political positions. In March 2011, Sophie Robert, FN's regional counsellor in the region Rhône-Alpes, blamed the Lyon Gay Pride Parade for the supposedly Christianophobia of this event.[22] Even though the 2017 presidential manifesto of Marine Le Pen did not contain the praise of the family 'based exclusively on the union of a man and a woman' included in the 2012 manifesto (FN 2012), it nonetheless showed a heteronormative imprint and stated Marine Le Pen's commitment to replace the gay marriage bill introduced in 2013 with an enhanced civil union (FN 2017, 12). During the electoral campaign, the FN's President also took the opportunity to remind her religiosity and her dissatisfaction with the Church for pushing forward a pro-migrant political agenda.[23] However, these positions did not lead the FN's leader to engage in extensive criticisms against religious authorities or to present herself as a better defender of the Catholic values of the people.

The 2017 presidential elections were a big disappointment for Marine Le Pen who was significantly defeated in the second runoff by the centrist candidate Emmanuel Macron.[24] Although Macron's permissive positions on gender, family, and bioethical issues alienated him the support of the Manif pour Tous,[25] Marine Le Pen was not endorsed by this organization. A kind of mutual distrust divided the Manif pour Tous from the leader of the major French right-wing populist party. While the former was suspicious toward a possible political appropriation of its anti-gender campaign for electoral purposes, the latter did not show any sign to leave aside the apparent secularism and the effort to modernize the public image of her party, which were core elements of the 'dédiabolisation' of the FN that Marine Le Pen had pursued since the early 2000s.

The change of the name of the FN in Rassemblement National (RN) in June 2019 was not followed by a revision of this party's stance on religion and LGBT+ issues, which continued to be affected by some degree of ambiguity, namely the defence of moral conservative positions bearing the imprint of Catholicism, but a refusal to become the political reference of Catholic traditionalist organizations. This ambiguous political strategy was also shown during the debate on the revision of the bioethical law in 2019–2020, when the RN's deputies contrasted new permissive measures proposed by Macron administration, notably the legalization of assisted reproductive technologies for single women and lesbian couples but most of them refused to demonstrate against these policies along with traditionalist Catholic organizations. The ongoing radicalization of several fringe Catholic organizations, following the controversies over gay marriage (Raison du Cleuziou 2019) may propel a reconfiguration of the relations between religion and politics in France, and possibly a repositioning of the RN on religious issues. However, the political history, ideological background, and party

---

[22] Quoted in Égalité LGBT, 2012.

[23] La Croix, April 14, 2017.

[24] Le Monde, May 7, 2017.

[25] Le Point, April 26, 2017.

leadership, which we have considered in the previous sections, make unlikely that the RN would become part of the French Catholic dissent or provide a political representation of its demands.

Concluding Remarks

This paper has shed light on the role of religion in the development of the political positions and discourses of the LN/Lega and FN/RN on LGBT+ rights from their foundation to the present day. These two parties have shared two key features relevant for this paper: strong ties with the conservative wing of the Catholic world; and the attitude to defend the legacy of a patriarchal worldview. In the last decade, both of them have undergone a renewal of their political images brought about by young leaders against the will of the parties 'founding fathers'. In the case of the LN, this has mainly implied the rejection of the old regionalist and anti-southern perspective to become a fully-fledged nationalist party (Biorcio 2015); while for the FN/RN, this process has meant the pursuit of a strategy of 'dédiabolisation' with the abandonment of the most radical positions and anti-Semitic stances (Camus and Lebourg 2015). Although neither the Lega nor the RN have become advocates of marriage equality, they have both partly softened their positions on LGBT+ issues, at least in terms of tones and language, if not of policies. This process is more evident for the RN, in which outspoken homosexuals have held senior party positions, while for the Lega LGBT+ issues are still seen with considerable hostility (also considering its strong reliance on the 'gender ideology' thesis and the party's relations with national and international conservative Christian organizations marked by very hostile stances towards the LGBT+ community).

Religion, notably a civilizational interpretation of Catholicism, focused on identity rather than belief and practices, has played a decisive role in shaping the development of the positions of the LN/Lega and FN/RN on LGBT+ issues. However, since in recent years both parties have partly mitigated their tones towards homosexual people mainly in the context of their anti-Islamic and anti-immigrant platforms, they are today affected by some degree of dyscrasia. Although their official discourses – especially the RN's ones – have partly been purged from patriarchal and politically incorrect overtones, their political proposals and the popular base of militants are – especially in the case of the Lega – still marked by conservative and 'traditional' views on genders and the family roles.

In any case, our historical analysis let us conclude that the positions of the LN/Lega and FN/RN do not seem to be primarily a phenomenon of religious dissent, although in the early phases of both parties their opposition to post-conciliary Catholicism expressed in the appreciation for Msg. Lefebvre ultra-conservative vision of Christianity. In the case of the LN, moreover, the adoption of neo-Pagan rituals and symbols was the manifestation of a political project aiming at creating a distinct northern Italian identity, also in religious terms. In this context, anti-clerical feelings even found a place, with the identification of the Catholic hierarchies as part of the "elite" opposed to the "pure people", in the context of the party's populist worldview.

In the twenty-first century, this situation has significantly evolved, particularly after the leadership changes that both parties have experienced in the early 2010s. This is particularly true in the French case as the RN has left aside the Catholic rhetoric that characterized Jean-Marie Le Pen's speeches (Alduy and Wahnich 2015) to present itself as a defender, if not the better defender, of the laïcité of the French Republic. The situation is more complex in the case of the Lega. On the one hand, the party's adoption of religious language and symbols and its defence of traditionalist positions on some religion and morality-related issues does not seem to be motivated by religious, but only by identity-driven and strategic concerns. On the other hand, the choice to harshly criticize the Vatican on immigration- and multiculturalism-related issues has aligned with the positions of some ultra-conservative Catholics who are not at ease with Pope Francis's management of the Church (and, more broadly, with post-conciliary Catholicism). This has undoubtedly catered on strains and polarization probably already existing within the Italian Catholic community, and exasperated them (Ozzano, 2019, 2016). As a consequence, this orientation has put the party – at least in some fields – in a position of competition with the Church hierarchies in defining what it means to be an engaged Christian in today's Italy. This is particularly true in the most recent phases, with Salvini's use of devotional language and symbols during his political rallies since the campaign for the 2018 elections, marking an upgrading of the religious rhetoric of the party which might turn, in the coming years, into a fully-fledged phenomenon of religious dissent.

References

Akkerman, Tjitske, Sarah L. de Lange, and Matthijs Rooduijn. eds. 2016. Radical Right-wing Populist Parties in Western Europe: Into the Mainstream? London: Routledge.

Alduy, Cécile and Wahnich, Stéphan. 2015. Marine Le Pen Prise aux Mots. Décryptage du Nouveau Discours Frontiste. Paris: Seuil.

Arato, Andrew, and Jean L. Cohen. 2017. "Civil Society, Populism and Religion." Constellations, 24 (3): 283–95. https://doi.org/10.1111/1467-8675.12312.

Baubérot, Jean. 2014. La Laïcité Falsifiée. Paris: La Découverte.

———. 2015. Les Sept Laïcités Françaises. Paris: Éditions de la Maison des Sciences de l'Homme.

Béraud, Céline and Portier, Philippe. 2015. Métamorphoses Catholiques: Acteurs, Enjeux et Mobilisations depuis le Mariage pour Tous. Paris: Éditions de la Maison des Sciences de l'Homme.

Brubaker, Rogers. 2017. "Between Nationalism and Civilizationism: The European Populist Moment in Comparative Perspective." Ethnic and Racial Studies 40 (8): 1191–226. http://dx.doi.org/10.1080/01419870.2017.1294700

Camus, Jean-Yves and Nicolas Lebourg. 2015. Les Droites Extrêmes en Europe. Paris: Seuil.

Congregation for the Doctrine of the Faith. 2003. Considerations Regarding Proposals to Give Legal Recognition to Unions between Homosexual Persons. http://www.vatican.va/roman_curia/congregations/cfaith/documents/ rc_con_cfaith_doc_19861001_homosexual-persons_en.html [Accessed 10 May 2020].

Crépon, Sylvain. 2015. "La Politique des Mœurs au Front National.' In Les Faux-semblants du Front National, edited by Sylvain Crépon, André Dézé, and Nonna Mayer, 185–205. Paris: Presses de la Fondation Nationale des Sciences Politiques.

Delwit, Pascal. 2012. "Les Étapes du Front National '1972–2011.". In Le Front National: Mutations de l'Extrême Droite Française, edited by Pascal Delwit, 12–36. Bruxelles: Éditiones de l'Université de Bruxelles.

DeHanas, Daniel N. and Marat Shterin. 2018. "Religion and the Rise of Populism." Religion, State & Society, 46 (3): 177–85. https://doi org/10.1080/09637494.2018.1502911.

De Lange, Sarah L. and Mügge, Liza M. 2015. "Gender and Right-wing Populism in the Low Countries: Ideological Variations across Parties and Time." Patterns of Prejudice 49 (1–2): 61–80. https://doi.org/ 10.1080/0031322X.2015.1014199.

Dezé, Alexandre. 2017. Comprendre le Front National. Levallois-Perret: Bréal.

Diotallevi, Luca. 2002. "Internal Competition in a National Religious Monopoly: The Catholic Effect and the Italian Case." Sociology of Religion 63 (2): 137–55. https://doi.org/10.2307/3712562.

Durand, Géraud. 1996. Enquête au Cœur du Front National. Paris: Grancher.

Francis. 2020. Encyclical Letter Fratelli Tutti. http://www.vatican.va/content/francesco/en/ encyclicals/ documents/papa-francesco_20201003_enciclica-fratelli-tutti.html. [Accessed 23 October 2020].

Front National. 2002. Pour un Avenir Français. Le Programme de Gouvernement du Front National. Paris: Godefroy de Bouillon.

———. 2012. Notre Project. Programme Politique du Front National. Available at: http://www.frontnational. com/pdf/projet_mlp2012.pdf [Accessed 10 November 2018].

———. 2017. 144 Engagements Présidentiels. Available at: https://www.marine2017.fr/wp-content/uploads/ 2017/02/projet-presidentiel-marine-le-pen.pdf [Accessed 09 March 2019].

Garbagnoli, Sara. 2017. "Italy as a Lighthouse: Anti-Gender Protests between the 'Anthropological Question' and National Identity." In Anti-Gender Campaigns in Europe: Mobilizing Against Equality, edited by Roman Kuhar and David Paternotte, 151–73. London: New York: Rowman & Littlefield International.

Garbagnoli, Sara and Massimo Prearo. 2017. La Croisade « anti-Genre ». Du Vatican Aux Manifs Pour Tous. Paris: Textuel.

Garelli, Franco, Gustavo Guizzardi and Enzo Pace, eds. 2003. Un Singolare Pluralismo. Indagine Sul Pluralismo Morale e Religioso Degli Italiani. Bologna: Il Mulino.

Guolo, Renzo. 2011. Chi Impugna La Croce. Lega e Chiesa. Roma/Bari: Laterza.

———. 2019. "La Chiesa di Papa Francesco e la Lega non Possono che Essere Nemici." Espresso, February 08.

Kuhar, Roman and David Paternotte, eds. 2017. Anti-Gender Campaigns in Europe: Mobilizing Against Equality. London: Rowman & Littlefield International.

Kuru, Ahmet T. 2007. "Passive and Assertive Secularism: Historical Conditions, Ideological Struggles, and State Policies toward Religion." World Politics, 59(4): 568–94. https://doi.org/10.1353/wp.2008.0005.

Haegel, Florence. 2012. Les Droites en Fusion: Transformations de l'UMP. Paris: Presses de la FondationNationale des Sciences Politiques.

Haynes, Jeffrey. 2019. "From Huntington to Trump: Twenty-Five Years of the 'Clash of Civilizations.'" The Review of Faith & International Affairs 17 (1): 11–23. https://doi.org/10.1080/15570274.2019.1570755.

Hennig, Anja. 2018. "Political Genderphobia in Europe: Accounting for Right-wing Political-Religious Alliances against Gender-sensitive Education Reforms since 2012." Zeitschriftfür Religion, Gesellschaft und Politik 2: 193–219.https://doi.org/10.1007/s41682-018-0026-x.

Ignazi, Piero. 2006. Extreme Right Parties in Western Europe. Oxford: Oxford University Press.

———. 2012. "Le Front National et les Autres. Influence et Évolutions." In Le Front National: Mutations de l' Extrême Droite Française, edited by Pascal Delwit, 37–55. Bruxelles: Éditiones de l'Université de Bruxelles.

Invaldi, Gilles. 2012 "Permanences et Évolutions de l'Idéologie Frontiste." In Le Front National: Mutations de l'Extrême Droite Française, edited by Pascal Delwit, 95–112. Bruxelles: Éditiones de l'Université de Bruxelles.

Lebourg, Nicolas, and Joseph Beauregard. 2012. Dans l'Ombre des Le Pen: une Histoire des Numéros 2 du FN. Paris: Nouveau Monde.

Le Bras, Hervé and Emmanuel Todd. 2013. Le Mystère Français. Paris: Seuil.

Le Pen, Jean-Marie. 1985. Pour La France. Programme du Front National. Paris: Albatros.

———. 1995. Le Contrat pour la France avec les Français. Paris: Albatros.

Marzouki, Nadia and Duncan McDonnell. 2016. "Populism and Religion." In Saving the People. How Populists Hijack Religion, edited by Nadia Marzouki, Duncan McDonnell, and Olivier Roy, 1–11. London: Hurst & Co.

McDonnell, Duncan. 2016. "The Lega Nord. The New Saviour of Northern Italy." In Saving the People. How Populists Hijack Religion, edited by Nadia Marzouki, Duncan McDonnell and Olivier Roy, 12–28. London: Hurst & Co.

Moscati, Maria Federica. 2010. "Trajectory of Reform: Catholicism, the State and the Civil Society in the Developments of LGBT Rights." Liverpool Law Review 31 (1): 51–68. https://doi.org/10.1007/s10991-010-9072-y.

Mudde, Cas. 2016. "The Study of Populist Radical Right Parties: Towards a Fourth Wave." Working Paper Series, no. 1, University of Oslo: Center for Research on Extremism: The Extreme Right, Hate Crime and Political Violence (C-REX).

Mudde, Cas and Cristóbal Rovira Kaltwasser. 2015. "VoxPopuli or Vox Masculini? Populism and Gender in Northern Europe and South America." Patterns of Prejudice 49 (1–2): 16–36. https://doi.org/10.1080/0031322X.2015.1014197.

Müeller, Jan-Werner. 2016. What is Populism? Philadelphia: University of Pennsylvania Press.

Occhetta, Francesco. 2018. "Alla Vigilia delle Elezioni Politiche in Italia." La Civiltá Cattolica, 4023 (3): 238–45.

Oggiano, Francesco. 2018. "Fontana, il ministro per la Famiglia contro aborto e coppie gay." VanityFair.it (blog). June 01, 2018. https://www.vanityfair.it/news/politica/2018/06/01/lorenzo-fontana-ministro-famiglia-gay-aborto-gender.

Ozzano, Luca. 2015. "The Debate about Same-Sex Marriages/Civil Unions in Italy's 2006 and 2013 Electoral Campaigns." Contemporary Italian Politics 7 (2): 144–60. https://doi.org/10.1080/23248823.2015.1041250.

———. 2016. "Two Forms of Catholicism in Twenty-First-Century Italian Public Debate: An Analysis of Positions on Same-Sex Marriage and Muslim Dress Codes." Journal of Modern Italian Studies 21 (3): 464–84. https://doi.org/10.1080/1354571X.2016.1169888.

———. 2019. "Religion, Cleavages, and Right-Wing Populist Parties: The Italian Case." The Review of Faith & International Affairs 17 (1): 65–77. https://doi.org/10.1080/15570274.2019.1570761.

———. 2020. "Last but Not Least: How Italy Finally Legalized Same-Sex Unions." Contemporary Italian Politics 12 (1): 43–61. https://doi.org/10.1080/23248823.2020.1715594.

Ozzano, Luca, and Alberta Giorgi. 2016. European Culture Wars and the Italian Case: Which Side Are You On? London: Routledge.

Passarelli, Gianluca and Dario Tuorto. 2018. La Lega di Salvini. Estrema Destra di Governo. Bologna: Il Mulino.

Prearo, Massimo. 2017. "Le Cadrage Religieux de la Mobilisation « Anti-genre » : Une Étude Micro-événementielle du Family Day." Genre, sexualité & société, no. 18 (December). https://doi.org/10.4000/gss.4100.

Raison du Cleuziou, Yann. 2019. Une Contre-Révolution Catholique: Aux Origines de La Manif pour Tous. Paris: Seuil,

Rémond, René. 2007. Les Droites Aujourd'hui. Paris: Seuil.

Rossi Barilli, Giovanni. 1999. Il Movimento Gay in Italia. Milano: Feltrinelli.

Rydgren, Jens. ed. 2018. The Oxford Handbook of the Radical Right. Oxford: Oxford University Press.

Scrinzi, Francesca. 2017. "A 'New' National Front? Gender, Religion, Secularism and the French Populist Radical Right.". In Gender and Far Right Politics in Europe, edited by Köttig Michaela, Bitzan Renate, and Petö, Andrea, 127–40. London: Palgrave-Macmillam.

Stavrakakis, Yannis. 2004. "Antinomies of Formalism: Laclau's Theory of Populism and the Lesson from Religious Populism in Greece." Journal of Political Ideologies 9 (3): 253–67. https://doi.org/10.1080/1356931042000263519.

Vaggione, Juan Marco. 2005. "Reactive Politicization and Religious Dissidence. The Political Mutations of the Religious." Religion and Politics 31(2): 233–55. https://doi.org/10.5840/soctheorpract200531210.

Verloo, Mieke. 2018. "Gender Knowledge, and Opposition to the Feminist Project: Extreme-Right Populist Parties in the Netherlands." Politics and Governance 6: 20–30. http://dx.doi.org/10.17645/pag.v6i3.1456.

Winock, Michel. 2017. La France Républicaine: Histoire Politique XIXe-XXIe Siècle. Paris: Laffont.

International Journal of Religion

ISSN: 2633-352X (Print) | ISSN: 2633-3538 (Online)

journals.tplondon.com/ijor

TRANSNATIONAL PRESS®
LONDON

International Journal of Religion
November 2020
Volume: 1 | Number 1 | pp. 61 – 76
ISSN: 2633-352X (Print) | ISSN: 2633-3538 (Online)
journals.tplondon.com/ijor

TRANSNATIONAL PRESS®
LONDON

First Submitted: 15 July 2020 Accepted: 1 November 2020
DOI: https://doi.org/10.33182/ijor.v1i1.1229

A Religious Movement on Trial: Transformative Years, Judicial Questions and the Nation of Islam

Sultan Tepe[1]

Abstract

The Nation of Islam (NOI) is one of the most controversial political-religious groups in the United States. Some define it as an exclusionary race-based group, while others see it as a genuine empowerment movement. Although it has been viewed as an unconventional fringe group, NOI represents an important syncretic movement of its time. Its approach to Islam was marked by a range of currents from the anti-colonial interpretive framework of the Ahmadiyya to Marcus Garvey's Universal Negro Improvement Association forging a highly dynamic narrative to explain the racial injustices and individual and collective requirements of future emancipation. Despite its strong anti-establishment discourse, NOI operates within the parameters legal and judicial system and seeks to reach out to new groups. As NOI faces the challenge of balancing its clashing inner currents rooted in its commitments to orthodox vs. vernacularized Islam or anti-systemic vs. accommodationist policies and often stigmatized by outside observers, it constitutes one of the most promising and precarious black movement.

Keywords: *Nation of Islam; Islam; dissent; internal religious change; political-religious groups.*

Introduction

The Nation of Islam (NOI or the Nation) is one of the most controversial political- religious groups in the United States. Some define it as an exclusionary race based group, while others see it as a genuine empowerment movement.[2] Despite its critical role in US history, the ideas and identity of the Nation's founder, Wallace Fard, remain mostly a mystery - a mystery that is both embraced and reinforced by the movement's own theology. Likewise, despite continuing scholarly and popular interest, the movement's history and the details of its theology remain largely under-researched. This analysis contends that although it has been viewed as an unconventional fringe group, the Nation of Islam represents an important syncretic movement of its time. Understanding its theology, just like other theologies of resistance, requires a careful placement of its ideas into its historical and ideational context. Such contextualization enables us to recognize that the movement's approach to Islam is rooted in a range of currents from the anti-colonial interpretive framework of the Ahmaddiya branch of Islam to other African-American movements such as the Moorish Science Temple and Marcus Garvey's Universal Negro Improvement Association, among others. Each movement put forward its

---

[1] Sultan Tepe,PhD, Associate Professor, University of Illinois at Chicago, United States. E-mail: sultant@uic.edu

Acknowledgement: The author thanks the Institute for Research on Race & Public Policy at the University of Illinois at Chicago for its support to this research. This analysis would not have been possible without Keith Simonds' meticulous assistance with archival research and careful review of the cited texts.

[2] Attesting to its clashing images the Nation is praised by the Chicago Mayor's office led by Rahm Emanuel due to its contributions to community safety on the south side of Chicago but also listed as a hate group by the Southern Poverty Law Center. Armstrong Williams, "The Nation of Islam Could Be Chicago's Savior," The Hill, October 5, 2015.

own distinct account to explain past injustices faced by those of African descent and offered narratives to explain their displacement as well as their future emancipation.[3]

Due to its multilayered theology and organizational model, both of which have been present since its inception, the Nation does not fit any easily into conventional social and religious categories. The movement has been assessed through some binaries (e.g., cult vs. religion, separatist vs. empowerment, colony vs. settlement) bringing the legitimacy of its ideas and practices into question. Being framed by such binaries strengthened the movement's appeal but also undermined its ability to operate. Below is the first analysis of a decisive court case (1977-1984) that sought to determine the rightful inheritors of the movement after the death of its second leader, Elijah Muhammad, in 1975. The analysis illustrates how those court deliberations captured the difficulties of demarcating different components of the movement, and that by doing so it inadvertently strengthened and legitimized the proponents of the more racialized and exclusionary tenets of the Nation of Islam. Due to the length of the trial, the "philosophical questions" the court felt compelled to address, and the emergence of the court as a main venue to settle distinct views among different parties within the movement, the final court decision played a crucial role in changing the internal dynamics of the movement. The types of questions and clashing answers draw our attention to why judicial processes cannot be seen as insulated. In fact, the ways in which social and popular questions surrounding the movement clearly made inroads into the court's deliberations have reinforced the movement's image as a private organization. Despite its specific questions, the court's deliberation and decision also manifested the resiliency of markers that defined the movement's early years as an ambiguous organization with questionable practices.

The conclusions illustrate how the court case took place at a critical juncture and played a pivotal role in changing the internal dynamics of the movement. Eliciting its findings from the court's proceedings and presenting some of its documents for the first time, the analysis shows below that the case, in effect, put the movement on trial and sought to determine if the Nation was a family-centered profit-making venture, or a true religious movement. The review argues that the court case captures the continuities and shifts in the treatment of the Nation of Islam that has situated itself at the intersection of black civil rights and Islamic movements. As the following review of the movement highlights, the blending of distinct racial and religious claims makes the analysis of the movement highly complex. Precisely due to this hybrid appearance, the court's treatment of the Nation offers a unique vantage point to assess the ways in which exclusionary and inclusionary forces interact and thereby define the abilities of social movements and new theologies of resistance to carve out new arenas of contestation.

The following discussion (i) offers a brief intellectual background of the movement, (ii) places its emergence in its historical context and introduces the early terms applied to the Nation in popular and scholarly circles, (iii) describes the main issues faced in the court case, (iv) argues how the same tensions that led to the movement's success also triggered internal divisions and external interventions, and (v) how the court case captured a critical turning point in the internal organization and theologies of the movement which changed the course of its national and local trajectories and the way they were perceived by outsiders as well as the ways it reinforced the binaries (e.g., cult vs.

---

[3] Ahmadiyya Islam was founded in India by Mirza Ghulam Ahmad in the late 19th century. It is treated as an unorthodox branch of Islam and not recognized by many mainstream Islamic groups. Unlike other branches of Islam, perhaps due to its marginalization and new ideas, Ahmadiyyans consider spreading the main ideas of the movement as one of their main devotional commitments. For more see Walter, H. A. *The Aḥmadīya Movement.* Oxford university press, 1918.

religion, family- centered vs. social, empowerment vs. separatist etc.) that continue to simplify the movement's complex ideas and local and transnational engagements.

Intellectual Background: Authentic Syncretism?

The Nation was born in Detroit under the leadership of Wallace Fard whose identity and background remains largely unknown and contested. Some accounts refer to Fard's work in Detroit as early as 1929.[4] A skillful salesman, Fard visited many houses to sell fabric and clothes and his "house meetings" became popular. Among the many topics he brought up for discussion, was why black Americans were mistreated in the US. His message resonated with many audiences, as Fard offered a broad historical explanation for the plight of the poor as well as for people's daily struggles in a rapidly changing country. Adopting conventional examples to better fit marginalized populations, Fard introduced new metaphors representing the African-American's experiences in the US as those of a dead-nation. A personal and spiritual awakening was needed to change the entire belief system (to abandon conventional religious beliefs and the "Poison book") and daily habits:

> I can sit on top of the world and tell everyone that the most beautiful Nation is in the wilderness of North America. But do not let me catch any sister other than herself in regards to living the Life and weighing properly.

> Big fields are awaiting for the wide Awake man to work out. Arise the Dead by the thousands!

> The dead Nation must arise - for the Time is at hand. Look in your Poison Book.

> Work cheerfully and fear not!

> You are the Righteous, the Best and the Powerful.[5]

Beneath its revolutionary appearance, Fard's rich symbolic language was eerily similar to the traditional American rhetoric that emphasized mastering the land, controlling circumstances and even American exceptionalism. What changed the impact of Fard's teaching was Elijah Muhammad's participation with the movement. Elijah Muhammad (born Elijah Robert Poole), the son of a slave Baptist minister from Georgia, became the next, and most important, leader of the movement. Elijah's own experience of racial oppression in the South, familiarity with the Bible and with Garvey Marcus' teachings and experiences in Detroit (at that time the fourth largest urban center in the country) made him an excellent articulator of the movement's ideas. Although many accounts describe the movement as anachronistic and insular, a closer look at the Nation of Islam shows that it incorporated the tenets of various theologies and movements that marked the late 1800s and early 1900s:

- Wallace Fard and Ahmadiyya Islam--Very little is known about Elijah Muhammad's mentor and the founder of the Nation of Islam-Wallace Fard. However, the version of the Quran adopted by the movement suggests that he was familiar with, or perhaps even a follower of the Ahmadiyya branch of Islam, an unorthodox version

---

[4] Polk, A. R. "The Best Knower: Mythmaking, Fard Muhammad, and the Lost-Found Nation of Islam." *International Journal of Religion & Spirituality in Society*, (10:1), 81–93, 2020.

[5] Elijah, Muhammad. (1957) *The Supreme Wisdom: Solution To The So-Called Negroes Problem*. Newport News, VA ; National Newport News.

of Islam which was formed in Punjab, British India, near the end of the 19th century. The founder of Ahmadiyya Islam, Mirza Ghulam Ahmad, articulated an Islamic anti-colonial discourse.[6]

- The Moorish Science Temple of America--Prophet Noble Drew Ali founded the Moorish Science Temple of America, one of the most influential black movements in the early 1900s. Drew Ali (formerly known as Timothy Drew) identified himself as "Noble" Drew Ali, the divinely inspired messenger and a prophet who used Islamic idioms to present his ideas. Among others, Ali proclaimed that black populations, "so-called Negroes", in the US were in fact Moorish Americans, descended from the ancient Moabites and that they shared a rich heritage that stretched from ancient Palestine to Arabia and the Muslim empires in Eurasia and Africa. The movement emphasized the importance of recovering the authentic self (which, among other things, meant acquiring new last names) and economic self-sufficiency. With these goals in mind, he established a factory to produce oils, incense, soaps, and other Moorish products, the sales of which buoyed the religion's financial base.[7]

- The Universal Negro Improvement movement-- Marcus Garvey founded another one of the most impactful black movements in American history, the Universal Negro Improvement Association (UNIA) in the early 1900s. The UNIA aimed to foster worldwide unity among all blacks while rejecting any notion of integration in the US or beyond. Instead, the movement focused on the philosophy of black consciousness, self-help, and economic independence. Garvey's weekly newsletter, *Negro World,* became one of the most popular publications, with millions of followers, and his investments under the Black Star Line caused many controversies.[8]

- The Black Hebrew Movements—Some, like William Saunders Crowdy (1895), promoted a new theology that described the black populations in the US as the descendants of the twelve biblical tribes of Israel. For such theologies America's recently emancipated slaves were God's chosen people, the true Hebrews. They were part of a "theological élan to give a positive interpretation to the black past." [9] In 1896 Crowdy was preaching on State Street in Chicago, gaining the nickname

---

[6] Jalal, A. (2005). *Self And Sovereignty: Individual And Community In South Asian Islam Since 1850*. London: Oxford University Press; Murphy, E. (2016). From Sufism to Ahmadiyya: a Muslim minority movement in South Asia. *Contemporary South Asia, 24*(2), 214-215.

[7] Vardat, Scott J. 2013. "Drew Ali And The Moorish Science Temple Of America: A Minor Rhetoric Of Black Nationalism." Rhetoric & Public Affairs 16, no. 4: 685-717; Mubashshir, Debra Washington. 2001. "Forgotten Fruit of the City: Chicago and the Moorish Science Temple of America." *Cross Currents* 51, no. 1: 6; Johnson, Sylvester A. 2010. "The Rise of Black Ethnics: The Ethnic Turn in African American Religions, 1916-1945." *Religion & American Culture* 20, no. 2: 125-163; Nance, Susan. 2002. "Respectability and Representation: The Moorish Science Temple, Morocco, and Black Public Culture in 1920s Chicago." *American Quarterly* 54, no. 4: 623.

[8] Dagnini, Jérémie Kroubo. 2008. "Marcus Garvey: A Controversial Figure in the History of Pan- Africanism." *Journal Of Pan African Studies* 2, no. 3: 198-208; Carter, S 2002, 'The Economic Philosophy of Marcus Garvey', *Western Journal Of Black Studies*, 26, 1, p. 1; *Negro with a Hat: The Rise and Fall of Marcus Garvey*. By Colin Grant. Ox- ford: Oxford University Press, 2008.

[9] Jones, Elias F. "Black Hebrews: The Quest for Authentic Identity." *The Journal of Religious Thought*, vol. 44, no. 2, 1988, pp. 35

of "Black Elijah." This new genre of theologies identified the Blacks as morally and racially superior to others while projecting their inevitable full salvation.[10]

II. Historical Context: "Dixie Exodus" and Racial Encounters

As the above brief review indicates, the Nation of Islam was born in an ideational and theological environment where black movements focused on *self-knowledge*, which meant explaining past wrongs; the road to *emancipation*, which meant mapping out specific processes for salvation, and *economic self-reliance* which meant creating black-ownership centered economic activities; and *political independence*, which meant creating an independent nation free of any type of outside control or undue influence. Beyond the impact of the above listed theological and social movements, it is also important to note that the Nation's ideas were fermented during the influx of migrants from the south to the north to work in the booming war industries.[11] In an effort to explain the race riots happening across the United States in industrial urban centers in the early decades of the 20th century, the Chicago Tribune presented the socially and religiously disruptive effect of the "Dixie Exodus" (or the Great Migration of 1916-1929 from the South to northern cities) and heightened social expectations as the most decisive determinants of racial clashes. The analyses reported an average of 1,000 people per month were leaving the south between 1937 and 1943. Sudden urbanization and the cultural impact of newly arrived rural whites who organized around religion created the context of the Nation of Islam's early years.

Although the population movement was important, what was also crucial was the increasing role of religion in organizing the migrants, particularly that with Southern-rural anti-Semitic tones. According to Dr. Claude C. Williams:

> "Along with them [the rural southerners] came 2,500 'working preachers' who are now employed in Detroit's war plants. These men are the real leaders of the southern masses in Detroit. They preach, not because they are ordained, but because they feel 'the call' to preach. Every Sunday and often during the week they speak and they lead groups ranging from 20 or 25 to 300 or 500 persons."[12]

Given the role of differing theologies in serving as the new organizational foundation for the large numbers of incoming migrants, the Nation's religious core was not an exception, but instead followed the pattern of the time. What made the Nation different from others was not its religious core, but the particular form of ideas it adopted and the level of success they found in institutionalizing its meetings and teachings. Diverging from the dominant Christian religious repertoire, the Nation instead turned to Islam.

Reflecting the confusion about, and reactions to the Nation's beliefs, one of the first scholarly assessments of the Nation published in 1938 described it as an African Voodoo Cult formed mostly by southern negro migrants who were relatively new arrivals to the industrial cities of the North.[13] Despite its valuable data collection, the terms and presentation of this early publication reveal how the nation was delegitimized from its very inception. It was presented as a cult rooted in foreign

---

[10] Fauset, Arthur Huff. *Black Gods of the Metropolis; Negro Religious Cults of the Urban North*. New York: Octagon Books, 1974.

[11] Hughes, F. "Experts Trace Race Conflicts to Dixie Exodus," *The Chicago Tribune*, (June 27, 1943).

[12] *ibid*

[13] Erdmann Doane Beynon, "The Voodoo Cult Among Negro Migrants in Detroit," American Journal of Sociology vol. 43 (July 1937 – May 1938). Pp. 894-907

cultures, a reincarnation of an African voodoo tradition, an uncivilized movement that was open to human sacrifice. References to other unacceptable acts (e.g., homeschooling with a teaching denouncing the dominant beliefs) put the movement firmly outside of the mainstream and questioned whether their existence was even compatible with civilization itself let alone an emerging urban life.

The Nation explained many social ills such as the illiteracy common among southern Negroes as an act of the devil. Elijah explained: "Why does the devil keep our people illiterate? So that he can use them for a tool and also a slave. He keeps them blind to themselves so that he can master them."[14] The movement's references to "devil" disturbed many observers, as the movement used this language to describe the white control of Black populations and the historical deployment of conventional Christian beliefs to enforce racial hierarchies. The exclusionary ideas of the Nation came to overshadow its other messages and thereby defined all of its distinct components. The analysis of the Nation often ended with a warning:

> "The Black Muslims have become a protest group-more militant than the Urban league and the N.A.A.C.P. could ever dare to be-and, for this reason, often more appealing to the disgruntled Negro man on the street... Every negro protest organization today is, in its own way, impatient. Each is learning to seize the moral initiative. Each is preparing to force America to a showdown. And sooner or later, Americans will have to yield--if not to the soft spoken, reasonable demands of the conservative organizations, then to the strident, extreme, and vengeful demands of the black nationalists. For the moment--a brief and fateful moment--the choice is still in our hands."[15]

III. Court Case: Who Owns the Movement?

Elijah Muhammad's death in 1975 led to years of litigation attempting to resolve multiple questions surrounding the various issues of who would be the rightful heirs to numerous funds and bank accounts, which also forced the court to weigh various philosophical and religious questions. In the court's own words "The issue was to determine for whom or what was Elijah's poor Fund (the main account for which the movement's donations were solicited and collected). And was it Elijah Muhammad's personal fund or did it belong to the religion, the Nation of Islam?" The court case coincided with a time when the movement's internal questions had brought it to a crossroads as important as at any point in their history. Under the leadership of the movement's new leader Warith Deen Mohammed (the elected successor of the movement and the son of Elijah Muhammad who was originally named Wallace D. Muhammad), the Nation moved towards a more orthodox version of Islam and started to revisit some of the tenets of their race-centered rendition of Islam.[16] While the movement's transition towards more mainstream Islam and gradual rejection of the categorical treatment of the white race as a singular group) was a welcome change for some; it also unsettled some members of the group who perceived the movement's emphasis on racial injustice as centrally important to its identity.

Sudden divergence from Wallace Fard and Elijah Muhammad's teachings, the critics argued, might conform the movement to an orthodox version of Islam but would undermine the movement's US specific core and its historical mission. Amidst these disputes the court case served as an important

---

[14] *ibid*

[15] Herb Nipson, "Astute Study of a hate group," *The Chicago Tribune*, May 15, 1961.

[16] Warith Deen, The Lost-Found Nation, *the Bilalian News*, Vol.1, no.1 November 14, 1975.

platform to reflect internal theological discussions and steer the competition playing out within the movement. One might argue that Elijah Muhammad was responsible for this internal crisis as he left no will to specify the process for splitting his assets. However, Elijah left a certain amount to his rightful inheritors and the lack of a will might also indicate that he perceived the property as the movement's and not as his own. The situation was further complicated by the fact that in addition to his legitimate children, others also claimed to be his children and therefore rightful heirs. Over the years, Elijah's polygamous practices came under scrutiny and led to no small amount of controversy within the movement. Yet, the main question facing the court was whether the family of Elijah Muhammad had a right to the money, as an individual as opposed to the Nation of Islam itself.

The first trial ended in 1982. After four months, it had produced over 6,000 pages of testimony based on 16 witnesses, and Cook County Circuit Court Judge Henry Budzinski ruled to distribute Elijah's property, thus treating the Nation of Islam as a private organization and all Elijah's children as rightful inheritors. Although the estate was awarded $4.6 million, the victory would be short lived. In 1984 the decision was reversed by the Illinois Appellate Court on appeal. The appeals court found that the funds and accounts in question were not clearly the property of Elijah Muhammad as an individual and that they may have belonged to the Nation of Islam as a religious organization. The central question had not been satisfactorily resolved. Judge Henry Budzinski heard the case again, with a new focus on the question of whether the money had been given to Elijah Muhammad the man or to the organization he led, the Nation of Islam. After four weeks and 1,500 pages of new testimony, Judge Budzinski ruled again that the property needed to be treated as personal not that of a movement.

The excerpts below exemplify how the court tried to distinguish different parts of the movement and clarify its identity:

Q: Are you here appearing sir pursuant to a subpoena? A: Yes, I am

Q: Did you Sir at any time have any contact with an organization known as the Nation of Islam?

Mr. Cook: I will object to the form of a question. There has been nothing in evidence to show the Nation of Islam is an organization?

Mr. Wilkins: I join in that objection.

The court: Sustained. Paraphrase the question counsel,

Mr. Lies: Are you familiar with the term Nation of Islam? A: Yes, I am

Q: When did you first hear that term?

A: I guess it's been many years: 1969, 1970

Q: There was a lot of publication about the mosque and I think it was referred to as the Nation of Islam at that time

A: Did you Sir, ever have any contact with persons purported to represent that organization?

Mr. Cook: I will object to the form of a question; there's been no evidence showing the Nation of Islam is an organization.

Mr. Lies: Judge, the witness has just testified that he is aware of the Nation of Islam since the late 1960s or the early 70s and was familiar with the mosque.

The court: Correct. He is objecting to the term organization in relation to the Nation of Islam. I will sustain the objection.[17]

Similar discussions were not rare but instead dominated the trial and raised the question of whether or not the movement was religious, prompting some to object. When he was told the Nation was not a religion, a member of the NOI brought as a witness objected in the following way:

Rahman: Yes, I don't know understand what is going on. I thought I belonged to a religion. I believe in God.

The court: No comment[18]

In 1988, the Illinois Appellate Court would again reverse the ruling made in favor of the children. Even if the money had been given to Elijah Muhammad as an individual, the court concluded, this did not mean that it wasn't meant as a donation to the Nation of Islam. The brochures and orientation materials used by the Nation of Islam became important evidence. Those materials stressed that as a religious leader Elijah Muhammad collected charity and used the funds to help the poor and the needy. Yet the question was in what capacity Elijah collected the funds.

Mr. Joyce: So, Your Honor. If the words of the Honorable Elijah Muhammad can be brought into evidence as the leader of the mosque or the religion then certainly the words national secretary at that time of that...Religious organization or religion whatever can be brought into evidence to show what was said and what was the intention of the parties. Now this is prefatory to what will come later to lay a foundation work for the actions of the individual but still in all it's because of the relationship of Elijah Muhammad as the individual and as the leader of that religion. You can't say he is only an individual in this lawsuit but also the leader of the religion. So, what the officer say is also germane and should be a part of the record.

The court: Now we are getting into the philosophical issues

Mr. Joyce: No, I am getting into the law of agency. I'm getting into the status of parties and the law of agency and binding of the agency. We intend to set up a groundwork for the action of this witness and what he actually did as the basis of ... he did and that is the sole purpose for which it is being offered. Even so John Ali being the national secretary of that religion of the Nation of Islam and the mosque, being No.2., even without that purpose it would still be admitted into evidence to assist this court in showing what is the ultimate issue in this case or what is the ultimate decision in this case and that hang up because Mr. Ali is not here or it is hearsay we submit that is not true. The fact of the matter is what is the ultimate issue in this case, what does it bear on?[19]

---

[17] From the proceeding of the court case, Estate of Muhammed, 463 N.E.2d 732 (Ill. App. Ct. 1984) Mar 22, 1984

[18] ibid

[19] From the court proceedings, re: Estate of Muhammad, 520 N.E.2d 795 (Ill. App. Ct. 1987)

The court argued that even if the money was also used by Elijah Muhammad and his family, this did not mean that the money was properly considered as personal gifts rather than religious or charitable donations. The court also noted that in the materials used to ask for donations, it told possible donors that their donations were income tax deductible, which would only be true if they were not contributions made to an individual.

Despite the evidence, the prolonged court case resulted in the distribution of the Nation of Islam properties between its two branches Warith Deen Mohammed (i.e., universal orthodox Islam-centered aspect of the movement) and the Farrakhan (i.e., race-centered aspect) side of the movement. While Deen lost most of the properties, Farrakhan reclaimed some of the main properties such as the movement's current headquarters, Mosque Maryam, thus ensuring the continuity of some of the most visible traditions that were introduced by Elijah. The changes in the moment were captured by the restoration of the internal appearance of Mosque Maryam to its original form under Elijah.

IV: Internal Tensions and External Interventions: Prophet or Profit?

As indicated above, although the court case was mainly about the distribution of the Nation of Islam properties, throughout the process the court had to address many societal, religious and legal questions surrounding the NOI and thus had the opportunity to assess many of the movement's unconventional positions. One of the questions that the court addressed was whether donations to the NOI were the property of the movement or its leader, Elijah. One group argued that the leadership status of Elijah was used in the solicitation of the support donations which were described as being tax exempt and thus meant to support the movement's social services. What complicated the issue however was that donations collected for the poor were used by the movement to invest in different properties and businesses. Consistent with its ideology, the movement wanted to create economic self-sufficiency. Thus, donations of all kinds were meant to be invested in different areas for profits that could then be reinvested into the movement. This framework created the question of if and how a religious group can be for profit, and if so, who would have rightful ownership of the profits?

Under Elijah's leadership, the movement rose from being a small Detroit based movement to one with national prominence. The movement's message resonated with an increasing number of people:

> I appeal to all Muslims, and to all the members of the original Black Nation in America, to sacrifice at least five cents from each day's pay to create an "Economic Savings Program" to help fight unemployment, abominable housing, hunger, and nakedness of the 22 million black people here in America who continue to face these problems.

> We hope to set up a committee to teach and force our people to be clean: The Committee of Cleanliness. We already have such a committee in effect among the Muslims. It compels our people to clean their bodies as well as their houses... Until we enforce cleanliness among the people of our Nation and get them into the spirit of self-respect and the spirit of making themselves the equal of other civilized nations of the earth we will never be recognized as being fit members of any decent society of those nations.

> Send your quarters every week to Muhammad's Mosque No. 2 in Chicago, Illinois. These quarters will be banked until we have a million dollars to begin building a banking system...

We are asking you to help us enlarge our educational system so that our people can be educated. This we refer to as re-education into the knowledge of self, our history and the knowledge of the good things of life, of which we have been deprived. You can also aid us by subscribing to the Muhammad Speaks Newspaper.

May Allah bless our poor dependent people in America with better homes more money and better friendships among the nations of the earth. (Elijah Muhammad, The Message to the Black Man, 1965)[20]

From 1934 to 1975 the movement's membership reached, according to some, 600,000 (based on the distribution of *Final Call*, though real numbers are always disputed) and the Nation's wealth included many properties including schools in 46 cities, restaurants, stores, a bank, a publishing company that prints the country's largest circulating black newspaper, and 15,000 acres of farmlands in three states that produce beef, eggs, poultry, milk, fruit and vegetables. Due to its personal and economic empowerment theology that tied individuals' empowerment to economic empowerment, the movement combined both profit and non-profit components. The movement's printed invitation for donations indicates how its theology and survival rested on the contributions of others and careful investments by the movement.

The Nation's calls for donations were encouraged as a religious injunction, social solidarity to help to those in need. Yet at some point separate donations were asked with the intention of covering the needs of the movement's leader and his family only. The movement's official solicitation below captures the complexity of the movement by including a carefully selected citation from the Quran (Surah Maryam verse 30-31) that praises both Jesus and charity and appeals to those who are new to Islam, giving an option to contribute to the leader directly and indicating that tax exempt status:

Charity is a principle of Islam second only to payer. Charity is a principle of every religion and we think it should be clearly discussed and understood as every other principle is.

In our life as negroes we are asked to contribute to everything under the sun but you can count on two fingers how many things we contributed to that really helped us to achieve freedom, justice, equality and recognition as a civilized people. In Islam under the divine guidance of the Honorable Elijah Muhammad for the first time we can see the benefits of charity.

Remember that charity wasn't something that was just added to Islam. It is as old as Islam itself and a quotation from the Holy Quran will bear out that all the prophets themselves were subject to the poor rate or charity: Jesus said: "Surely I am a servant of Allah: he has given to me the Book and me a prophet (not his son) and He has made me blessed wherever I may be and He has enjoined on me prayer and poor rate as long as I live" (19: 30-31). Enclosed here is a charity slip. This slip is actually a receipt for whatever moneys you contribute to the growth of your chosen religion and it is income tax-deductible. You should, therefore, save these slips to substantiate your deduction.

There are several charitable items listed which should have our support: No. 2 Poor: This treasury is for the use of our leader and teacher. With it the Honorable Elijah Muhammad sees to it that the poor and needy of our nation are looked after. This treasury is also designed

---

[20] Elijah Muhammad, *The Message to the Black Man*, Chicago:Final Call, 1965.

to see to it that our leader and teacher himself and his family want for nothing. The generosity of our leader is so well known that stories are told about his gifts throughout the Nation. For a man who has given his very soul and health to see to it that his people hear the truth, we cannot give too much.[21]

As the above text used by the movement shows it carefully situated itself at the intersection of Abrahamic faiths. Referring to the Quran where Jesus was mentioned appealed to the sensibilities of those who were new or old to Islam and had upbringing in different faiths. The intricate language used it the Nation's calls for contributions was not discursive. In fact, the Nation of Islam created an institutional framework that corresponded to the distinct parts of its ideology and included three parts:

- Poor Funds-- captured the movement's charity side and received donations

- Progressive Land Developers Inc. --captured movement's business side that sought to strengthen the movement's financial capacity through economic activities

- Temples-captures the movement's religious services

In order to under to understand Elijah's role in maintaining these three parts it is important to recognize the various roles assigned to his carefully crafted personality. The *Nation's Orientation Brochure* captures how Elijah's role was introduced to new members in terms that evoked the various roles of a civil rights activist or leader, a holy- person or a religious leader simultaneously:

The messenger has been a solitary man fighting for his ideas and principles but he has never become discouraged or embittered for his eloquence, wisdom and inspirations are derived from the triumphant Lord of the Worlds—ALLAH. Today the Honorable Elijah Muhammad stands alone as the unacclaimed leader of the American Negro and the beloved leader of we who follow him. In those of us who know him intimately he has inspired loyalty, given meaning to our lives, and articulated our aspirations for a "UNITED FRONT OF BLACK MEN." To us he is indeed an Anointed leader.

The messenger is a remarkable person, though he is the most self-effacing and modest of public men. He has lived and suffered in the midst of the hurly-burly of the American Negro's problems, and knows the hopes and aspirations of his people exceedingly well. Our leader and teacher is totally free from scheming and duplicity, honest to enemy and friend alike. For him we will lay down our lives. We swear allegiance to no other leader or combination of leaders.

Remember that! (Orientation Brochure)[22]

Although the court expected the movement's three parts (the charity, the investment and temple/religious services) to be clearly distinguished and managed, these three components were not separated, particularly during the early years of the movement. While the court described the lack of separation among the movement's different parts as "co-mingling", what was neglected was that the failure of the movement to separate its profit side from its non-profit side was due to its theological

---

[21] From the exhibition material of Estate of Muhammed, 463 N.E.2d 732 Ill. App. Ct. 1984.

[22] From the exhibition material of Estate of Muhammed, 463 N.E.2d 732 Ill. App. Ct. 1984.

and social commitments. It is important to note that the establishment and emergence of the movement coincided with the creation of the modern tax system in the US which regulated the declaration of non-profit status. The movement developed as the regulatory terrain was changing to meet new challenges and demands.[23]

V. Turning Points: Quests for Legitimacy and Unexpected Trajectories

Throughout its history, the Nation had always moved on two separate, yet intertwined, tracks in terms of its relationship with mainstream society and its rules and expectations. The nation described itself as "a nation within a nation," and carried with it a strong anti-establishment discourse while simultaneously choosing to operate within the parameters made acceptable by the legal and judicial system. In contrast to, or perhaps because of, the discourse that often described the Nation as illegitimate, the movement's discursive practices have carefully pushed the boundaries yet remained within the systemic boundaries. For instance, although the movement rejected the "draft," it opted for civil disobedience to protest the war/conscription, and accepted jail sentences for such actions. It sought legitimacy according to the standards laid out by the system it critiqued so vociferously, but that legitimacy always came with costs and new complications. Additionally, the legitimacy was coming from the institutions of a system whose legitimacy the members themselves questioned.

Beyond the surface of its highly contentious and polarizing language, the movement had a rather unexpected outlook that made inroads to its formal policies. For instance, although the nation adopted a strong anti-systemic language, it also sought to operate within the system and acquire legitimacy through multiple avenues. Given its multi-faceted appeal as a race, social-welfare, rights and religious movement, the movement's language has lent itself to different and contradictory interpretations. Perhaps due to diverse interpretations, some notes clearly stated that the movement did not challenge or denounce existing policies confronted as a movement.

For instance, in its solicitation for donations, the Nation's note included the following:

> "This [the nation's efforts] will not interfere with, the government's program for better housing conditions at all; it will only aid those who have never known anything in the way of help and those who do not even know that there is a government housing act to help dependent people. There are thousands of our people living in worse conditions than dogs and pigs. At least dogs are not bothered with too many rats and roaches in their houses because they kill them to keep out the uncleanliness and filth which dominate and create bad housing conditions." [24]

The tone of the announcement above was not exceptional. Despite the movement's sharp denouncements of the "white" establishment for putting shackles on the black community it still accepted the state's policies and powers. The movement declared many times it sought not to undermine but to improve the living conditions of its followers by building upon existing programs and filling the needs not adequately addressed by the state. It is not surprising therefore, that considering itself a religious group working in the name of public interest, the movement tried to acquire tax-exempt status for its temples and started its businesses by following acceptable business practices. Elijah's letter to his lawyers captures the movement's dual discourse that conveys distrust

---

[23] Paul Arnsberger, Melissa Ludlum, Margaret Riley, and Mark Stanton, "A History of the Tax-Exempt Sector: An SOI Perspective," *Statistics of Income Bulletin*, Winter 2008.

[24] From the exhibition material of Estate of Muhammed, 463 N.E.2d 732 Ill. App. Ct. 1984.

and seeks to gain legitimacy at the same time. It captures the movement's conviction that it would not be granted this status due to the social and political biases against it. Yet, instead of denouncing the tax policies, the movement declared its commitment to maintain its legitimacy at the expense of paying more in taxes. A letter typed by Elijah on February 1, 1971 to the movement's lawyer Newton Brozan based in New York indicated the Nation's overall sentiment about the movement's treatment:

> Thank you for your letter of January 8, 1971. Let us forget about this tax appeal for exemption. The government is not, by any means, willing to show me and my followers any favor. This, I am well aware of, and will not try again; even if takes half our income to pay tax, we will pay it.
>
> Thank you for your efforts that you have made over a year. I appreciate it. Please send me your bill for what you have been trying to do in the way of getting us tax exemption.
>
> Sincerely Elijah Muhammad [25]

Although the ultimate goal of economic separation was declared, one of the appeals of the movement has been its insistence on economic empowerment as inherent to political and spiritual independence. Thus, although the Poor Funds (the charity aspect of the movement) and Progressive Funds (investment side of the movement) are seen as contradictory by others, for the movement they were necessarily related projects. Given the complicated nature of the movement, the court consistently tried to determine if the nation of Islam was a religion (thus its property needed to be inherited by the movement), or a private venture or organization under the leadership of Elijah. Facing the various components of the Nation, the following excerpt from the court proceedings offers an example of how the court sought to make sense of the identity of the movement and reflected on one definition of the movement as a religious organization:

> Court: To be honest it was more than a religious organization.
>
> Mr. Heinz: Certainly was. I can see that
>
> Court: That's where we have a problem because if we merely say that the Nation of Islam is a just religious organization we are not being accurate.
>
> Mr. Heinz: I can see that it was more than religious organization your Honor.
>
> Court: Because as he has indicated in the orientation brochure and all of the evidence indicated the nation of Islam really was a nation within a nation, intended to create a nation composed of black people.[26]

The exchange above, and other similar lines of questions, dominated the court's questions and that "nation within a nation" concept was suggested by Judge Budzinski as the working definition of NOI without answering any of the questions about what "religious organization plus" meant institutionally and legally. For instance, would Nation of Islam INC. be considered as an organic expansion of the movement due to its theology and goals? Devoid of a thorough review of the movement's theology, perhaps it's not surprising that the circuit and appellate courts delivered four distinct decisions declaring the movement a private organization and a religion.

---

[25] *ibid*

[26] *ibid*

Although its policies were contentious, the Nation's efforts were officially recognized by Mayor Richard J. Daley and Governor Dan Walker. In fact, the last Savior Dinner (a yearly traditional dinner for the movement) held before Elijah Muhammad's death, was endorsed by official representatives of the Mayor and Governor and participation was encouraged to raise funds for the movement's Southside hospital project.[27] That recognition continues to be an important part of the movement's discourse especially when its legitimacy is questioned. Along with its motto "we turn boys to men", the movement presents it mission as creating model US citizens. In fact, Elijah described his followers:

> "Despite the unfavorable attitude of those in power (Government) toward my followers, I must emphatically deny their being "subversive" in any way or manner whatsoever. How could anyone expect trouble of any kind from a peace-loving people who aren't even allowed to carry a pen-knife on them at any time? My followers, in fact, are the BEST CITIZENS this country has got, because they are believers in Islam, the Religion of Peace, and in Righteousness, not evil, and they can do no wrong to anyone."[28]

Although the followers of the Nation might be defiant, Elijah Muhammad argued, they remain defiant within the boundaries of the law.

Conclusion

The sudden rise of the Nation from the preaching of two individuals, Ward (1929-1934) and later Elijah (1934-1975), to an organization with national prominence came with many theological adaptations and organizational challenges. Due to its theology, the nation focused both on spiritual and economic independence, and did not see any difference between the two. Although its theology was anti-systemic, it consistently sought to legitimize itself through carving out a place in the market system and developing a theologically hybrid language. In its theology, the movement combined the tenets from (i) orthodox (universal) Islamic claims (which denounce any discrimination based on race) and (ii) racialized discourse that claims the root of black problems is the internalization of the slave mentality and lost sense of the self and the original status. Due to the fact that economic empowerment is inherent to its theological empowerment, The NOI did not fit any institutional template (non-profit vs. profit, organization vs. religion) that typically helps guide judicial decisions.

The Nation of Islam's trial posed the question of if and when a group is considered as religious. Given the Supreme Court's decisions on religion one might ask if and how the court defined its own criteria of what it means to be a religious group. For instance, in the United States v. Seeger (1965) the court treated any beliefs as religious if a given belief was sincere and meaningful and occupied a similar place in the life of its possessor parallel to that filled by the orthodox belief in God.[29] In Welsh v. United States (1970) the court let followers say the final word by describing religion as "deeply and sincerely held moral and ethical beliefs" and thus granting those groups holding such beliefs the status of religious.[30] The court's decision to treat Elijah Muhammad's properties as his personal property suggests that the court gave more weight to the claims that reduced the nation to a private venture;

---

[27] Chicago Tribune, *No Elijah but Dinner is a Success*, March 3,1974.

[28] Elijah, Muhammad. (1957) The supreme wisdom: solution to the so-called Negroes problem. Newport News, VA ; National NewportNews.

[29] United States v. Seeger, 380 U.S. 163 (1965) United States v. Seeger, No. 50 March 8, 1965 (380 U.S.163).

[30] Welsh v. United States (No. 76) January 20, 1970 (398 U.S.333)

whether the supporters treated the group as religious or the nation considered itself a religion did not change the result.

Although the Nation of Islam's theology remains controversial and it is often assessed in a vacuum, it is important to notice that since its inception the movement has incorporated some monotheistic, Abrahamic religious beliefs as well as non-monotheistic ideas from its immediate intellectual environment. Self-reliance and emancipation against historical and present injustices took priority over religious puritanism. Given its hybrid theology and organizational structure, the lower court's decision to redistribute the Nation's wealth resulted in the overall decline in its organizational capacity and the dominance of one branch over the other. The decision also reinforced the impact of the well entrenched dichotomies or markers that rendered the movement as an anti-systemic fringe group. The court decision confirmed that the movement fell in a gray area left by the boundaries drawn by the binaries of Religion vs. Cult, Native vs. Migrant, City vs. Colony, Separatist vs Integrationist. While the movement's financial success raised many questions about the proper uses of funds, the nation's projects took many distinct forms.

It is important to note that two years prior to the beginning of its court case, the Nation was soliciting funds to complete its south-side Chicago project. Due to the impact and necessity of such a project, the nation garnered a wide range of support. As noted above, the 1974 Savior Day was recognized by the city's mayor and all residents were invited to support the nation's efforts. Such endorsements were based on the Nation's practices and its social projects, especially its Southside Chicago Hospital. Not only did such projects become defunct due to the redistribution of the funds but also the movement lost its social appeal. Given the decline in the movement's branch that sought to promote a more inclusive theology, one might argue that the court decision both reflected the corrosive social image of the Nation (e.g., cult promoting private profit) held by some in the 'mainstream' and served as a block thwarting the movement's development as a more inclusive and universal social movement working to better the lives of a marginalized community. Such an assessment indicates that instead of viewing unconventional movements like the Nation as in tension with the state, we might see them as the output of some state policies. In other words, neither the Nation's emergence nor the decline in its power after the early 1980s is a process beyond the societal and state dynamics; instead they are the outcome of the negotiations between the state and multiple actors that came to speak on behalf of the Nation with different outcomes.

References

Carter, Shawn. 2002, 'The Economic Philosophy of Marcus Garvey', Western Journal Of Black Studies, 26:1.

Dagnini, Jérémie Kroubo. 2008. "Marcus Garvey: A Controversial Figure in the History of Pan-Africanism." Journal Of Pan African Studies 2, no. 3: 198-208.

Deen Warith, "The Lost-Found Nation," The Bilalian News, Vol.1, no.1 November 14, 1975.

Erdmann Doane Beynon, "The Voodoo Cult Among Negro Migrants in Detroit," American Journal of Sociology. Vol. 43 (July 1937 – May 1938). Pp. 894-907.

Grant, C. Negro with a Hat: The Rise and Fall of Marcus Garvey. Oxford University Press, 2008.

Hughes, Frank. 1943. "Experts Trace Race Conflicts To Dixie Exodus." Chicago Tribune.

Jalal, A. 2005. Self and Sovereignty: Individual and Community in South Asian Islam since 1850. London: Routledge.

Johnson, Sylvester A. 2010. "The Rise of Black Ethnics: The Ethnic Turn in African American Religions, 1916-1945." Religion & American Culture 20, no. 2: 125-163

Jones, Elias F. "Black Hebrews: The Quest for Authentic Identity." The Journal of Religious Thought, vol. 44, no. 2, 1988, pp. 35.

Mubashshir, Debra Washington. 2001. "Forgotten Fruit of the City: Chicago and the Moorish Science Temple of America." Cross Currents 51, no. 1: 6

Muhammad, Elijah. 1957. The Supreme Wisdom: Solution to the So-Called Negroes Problem. Newport News, VA; National Newport News.

Elijah Muhammad, 1965. The Message to the Black Man, Chicago:Final Call.

Murphy, E. 2016. From Sufism to Ahmadiyya: a Muslim minority movement in South Asia. Contemporary South Asia, 24(2), 214-215.

Nance, Susan. 2002. "Respectability and Representation: The Moorish Science Temple, Morocco, and Black Public Culture in 1920s Chicago." American Quarterly 54, no. 4: 623.

Nipson, Herb. 1961. "Astute Study of a Hate Group". Chicago Tribune. May 15.

Page, Clarence. 1974. "No Elijah but Dinner is a Success." Chicago Tribune. March 3.

United States v. Seeger, 1965. 380 U.S. 163

Vardat, Scott J. 2013. "Drew Ali And The Moorish Science Temple Of America: A Minor Rhetoric Of Black Nationalism." Rhetoric & Public Affairs 16, no. 4: 685-717.

Walter, H. A. 1918. The Aḥmadīya Movement. Oxford University Press.

Welsh v. United States, 1970. 398 U.S. 333

Williams, Armstrong. 2015. "The Nation of Islam Could Be Chicago's Saviour." The Hill. October 5.

Wynia, Elly. 1994. The Church of God and Saints of Christ: The Rise of Black Jews. Milton Park: Taylor and Francis.

International Journal of Religion
November 2020
Volume: 1 | Number 1 | pp. 77 – 90
ISSN: 2633-352X (Print) | ISSN: 2633-3538 (Online)
journals.tplondon.com/ijor

TRANSNATIONAL PRESS®
LONDON

First Submitted: 31 July 2020 Accepted: 1 November 2020
DOI: https://doi.org/10.33182/ijor.v1i1.1106

Finding the Right Islam for the Maldives: Political Transformation and State-Responses to Growing Religious Dissent

La Toya Waha[1]

Abstract

At the first glance, the Maldives appear not to be prone to religious conflict. The archipelago state comprises a religiously and ethnically homogenous society, the different islands have been subject to shared Islamic rule for centuries and even constitutionally religious homogeneity is granted by making every citizen a Muslim and religious diversity prevented by limiting naturalisation to a specific Muslim group. Yet, today allegations of a threat to Islam play a major role in political mobilisation, the Maldives are faced with Islamist violence, and Maldivians have joined the Islamic State and al Qaeda in disproportionally high numbers. The paper seeks to find an answer to the question of how the repression of dissent under the Gayoom regime and the expansion and rise of violent Islamism relate in the Maldivian context. Next to the theoretical model, the paper will provide an introduction to the Maldivian political culture and the reasons for changes therein. It will shed light on the emergence of three major Islamic streams in the Maldivian society, which stood opposed to one another by the late 1990s and early 2000s, and show how Gayoom's state repression of dissent initiated an escalation process and furthered Islamist violent politics. The paper will argue that while state repression of dissent played a significant role in the repertoire selection of Islamic non-state agents, the introduction of fundamentalist Islamic interpretations through migration, educational exchange programmes and transnational actors have laid the ground for violence in the Maldives.

Keywords: *Transnationalism; political violence; Maldives; contentious politics; state repression; migration; Islamic fundamentalism.*

Introduction

The Maldives have long been regarded not only as paradise for tourists from all over the world, but also as a paradise for adherents of a moderate and non-violent Islam; a place where fundamentalist interpretations of Islam have not been put into practise and where women enjoy rare freedoms from religiously sanctioned suppression. Moreover, the population's relative ethnic, linguist and religious homogeneity laid ground to the hope that Maldivians would be spared from intercommunal violence and terrorism, which plagued the diverse neighbouring South Asian states. Several internally initiated political reforms were evaluated as positive steps towards a modern state, for example, the introduction of a constitution and a parliament (*Majlis*), which terminated the hereditary handover of power and turned the Sultanate into a constitutional monarchy in 1932, or the creation of the first Maldivian republic in 1953. Despite a period of increased political tension and turmoil from 1954 to the creation of the second republic in 1968, which comprised a violently ended secessionist movement of the southern atolls and the independence from British protectorate in 1965, the Maldives were not considered a negative exception of the South Asian rule. The Maldives opened to the world by inviting tourists in the 1970s and by joining several multilateral organisations, including

---

[1] La Toya Waha, PhD, Konrad-Adenauer-Stiftung, Singapore. E-mail: latoya.waha@kas.de

the United Nations, the Non-Alignment Movement, and – even as a founding member – the South Asian Association for Regional Cooperation (SAARC). In the 1980s, the Maldives sought greater visibility in the world and engaged actively in organisations, such as the Organisation for the Islamic Conference (OIC). And despite several foreign attempts to use Maldivian islands as military posts, Maldives managed not to be drawn directly into great power rivalry in the region, first between the US and the USSR and later India and China (Phadnis and Luithui, 1981). With the transition from the authoritarian president Maumoon Abdul Gayoom to Maldivian Democratic Party (MDP) head Mohamed Nasheed in 2008, the Maldives have moreover raised the hope for a functioning Muslim democracy, in which dissent and the acceptance of human rights were possible.

Today, the Maldives are drawn to authoritarian regimes; Maldives joined the Chinese Belt and Road Initiative (BRI) and received large funds from Saudi Arabia (Naseed, 2015: 108). The Maldivian society is polarised, which frequently shows in the contention around the implementation of *hudud* punishments.[2] Maldivians travelled to join the Islamic State (IS) in Syria in disproportional numbers, and are frequently found involved in Islamist attacks in the region and engaging in transnational terrorist networks, such as al Qaeda or Lashkar-e-Taiba (LeT) (Hafeez, 2008: 253). Women wear the burqa and the numbers of female circumcision have increased significantly.[3] Secular bloggers are murdered[4] and religions other than Sunni Islam violently suppressed (ACFHR, 2005). And despite the hope which arose from the surprising electoral success of MDP supported presidential candidate Ibrahim Mohamed Solih in 2018, the influence over key institutions by supporters of former authoritarian rulers appears unbroken. Even worse, the Islamic State (IS) has laid hand on the islands state and conducted its first terrorist attack in the country in April 2020. While writing, anti-government protests challenge the democratic forces currently in power, like, in the protest leading to the resignation of President Nasheed in 2012, with increasingly religious overtones.

This paper seeks to explain the expansion of violent Islamism in the Maldives by analysing how state responses to religious dissent have influenced the transformation of Maldivian politics and non-state actors' repertoire from non-violent to violent means of contention. Thereby, the paper draws on a theoretical model explaining shifts in political behaviour – repertoire – of non-state actors. Based on the analysis of the core hypothesis and its results, the paper shows how and why the repertoire of the fundamentalist religious-political agents has changed. Placing the analysis of the Gayoom presidency into context, the paper will first give a short introduction into the political culture of the Maldives and the changes herein introduced by the long-term powerholder Maumoon Abdul Gayoom. It will then show the emergence of three major Islamic streams in the Maldivian society, which stood opposed to one another by the late 1990s and early 2000s. It will be shown how Gayoom's state repression of dissent initiated an escalation process and the developments towards Islamist violent politics before and during the regime change in 2008 will be outlined. Finally, a conclusion will be drawn.

---

[2] See for example the controversy about the punishment of the raped teenage girl in 2013 (Elliott, 2013).

[3] According to Dawson et al., "In 2011, Dr Iyaz Abdul Latheef, the Vice President of the Fiqh Academy, the primary religious academy in the Maldives, encouraged the practice during a broadcast on national radio" (Dawson et al., 2020: 9).

[4] The rationale for killing the secular blogger Yameen Rasheed in 2017 was that the victim was believed to have "mocked religion" (Maldives Independent, 2017).

Theory and Method

The paper seeks to understand the impact of state responsiveness on agents' repertoire. What is to be explained, thus, is the change of behaviour of a certain, here religious, political agent towards the application of violence[5]. The theoretical model, which serves as the basis for this analysis, is based on rational choice theory and has been investigated on in the case of violent Buddhist monks in Sri Lanka (see Waha, 2018). It assumes behaviour to be the result of a decision making process. Related to the theory of human motivation, it is assumed that in such a process, the agent elaborates aims based on basic desires, in line with an overall aim, analyses his current conditions, including the constraints for the achievement of the desired end, and selects the behavioural alternative relating the current condition and the desired end, which, based on his cognitive models, he thinks serves his ends best. In the course of decision making, the agent weighs costs and benefits with regard to 1) the value of the aim, also in relation to his overall aim ('the good life'), 2) the incentives provided by the opportunity structure as by the agent's evaluation which is grounded in the agent's 3) cognitive models (worldviews).

Violence as a costly form of behaviour is considered to be chosen in situations, in which an agent seeks to prevail. This is often the case when an agent pursues a high-valued aim or perceives important values to be severely threatened. In situations of contention, where agents seek to and/or need to prevail escalation – that is the step-like increase in the costs of behaviour[6] – is likely. At the same time, the opportunity structure, which includes the opponent, sets incentives for certain behaviours (Waha, 2018: 553).

It is hypothesised that if in the context of contention of identity – here Muslim identity in the Maldives – state elites lack to be responsive, collective identity elites – here elites of the three relevant streams – are likely to enter a process of escalation/escalate. Based on the conceptualisation by Tilly and Tarrow, *contentious politics of identity* is defined as interactions, in which agents make claims bearing on someone else's identity interests, leading to coordinated efforts on behalf of a shared collective identity, in which governments are involved as targets, initiators of claims, or third parties (see Tilly and Tarrow, 2007: 4). The operationalisation thereof is collective action in the name of an Islamic community which bears on the identity-interests or programmes of another agent, who makes an own value-proposal for the Islamic community in the Maldives, whereby the government is involved as a target, initiator of claims, or third party.

The independent variable (IV) of the given hypothesis is state responsiveness. *State responsiveness* refers to the ability or willingness of the state elites, in this case particularly the Maldivian president, to allow for the accommodation of the claims considered as important by the contending opponent within the state. The operationalisation thereof are actions which indicate accommodation, like making concessions to another stream's demands, etc.; lacking state responsiveness refers to the lack of such behaviour and/or actions which are directed against the claims made by the contending opponent (see Waha, 2018: 546). The dependent variable (DV) is escalation. *Escalation* is defined as the "step-like increase" in (the costs of) means (see Zartman, 2008: 195). It shall be operationalised as the application of increasingly costly means, ranging from 1) means allowed to means tolerated to means

---

[5] Violence is defined as "the intentional use of physical force by an agent or agents [...] threatened or actual, against the self, another person, against a group or community, or an object in order to damage, hurt or injure physically and/or psychologically, or kill" (Waha, 2018: 75), and considered to be a form of human behaviour.

[6] Based on the definition of escalation as "a step-like increase in the nature of conflict" (Zartman, 2008: 195).

prohibited by the state order[7]; ranging from 2) means with no or little risk to means with high risk for the participating agents; and 3) means ranging from non-violence to violence in the political sphere, and within violence 4) ranging from threats to apply violence to attacks against things and finally to attacks against beings, which are ranging from 5) damage to destruction and from harm to killing (Waha, 2018: 546f.).

The *opportunity structure* shall be, based on an extension of Tilly and Tarrow's concept, defined as features of an agent's environment that facilitate or inhibit an agent's actions and changes in those features, offering the agent opportunities and risks (Tilly and Tarrow, 2007: 49). Opportunity structure is operationalised as an agent's statement regarding his evaluation of the environment's opportunities and risks, and claimed or actual changes therein. Thereby a special focus is put on the evaluations of relations to the Maldivian ruling elite and to the members of their community, the evaluation of features of their organisation or networks, of the society as well as of the international community as favourable or unfavourable to the Islamists' aim achievement (Waha 2018: 553). *Means selection* is meant to be the rational decision for a behaviour as a means towards an end. It is operationalised as applied (collective) behaviour by members of the group.

The qualitative method which unifies the rational choice theory-based modelling with the closer analysis of the contextual givens of a case is the method of "analytic narrative" presented by Bates et al. (1998). The analytic narrative follows a micro-level approach towards the analysis of political events and outcomes. The central characteristics of this approach are the focus on agents and the accommodation of "the actors' preferences, their perceptions, their evaluation of alternatives, the information they possess, the expectations they form, the strategies they adopt, and the constraints that limit their actions" into the analysis (Bates et al., 1998: 11). According to Bates et al., the aim of the method is to "piece together the story that accounts for the outcome of interest" (Bates et. al., 1998: 11) and "to cut deeply into the specifics of a time and a place, and to locate and trace the processes that generate the outcome of interest" (Bates et al., 1998: 12). The narrative begins with a general introduction into the local specifics, and then introduces the sequence under investigation. The focus of the present sequence is the 1990s and early 2000s until the power transition in 2008.

The access to data in the Maldives is limited as is the academic treatment (Naseem, 2015: 99). Most research is conducted from outside the Maldives, potentially a consequence of the lack of higher education institutions which treat other subjects than Islam. For the sources, the author draws mainly on newspaper articles in newspapers from the Maldives and neighbouring countries as well as international news agencies. Beyond that, primary sources of political agents, like publications, interviews in the national or international media and social media comments – when already available at the time – are used. During repression, some Maldivian dissidents have published comments in newspapers in neighbouring countries, most notably in Sri Lanka (e.g. The Island). These sources are drawn on as well. The information provided by the sources is then triangulated.

Islam, Authority and Political Culture in the Maldives

Since the establishment of the Sultanate on the Maldivian islands, the subsequent expansion of state structures and enforcement of Islam for social and political control over the vastly dispersed Maldivian islands, there was little space for religious and political diversity. With the conversion of

---

[7] Tilly and Tarrow present different sorts of episodes of repertoire based on their reviewed literature. These are 1) legal, illegal but tolerated, illegal but tolerated in some circumstances, repressed and new means of claim making, and 2) conventional, confrontational and violent means of claim making (see Tilly and Tarrow, 2007: 50-51).

the last Buddhist king, powerholders sought to destroy the Buddhist religious structures and social institutions on the islands. Buddhist monks were killed, temples and shrines destroyed, and the population forced to convert (Maloney, 1980). The adoption of Islam did not only serve as a bridge to the Arab traders but has been a central element of the Sultanate's rule and its upholding of social and political order.

The geography of the Maldives poses a special challenge to the establishment of centralised control due to the wide dispersion of atolls and islands, among others given the time it takes to reach from one to the other by boat. In this context, Islam has become a framework for social and political order, next to the islands' and atolls' headmen, who could reinforce the centre's control locally. The tight religious rules and compulsory participation in daily religious rituals enabled the control of individuals even in the remote islands far away from the capital. Furthermore, the shared religion enabled a shared sense of belonging among the population, whose contact to one another was widely limited to the own island community. Islam further helped to keep the sense of belonging and social cohesion among the Muslim Maldivians as it allowed for a cultural barrier to the neighbouring powers, Hindu India and Buddhist Sri Lanka, and as such as the means to prevent foreign control and influence over the islands on religious lines (Maloney, 1980). Stories of Muslims, who were claimed central in defeating the Portuguese' attempt to colonise the Maldivian islands, project Islam as the reason for the strength to prevent Christian invasion. Given that the neighbouring states were colonised, while the Maldives were widely left unimpacted from foreign control over internal affairs, Islam was considered the force enabling the sovereignty of the country.

Despite the distinct religious and linguistic homogeneity, Maldivian politics were factious. Although the Sultanate lasted several hundred years, it was characterised by political intrigues at the court. To a large extent, political participation by selected members of the society was given through the installation of political leaders, like the island's and the atoll's headmen, to a certain extent even the Sultan, and political dissent was mainly expressed through the removal of political figures through popular protest or court intrigue. In the 'modern' Maldives, petitions were political means of interest expression. By and large, however, once a political leader was selected and installed, Maldivians accepted his authority and his decisions (Maloney, 1980). Dissent was expressed through the removal of people from office rather than demanding to change the content of policies and decisions. This practice did not change despite the introduction of a constitution in 1932, the abolishment of the monarchy, or the establishment of the first republic in 1953. Coups are found in the different regimes and remain part of Maldivian politics until today.

Particularly during the presidency of Gayoom (1978-2008) and the contentious situation of the foreign affairs in the Indian ocean at the time, shaped by the great power rivalry between the USSR and the United States, India's growing hegemonic interests, and later Chinese search for influence in the region (Phadnis and Luithi, 1981; Malik, 2001), the need was felt to secure Maldivian sovereignty and interests through balanced international relations on the one hand, and internal hegemony and control of politics and religion alike on the other. Foreign presence and exchange with the local population were sought to be kept at a minimum.

The secessionist movement (1956-1964) following the British presence on Gan thereby served as a poignant example. The most southern atolls had retained their own specific identity and sought to independently benefit from the wealth the British military base in Gan generated. However, the secession movement was defeated by police action from 1959 to 1960 and thereafter withered away. The impact of the British on local affairs was resented (Maloney, 1980: 203-206). Strength was a central requirement in the political realm. As mentioned earlier, Maldivian politics have been shaped by political intrigues throughout the Sultanate and the constitutional times alike. Coups and overthrows have been frequent, the weakness of a leader was quickly exploited and likely to end his term. The projection of strength became an important way to retain power and office. Also, Gayoom's three decades of authoritarian rule have witnessed several coup attempts. Most notable was the coup, which could only be ended by Indian forces in 1988. A Tamil militant organisation from Sri Lanka, the People Liberation Organisation of Tamil Eelam (PLOTE) served as a 'private' force of a Maldivian businessman living in Sri Lanka. Indian Special Forces had ended the coup which had severely challenged the Maldivian government (Haider, 2017: 45-46).

Since the Sultanate and beyond, Islam has legitimised power, served as a basis and the justification of authority and rule. Sharia was the basis for law and social order. Islam was considered the guarantor of political power, social control, as well as national unity and independence from foreign influences and control, most notably from the European colonial powers (Amir, 2011). Islam, thus, was understood as an instrument for unity and security in and of the Maldives (ACFHR, 2005: 4).

These aspects of the Maldives' political culture, Gayoom has carried to extremes, and has united the secular and religious power onto himself. Throughout his thirty-years lasting presidency, Gayoom has brought under his control the executive, legislative, judiciary, and religious pillars of power in the Maldives.

Where does the Dissent come from? The Three Major Streams of Islam in the Maldives

The first stream builds on the culturally grounded and widely practised Islam in the Maldives. This form of practice was described as dominant in the 1970s by Maloney (1980). Traditionally, sharia took a central role in state and social rules, but there were little Islamic teaching and knowledge of the scripts in the Maldives (Amir, 2011). While local officials were required to learn Arabic and to take basic courses for Quran and sharia, deeper Islamic education was rare on the islands state. Pre-Islamic traditions continued to influence the rather ritualistic practice of Islam, rites as well as the belief system. Myths from pre-Islamic times, like the Rannamaari (a myth about a sea goddess) or the inclination towards non-violence – including the aversion towards violence against animals – remained part of Maldivian life (Maloney, 1980). Certain social structures and practices, too, found continuation in the Muslim Maldivian society. As such, women were neither required to cover themselves completely nor to wear any form of veil, despite frequent attempts by foreign religious scholars to change it. While women in their older age covered their hair, this was less for religious purposes or requirements. Despite frequently practised rituals of female circumcision and the possibility for women to get married – and divorced – without their own presence in the respective ritual, relative to other Muslim countries at the time and today women enjoyed wider liberties and rights in the Maldives; their participation in certain areas of social life – except for religious rituals – was possible and the mixing of sexes for festivities and evening meetings was allowed on some islands. Although there were variations in the strictness of the application of religious rules, the formal, ritualistic practice of Islam was upheld. As such, for example, men's participation in the Friday prayers in the mosques prescribed by the state was mandatory and violations were punished. Sharia law was the basis of social and political life and physical punishment was practised. However, *hudud* punishments, like cutting off hands, were not welcomed by the wider society and rejected for the violence (Maloney, 1980). While Islamic rituals took a prominent role in the everyday life of the people, the collective identity was widely shaped by the belongingness to an island and atoll; being a Muslim, in turn, was taken as a given. Muslim identity was however stressed in delineation to foreigners. Christians were particularly disliked and pride was taken in the Maldivians' resistance towards Portuguese attempts to colonise the islands, seen as a victory of Islam over Christianity (ibid.). This outlined a culturally-grounded Islam, which might be considered as the indigenous "Maldivian Islam".

The second stream resulted from a kind of Islamic revivalism in the Maldives and was heavily influenced by then-president Gayoom. Gayoom lived longer parts of his childhood and young adult life abroad, first for schooling in Sri Lanka (length unplanned) and then for most of the time for Islamic education and studies in Egypt, most notably the Al-Azhar University. When Gayoom returned to the Maldives, the country's wider population and good parts of the political elite lacked deep knowledge and grounded education in Islam – despite political authority and the state's legitimacy had been built on Islam. Gayoom, who had gained a degree in Islamic studies and taught Islam in Nigeria, thus brought with him superior religious credentials. Selected by *Majlis* as the sole candidate, Gayoom became president in 1978. After assuming office, Gayoom promoted religious education and education programmes to other Muslim countries (Naseem, 2015: 114). Like in other countries in the region, the Maldives' economic situation provided little opportunities for self-actualisation and economic success. The Maldives under Gayoom's presidency, however, provided little or no opportunity for higher education, and, despite some English medium schools, instead, a focus was largely placed on religious education. The country's best students were provided with scholarships, often funded by other Muslim majoritarian countries like Pakistan and Saudi Arabia, and were sent abroad for madrassa education. A sort of Islamic revivalism in the Maldives accompanied Gayoom's drive for religious education and was furthered by Islamic educated figures, who, like Gayoom, had been educated abroad (Van Es, 2008). Gayoom united the secular and religious powers and authority in the country in the office of the president, which he held for thirty years. He turned himself into the Supreme Authority of Islamic Affairs and as such sought to determine the "right" Maldivian Islam. In delineation to foreign and domestic contenders of his position, he forged a Maldivian national identity mostly based on Islam (Van Es, 2008). As the religious and secular authority, it was on Gayoom to decide what was the right Islam and who was allowed to discuss it. Only a small circle was authorised to discuss Islamic issues, only authorised circles were allowed to preach Islam, and only according to Gayoom's interpretations. Dissenters, irrespective of them speaking up for more moderate or more fundamentalist interpretations, were silenced and severely punished (ACFHR, 2005). The merger of secular and religious authority, the equalling of Islamic and Maldivian identity, and the exclusivity of religious interpretation have resulted in Gayoom's widely believed and dispersed narrative of a homogenous Maldives and the special moderate Maldivian Islam. Gayoom's drawing on the teachings, the rejection of inner-Islamic plurality – let alone religious diversity –, the streamlining of thought, practice and interpretation, which included the denying of pre-Islamic traditions and influences, has turned the "moderate Maldivian Islam" in a mere catchword.

A third stream emerged in the Maldives in the course of the late 1980s and 1990s. On the one hand, the Maldivian students who had studied Islamic studies abroad were returning to the islands state. Educated in madrassas and Islamic universities in Pakistan, Saudi Arabia, Yemen, Qatar, Kuwait, Libya or Egypt (Van Es, 2008), the graduates brought back different interpretations of Islam. Rejecting the president as the major religious authority, they not only questioned Gayoom's religious orders but claimed the sole truth for their learned interpretations. While themselves dissenting the country's authority, they rejected any dissent from their interpretation themselves. On the other hand, foreign international agents inspired by the pan-Islamic movement came to the Maldives. With them came a transnational Islamic identity, which promoted Islamic unity beyond nations and state boundaries. The unity of Muslims is entailed in the Quran by the concept of the *umma* (the community of believers), similarly, pan-Islamism aimed at creating a "formal political unity in the Muslim world" dates back to Islamic thinkers in the late nineteenth and early twentieth century (Hegghammer, 2010: 17). It was, however, revived in the 1960s and 1970s in Saudi Arabia, based on "Saudi King Faisal's call for coordination and mutual aid between Muslim countries" and furthered the "notion of 'Muslim solidarity' (*al-tadamun al-islami*)" (Hegghammer, 2010: 17). "To promote pan-Islamism, King Faisal established a number of institutions at the […] supranational level which worked to promote cooperation, mutual solidarity and religious awareness in the Muslim world" of which the two most important were the Muslim World League (MWL) and the Organisation of the Islamic Conference (OIC) (Hegghammer, 2010: 18). The populist manifestation of pan-Islamism was fostered by the activities of such international Islamic organisations and was characterised by "a particularly alarmist discourse about external threats to the umma and the need for grassroots inter-Muslim assistance" (Hegghammer, 2010: 18). In the course of time, the issue was securitised and the threat to Islam and the Muslims – most notably by Christians – and the need to protect them became a prominent feature of their rhetoric and propaganda. Such populist pan-Islamists received funding from Saudi Arabia, engaged in different regions in the world and only cooperated with local governments where convenient (Hegghammer, 2010: 18). The Maldives had joined the OIC already in 1976 (Ministry of Economic Development) but became an active member only during Gayoom's regime in the 1980s (Amir, 2011). In the 1990s, the first MWL office opened in the capital Male, but remained largely inactive, until a new permanent office was opened in 2013 (Minivan News, 2013). But at the subnational level, religious teachers, preachers and Islamic NGOs with such populist pan-Islamic background have come to and established themselves in the Maldives in the course of the 1990s. They are fundamentalist, i.e. demand a literal reading of the Quran, Salafi, i.e. seek to live like in the times of the prophet Mohammad, and, given they receive funds from Saudi Arabia, promote Wahhabism. During the late 1990s and particularly in the consequence of the tsunami in 2004, which was followed by a flood of Islamic relief organisations with own political agendas, Islamic transnational organisations established themselves and took guidance over entire islands.[8] As a consequence, many new "solely right and true" interpretations of Islam emerged.

Lacking State Responsiveness and Escalation

When Gayoom took power in 1978, his religious credentials were hardly met, and few would contend his views on a religiously educated basis. While his views and interpretations trespassed the Maldives' religious-cultural traditions and went against the in fact existing religious diversity (including non-believers and cultural practitioners), due to his religious credentials he was able to underpin the legitimacy of his decisions and authority. This, however, changed particularly in the course of the 1990s, when Maldivian students, educated abroad, returned home and foreign graduates came to the Maldives to do Islamic "service". Gayoom's – and with him the Maldives' political system's – legitimacy was challenged. Even more, due to Gayoom's merger of religious and secular authority, each challenge to his religious views equalled a challenge to his secular power.

The contention of religion significantly increased throughout the late 1990s. To secure his position, Gayoom, who also controlled security forces and judiciary through established networks of supporters (Naseem, 2015: 101), employed substantial force to repress religious as well as political dissent. Through the arrival of new ideals of state and society accompanying the pan-Islamist fundamentalists, simultaneously rising demands for freedom and democracy, and the overall growing

---

[8] Based on a conversation with a Maldivian representative in March 2020.

rejection of Gayoom's style of governance, political and religious dissent increasingly became inseparable. The building pressure from below was met with state repression rather than responsiveness. According to a report by local journalists, men were detained for publicly following other forms of Islam (ACFHR, 2005). Many claim to have been tortured. The torture, according to an alleged victim included, among others, forcible shaving, while "using chilli sauce as shaving cream" (Van Es, 2008).

Contention crystallised on the female covering and the burqa. As mentioned above, the burqa and full coverage were not required in Maldivian Islamic practice. In the fundamentalist Salafi and Wahhabi circles, however, the covering of the whole female body was claimed to be mandatory. Increasingly, women across several islands, including in the capital Male, began to wear the burqa. This has been – and is – a public contestation of both, the state's religious authority as well as the traditional culturally-grounded Maldivian Islam. In response to this challenge to authority, the government legally prohibited wearing a burqa. The government justified this decision with security reasons. The alleged secular cause to prohibit the implementation of a – according to their view – religious rule, instilled anger in such fundamentalist groups. While men, who publicly rejected Gayoom's form of Islam, were frequently arrested in the course of the 1990s and early 2000s the wearing of the burqa has continued and in some places increased significantly. For men expressing their dissent, yet, punishment was harsh.

To serve the aims elaborated by the fundamentalists' cognitive models new and alternative means of action were sought. One alternative to the engagement within the Maldives was provided by the transnational Islamist networks with which Maldivian youth had come in touch through the madrassa education programmes abroad. These networks gained publicity in 2002 when Maldivian Ibrahim Fauzee was arrested in Karachi for his links to al Qaeda and his subsequent imprisonment in Guantanamo Bay (Hafeez, 2008: 253).

Within the Maldives, tourism moved to the centre of contention between the three streams, next to females' freedoms, dresses and role within the society. The Maldives' lack of natural resources or industries, and dried fish as the only export good at the time, demanded a strategy to generate income for the Maldivian population. With the rising tourism industry in the 1970s, the Maldivian government had begun to allow the construction of resorts (Amir, 2011). President Gayoom, however, significantly elaborated this economic sector, turning the Maldives into a luxury holiday destination, and thus lifting the country from its status as a least developed country. The tourists, who mostly came from Western countries, yet, posed a challenge to Gayoom's ideal of the Islamic society. While tourism would not flourish without the ability to pursue a Western lifestyle, including drinking alcohol and the mixing of sexes, this lifestyle contradicted the pious Islamic society Gayoom sought to build. Gayoom thus created a wall of separation between Maldivians and the tourists; mainly foreigners would work in the resorts, things that were allowed in the resorts – such as alcohol – were prohibited on the inhabited islands, and tourists were prevented from meeting the local population. As a consequence of this separation, the income generated by tourism did not benefit wider parts of the society, and the discrepancy between the liberties in the resorts and the regulations in the inhabited islands was frowned upon. Even more, the migration of foreign workers to the Maldives, mainly from Bangladesh but also from non-Muslim countries like the Philippines, raised the fear of growing foreign influence. While the Maldivian constitution protects Sunni Islam by allowing only the naturalisation of Sunni Muslims, forbidding the practice of all other religions and even prohibiting the import of other religions' books, symbols or idols, fear of losing Islam was promoted by fundamentalist agents. The fear of losing Islam furthered the escalation as it allowed for the application and acceptance of costlier means.

In 1999, for example, protests against the millennium celebrations escalated into attacks against the regime when protesters claimed these celebrations to be a plot to spread Christianity (Hafeez, 2008: 253). Despite the expectable violent repression of dissent by the state, people nevertheless were ready to openly contest the government's decision.

Changing Opportunity Structure and Escalation

The state's suppression of religious and political dissent had increased in the course of Gayoom's presidency since 1978. In 2003, however, the political conditions within the Maldives changed, when within diverse spectrums of the Maldivian society the rejection of Gayoom's government mounted. Calls for more democratic liberties as well as for a more strictly practised "true" Islam alike became louder. While the political aims of the diverse contenders of Gayoom's rule were quite different and to a large extent even incompatible, the contenders shared the rejection of Gayoom's treatment of dissenters.

While some continued to seek opportunities to fight for their religious-political aims abroad, as the documented travel attempts of Maldivian youth to training camps in Pakistan (Amir, 2011) suggest, others increasingly expressed their support for religiously sanctioned political aims within the country. As such, for example, Osama bin Laden posters praising the al Qaeda leader were hung in Edjyafushi Island (Hafeez, 2008: 253). In these circles of support for al Qaeda and *jihad* violence increasingly became considered as legitimate tool of politics, even within the Maldives.

While supporters of the traditional Maldivian culturally-grounded Islam sought political reform and non-violent protest, fundamentalist groups, in turn, sought the uncompromisable transformation of the country into an Islamic state according to their ideals. Although these two streams' political aims and ideals could hardly be further apart, they nevertheless shared the rejection of Gayoom's political and religious aims and views.

In the context of the growing challenge to his authority from the other streams, Gayoom revoked the narrative of a threat to Islam in the Maldives. In the collective 'national' identity, Islam was the central factor unifying the Maldivian population. To fan fears, Gayoom drew on an old folk tale of a sea demon, Rannamaari (Van Es, 2008). The folk tale[9] stems from a pre-Islamic myth and was later supplemented with Islamic elements. The Islamised version claims that reading from the Quran had once defeated a demon, which frequently ascended from the ocean to accept human sacrifice from the infidel population. This story was transformed to fit Gayoom's needs to create both a threat and an enemy. The new Rannamaari story went that the Portuguese attempted to force pious Maldivians to drink alcohol. "Three brothers from the island of Utheemu – Mohamed, Ali and Hasan Thakurufaanu – then intervened heroically, in a tale of cunning and tact, to overthrow the infidel Portuguese, and became heroes of Islam who saved our pious nation from the alcoholic, Christian invaders" (The Daily Panic, 2013). The threat to the Maldives and Islam was mainly kept vague, and the threat to traditional moderate Maldivian Islam (by fundamentalists) not mentioned. Only the

---

[9] The story goes as follows: a demon coming from the ocean demanded virgin girls. Once a month the demon came to the island and a virgin girl was sacrificed for him by the "infidel" population. She was brought to the idol temple to stay there for the night and was to be found "dishonoured" and dead at the next morning. A saint from the Maghreb became witness of this ritual and by reciting the Quran at night, defeated the demon. As a consequence, the king and his people embraced Islam, broke the idols and destroyed the temples and sent messages to the other islands to convert to Islam, too (Romero-Frias, 2012: 74-75).

narrative of a Christian threat was continuously revoked. Yet, such claims of threat changed the political discourse in the Maldives to such an extent that all contenders of power were judged by their religious credentials rather than the quality of their arguments.

Subsequent to the death of a political prisoner in custody in September 2003, anti-government demonstrations were accompanied by civil unrest in the capital Male (ACFHR, 2005: 4-6). The state's response was the imposition of the state of emergency. But national and international pressure had built up to such a degree that Gayoom was forced into political reform (Naseem, 2015: 100). A new constitution, which allowed for political parties, was prepared and two years later, the formation of political parties was permitted. Major contenders of Gayoom's rule were the Maldivian Democratic Party and from the rather fundamentalist stream the Adalaath Party[10]. In the course of increasing contention, particularly the MDP was turned into the "threat" to Islam. The political contention was drawn into the question of the security of Islam, which required all political agents to prove their religious credentials and political plans to find a legitimisation by Islam. Political agents who sought a separation of political and religious authority, the implementation of democratic principles and human rights, were sidelined and defamed by Gayoom and the fundamentalist streams, who both neither respected nor accepted dissent.

The 2004 Indian Ocean tsunami, which had a devastating effect on the Maldivian islands, served as a catalyst for the already emerging societal developments. Particularly the influx of a variety of relief organisations and NGOs from Muslim majoritarian countries, often related to the populist pan-Islamism (Amir, 2011), changed the power balance and capacities of fundamentalist streams in the Maldivian society to their favour.

With the changed opportunities to express diverging (Islamic) views – if not completely freely, than at least less suppressed – on the one hand, and the increasing perception of threat to Islam on the other hand, agents representing the fundamentalist streams in the Maldives gained broader support within the society. In 2006, a group of fundamentalists had established full control over an entire island, Himandhoo, in the Alif Alif Atoll. The state prescribed mosque remained unused and religious service was performed in a newly and illegally built mosque headed by fundamentalists. When the government agents sought to close down the illegally constructed mosque, they met with stiff resistance (Hafeez, 2008: 254). In the course of this contention, a state official was murdered on the island – in a country in which for long murders had been extremely rare (The Diplomat, 2020; Maloney, 1980). The willingness to escalate further was encouraged by strong local and transnational support networks which increased the agents' capacity on the one hand, and the simultaneous decline in state capacity, on the other hand, which furthermore limited the president's ability to use the state institutions to easily repress dissent according to his wish.

In 2007, the first Islamist attack took place in the capital Male. It was directed against foreign tourists – who had been made the symbol of the "threat to Islam". The attacks with a homemade device became to be known as the Sultan Park Bomb Incident and injured twelve tourists (Amir, 2011). The attack had been loaded with symbolism and underlined the attackers' claims as much as they had pointed towards their political aims. The attack was perpetrated on the 17th day of Ramadan, Mohammed's first 'victory' in battle, and was directed against tourists considered as infidels and a threat to Islam in the Maldives. Transnational links were found to Jamia Salafiya Islamia (Faisalabad)

---

[10] In 2017, the Adalaath Party posted on their twitter account an own interpretation of the Rannamaari story, in which the conversion to Sunni Islam and the castration of a non-Sunni king by a Sunni Muslim ended the former rule during which, disguised as Rannamaari, he had raped more than 150 girls below 13 years of age. See Adhaalath @adhaalath, 20. Dezember 2017. Last accessed 15 July 2020.

which stands in connection with Lashkar-e-Taiba, and to Saudi Arabia (Jamiat Ahl-e-Hadees) and the UK (Jamaat-ul-Muslimeen) (Dharmawardhane, 2015: 65; Hafeez, 2008: 254, 255; 261). Links were also found to local Wahhabi prayer meetings, and to the illegally constructed mosque in Himandhoo. Police were sent to the mosque and suddenly confronted by an "organised mosque militia", a group of fully masked men, wearing red-helmets and holding wooden planks (Amir, 2011: 55). The security forces clashed violently with the Islamists so that the Maldivian National Defence Force (NMDF) had to move in (ibid.). In the course of the year, the Islamists, who retained their grip on Himandhoo islands despite police action, themselves suppressed any form of dissents. Death threats were sent to inhabitants of the island in case they did not collaborate, children were prevented from going to the local school due to alleged "impure" influences by foreign teachers as they taught English and subjects beyond Islam, and women now were required to fully veil themselves (Hafeez, 2008: 254).

Himandhoo is just one extreme example of fundamentalists' influence on Maldivian islands (Borri, 2017). The escalation of repertoire, however, becomes increasingly visible in other places as well. Even with Gayoom voted out of office, this trend has not been stopped. International influences and transnational organisations have taken ground in the Maldives – and expanded it. In 2009, for example, Jamiat-ul-Salaf and the Islamic Foundation of Maldives (IFM) were formally established (Amir, 2011: 47). In the same year, too, an al Qaeda propaganda video featured a Maldivian, and another Maldivian's link to the Mumbai attack was uncovered (ibid.). Just a year later, nine Maldivians were arrested in North Warziristan, Pakistan. In 2011, shortly before the then-president Nasheed was forced to resign in the course of protests, which gained in religious overtones over time, Gayoom's and the fundamentalists' streams, represented by different groups and organisations, forced the temporal closure of spas and resorts on the basis of allegedly compromising Islam by furthering prostitution (The Guardian, 2011). Since then, fundamentalists have taken ground. Transnational, fundamentalist and often militant organisation established themselves and receive increasing popular support. In 2014, 200 people protested while carrying the IS flag demanding the full implementation of the sharia and the end of secular rule in the Maldives (Dharmawardhane, 2015: 64). One year later hundreds protested for the IS in Male (The Diplomat, 2019). In 2015, a YouTube video titled "A Message to the Maldives Government" appeared. Therein three masked men with riffles threatened "to kill the Maldivian President Abdulla Yameen and Vice President Mohamed Jameel Ahmed and carry out attacks in the country", to target the economy by attacking tourist resorts, if demands were not met within 30 days (Dharmawardhane, 2015: 64). Although they carried IS flag, the affiliation was not confirmed. Just two years later, however, an Islamic State bomb plot was foiled (The Diplomat, 2019). Finally, in April this year (2020), the first confirmed and 'successful' IS attack in the Maldives was perpetrated in Mahibadhoo island (The Diplomat, 2020).

Dissent from fundamentalist versions of Islam or people claimed to engage in "un-Islamic behaviour" are threatened, hurt, and punished by death at the hands of non-state actors. Assassinations of moderate clerics, political figures, journalists and bloggers took place in 2012, in 2013, in 2014, and in 2017. With that, the fundamentalists in the Maldives seek to change their opponents' behaviour and threaten them into compliance. They have escalated to violence and are willing to prevail.

Conclusion

This paper sought to find an answer to the question of the relation between the repression of religious dissent under the Gayoom regime and the expansion and rise of violent Islamism in the Maldives. The paper hypothesised that in the context of the contention of the Islamic identity in the Maldives,

Gayoom failed to be responsive to diverging interpretations and therewith furthered an escalation process.

It was found that Gayoom's merger of religious and secular authority, the exclusive linking of Muslim and Maldivian identity, and the violent repression of religious dissent have set the stage for violent protest against the Maldivian state and regime. Yet, the repression of dissent alone did not lead to the increase of Islamist violence in the Maldives. The expansion of Islamic education programmes in Mulsim majoritarian states and the increased influx of populist pan-Islamic organisations in the course of Gayoom's foreign policy as well as following the 2004 Indian Ocean tsunami promoted a transnational Islamic identity, "purified" from local traditions and directed towards the creation of an Islamic state and society based on the literal interpretation of Islamic teachings. The global securitisation of pan-Islamism had resonated well with Gayoom's claim of "Islam under threat". The violence directed against foreigners as well as "dissenters" within their own community, as the case of Himandhoo island shows, as much as the support of Islamist organisations abroad were not the result of escalated contention with the state, but the ruthless pursuit of religious-political aims built on certain transnational and fundamentalist cognitive models.

With a changing opportunity structure between 2002 and 2008, including political liberalisation and reform, the Islamisation of the political discourse and the increased influx of populist pan-Islamic organisations, Islamists were incentivised and enabled to pursue their political aims by violent means. The "purification" of Islam from its local cultural traditions has furthered the rise of violent Islamism in the Maldives and Maldivians' participation in foreign conflicts as foreign fighters. Gayoom's repression of dissent has furthered the spread of fundamentalist interpretations in several regards. While his suppression of dissent, thus, has provided a significant part of the agents' opportunity structure enabling an escalation process, the use of violence as a political tool is not solely grounded therein.

References

Amir, H. (2011). Islamism and Radicalism in the Maldives. Thesis, Naval Postgraduate School.

Asian Centre for Human Rights (ACFHR) (eds.) (2005). Maldives: The Dark Side of Life. New Delhi: Asian Centre for Human Rights.

Bates, R. H., ed. 1998. Analytic narratives. Princeton, NJ: Princeton University Press.

Borri, F. (2017). In Himandhoo Where Islam is Not a Religion, it's Politics. (https://www.ilfattoquotidiano.it/2017/10/12/maldives-in-himandhoo-where-islam-is-not-a-religion-its-politics/3908351). Last accessed 15 July 2020.

Dawson, A., Rashid, A., Shuib, R., Wickramage, K., Budiharsana, M., Martua Hidayana, I. and Marranci, G. (2020). "Addressing female genital mutilation in the Asia Pacifc: the neglected sustainable development target", Australian and New Zealand Journal of Public Health, 44 (1): 8-10.

Dharmawardhane, I. (2015). Maldives. Counter Terrorist Trends and Analysis, 8 (1) (December 2015 –January 2016): 63-69.

Elliott, F. (2013). "Raped Girl, 15, Sentenced to 100 Lashes for Premarital Sex in Maldives", The Times, 28 February 2013.

Hafeez, M. (2008). Growing Islamic Militancy in Maldives. Strategic Studies, 28 (1) (Spring 2008): 251-256.

Haider, Z. (2017). "Locating the Loopholes of South-South Cooperation in South Asia: Can SAARC Deter Hostilities and Promote Cooperation?", Journal of South Asian and Middle Eastern Studies, Vol. 40 (3): 35-56.

Hegghammer, T. (2010). Jihad in Saudi Arabia: Violence and Pan-Islamism since 1979. Cambridge: Cambridge University Press.

Kumar, A. (2016). Multi-party Democracy in the Maldives and the Emerging Security Environment in the Indian Ocean Region. New Delhi: Pentagon Press.

Maldives Independent. (2017). "Maldives blogger killed for 'mocking Islam', say police", 10 August 2017. (https://maldivesindependent.com/crime-2/maldives-blogger-killed-for-mocking-islam-say-police-131974).

Malik, J. M. (2001). "South Asia in China's Foreign Relations", Pacifica Review: Peace, Security & Global Change, 13 (1): 73-90.

Maloney, C. (1980). People of the Maldives Islands. Bombay et al.: Orient Longman.

Ministry of Economic Development, Republic of Maldives. See (http://www.trade.gov.mv/page/oic). Last accessed 07 May 2020.

Minivan News. (2013). Saudi Arabia's Muslim World League opens office in Maldives Islamic Ministry. 1 July 2013. https://minivannewsarchive.com/news-in-brief/saudi-arabian-muslim-world-league-opens-office-in-maldives-60583. Last accessed 31 July 2020.

Naseem, A. (2015). The Honeymoon Is Over: Maldives as a Growing Security Threat in the Indian Ocean. Irish Studies in International Affairs, 26, 99-119.

Phadnis, U., Luithui, E. (1981). The Maldives Enter World Politics. Asian Affairs: An American Review, 8 (3): 166-179.

Romero-Frias, R. (2012). Folk Tales of the Maldives. Copenhagen: NIAS Press.

The Daily Panic. (2013).(https://thedailypanic.com/2013/11/maldivian-history-a-mockery-of-past-and-present/). 8 November 2013. Last accessed 15 July 2020.

The Diplomat. (2019). Violent Extremism in the Maldives: The Saudi Factor. 24 December 2019.

The Diplomat. (2020). Islamic State Terror in the Maldives as COVID-19 Arrives. 18 April 2020.

Tilly, C. (2006). The Politics of Collective Violence. Cambridge [u.a.]: Cambridge University Press.

Tilly, C.; Tarrow, S. (2007). Contentious Politics. New York: Oxford University Press.

Van Es, M. (2008). Gayoom's Abuse of Faith. Himalmag. (https://www.himalmag.com/gayooms-abuse-of-faith/). Last accessed 15 July 2020.

Waha, L. (2018). Religion and State-Formation in Transitional Societies. Baden-Baden: Nomos.

Zartman, W. (2008). Negotiation and Conflict Management: Essays on Theory and Practice. Oxon: Routledge.

International Journal of Religion
November 2020
Volume: 1 | Number 1 | pp. 91 – 104
ISSN: 2633-352X (Print) | ISSN: 2633-3538 (Online)
journals.tplondon.com/ijor

TRANSNATIONAL PRESS®
LONDON

First Submitted: 4 May 2020 Accepted: 1 November 2020
DOI: https://doi.org/10.33182/ijor.v1i1.982

Islam, Catholicism, and Religion-State Separation: An Essential or Historical Difference?

Ahmet T. Kuru[1]

Abstract

There exist severe restrictions over religious dissent in most Muslim-majority countries. This problem is associated with the alliance between religious and political authorities in these cases. I argue that the alliance between Islamic scholars (the ulema) and the state authorities was historically constructed, instead of being a characteristic of Islam. Hence, the essentialist idea that Islam inherently rejects religion-state separation, whereas Christianity endorses it, is misleading. Instead, this article shows that the ulema-state alliance in the Muslim world was constructed after the mid-eleventh century, as well as revealing that the church-state separation in Western Europe was also historically institutionalized during that period. Using comparative-historical methods, the article explains the political and socioeconomic backgrounds of these epochal transformations. It particularly focuses on the relations between religious, political, intellectual, and economic classes.

Keywords: Islam; Catholicism; separation; ulema; state.

Introduction

Most Muslim-majority countries have serious problems regarding freedom of religious dissent.[2] Two-thirds of 49 Muslim-majority countries in the world have laws punishing apostasy or blasphemy (leaving or insulting Islam) in various ways, from prison to execution (Kuru, 2020). In a recent report, Pew Research Center documents religious restrictions around the world. Although Muslim-majority countries constitute only about a quarter of all cases in the report, they constitute over three-quarters of the cases "with most restrictive laws and policies toward religious freedom."[3]

Religious freedom requires a certain level of religion-state separation. If the state fully establishes a particular religion, this inescapably means legal, financial, and discursive discriminations against those who do not follow that religion. Such an establishment implies restrictions even upon those who believe in and practice the established religion, but in a different way than defined by the state. According to a well-known perception, Islam inherently rejects religion-state separation. If this is true, it is impossible to fully achieve religious freedom, particularly for those who hold dissenting views, in the Muslim world.

According to this perception, Christianity essentially embraces religion-state separation, whereas Islam rejects it. Those who promote this perception provide some textual evidence. They quote a

---

[1] Ahmet T. Kuru, PhD, Professor, San Diego State University, California, United States. E-mail: akuru@sdsu.edu

[2] The research for this article has been funded by the Religious Freedom Institute under the Freedom of Religious Institutions in Society Project, a three-year initiative funded by the John Templeton Foundation. Portions of this article were adapted from Kuru 2019; they were used with permission.

[3] Eighteen out of twenty-two cases with the most restrictive laws and policies are Muslim-majority. Pew Research Center, 2019. See also Philpott, 2019; Fox, 2020.

Biblical phrase, "render unto Caesar the things that are Caesar's, and unto God the things that are God's" (Luke 20: 25), to show church-state separation in Christianity (Lewis, 1991: 15; Huntington, 1996: 70). And they misquote Prophet Muhammad by attributing a maxim to him: "Religion and royal authority are twins. Religion is a foundation and the royal authority is a guard. Anything that has no foundation collapses and that has no guard perishes" (Rosenthal, 1958: 8, 39). In reality, this maxim belongs to the founding king of the Sasanian Empire, Ardashir I (r. 224–42) (Maçoudi, 1863 [947]: 162; "Le Testament d'Ardasir," 1966: 49; Nizam al-Mulk, 1978 [c. 1090]: 60). Several of Ardashir's sayings were translated into Arabic and this particular one has been used to justify the partnership between Islamic scholars (the ulema) and Muslim rulers, or what I call the ulema-state alliance (al-Ghazali, 2013 [1095]: 231).

Even if this statement had been a true hadith—a record about Prophet Muhammad's words and actions—it would not have mattered much, because religion-state relations in both Christianity and Islam are too complex to be explained by a Biblical phrase or a hadith. This article will show this complexity by exploring the changing characteristics of religion-state relations in the Muslim word and Western Christendom with a focus on the transformations that began in the mid-eleventh century in both regions.

In reality, Islam had a history of a certain religion-state separation. Between the eighth and mid-eleventh centuries, Islamic scholars generally regarded close entanglements with political authorities as corrupt. The ulema preferred to be funded by the private sector, especially commerce. Only a small minority of them worked as state servants. During that period, the Muslim world produced creative scholars in both religious and non-religious sciences. Western Europe, in contrast, was under the hegemony of the Catholic clergy and the military aristocracy. Unlike the Muslim world, Western Europe lacked influential intellectual and merchant classes.

Around the year 1050, however, a new political system emerged in the Muslim world. Instead of the old system, which allowed a certain level of private economic entrepreneurship and religious diversity within Islam, the new political system—represented primarily by the Seljuk Empire (1040-1194)—centralized both the economy and Islamic educational institutions. A major characteristic of the new system was the alliance between the ulema and the military rulers. The ulema-state alliance declared "unorthodox" views of Muslim philosophers apostasy. An institutional basis of this alliance was a new network of madrasas—schools of Islamic law and theology (Kuru, 2019: 71-116).

Again, around the year 1050, Western Europe began to experience a process almost in the opposite direction. From the mid-eleventh to the mid-twelfth century, the Catholic Church and various kings tried to dominate one another. The failure of these attempts led to the institutionalization of the church-state separation. This contributed to the increasing balance of power among various institutions in Western Europe, which eventually led to philosophical and religious diversity (Berman, 1983; Bloch, 2014 [1940]; Tierney, 1988 [1964]).

This article will explain that the ulema-state alliance was not an essential part of Islam; instead, it was constructed during and after the mid-eleventh century. Similarly, the church-state separation in Western Europe was a result of a historical process, which began in the mid-eleventh century. In social science terminology, for both Muslim and Western worlds, the second half of the eleventh century was a "critical juncture" (Mahoney and Rueschemeyer, 2003; Kuru 2009, 27–28), which left a "path-dependent" legacy for subsequent centuries. This legacy has had major implications for religious and political systems in both regions.

The Muslim World: The Ulema-State Separation

Scholars, Rulers, and Merchants

Between the eighth and mid-eleventh centuries, the ulema were largely trying to keep their financial independence from state authorities and regarded close relations with them as corrupt. This attitude had a historical background. In the mid-seventh century, there occurred a civil war between Ali, the fourth caliph and the son-in-law of the Prophet, and Muawiya, the governor of Damascus. This and the subsequent tragedies, including the death of thousands and the murder of Ali and his son Hussein, led Shii and many Sunni Muslims to be disenchanted about the relationship between political power and religious morality (Hodgson, 1974a: 212-223; Morony, 1984: 467-506).

Muawiya established the earliest dynasty in Islamic history—the Umayyads (661-750)—based on the persecution of the Prophet's family members. Unlike the charismatic, personal, and religious authorities of Prophet Muhammad and four succeeding caliphs (Abu Bakr, Umar, Uthman, and Ali), the authority of Muawiya was institutionalized and largely "secular." Muawiya was the first in Islamic history to use a throne and bodyguards (Ibn Khaldun, 2005 [1377]: 216; Morony, 1984: 93). Several scholars define Muawiya as the first real state-builder in Islamic history, and most Umayyad rulers as those who secularized political authority by prioritizing the *raison d'état* (Abdel Rezak, 2012 [1925]; Rahman, 1968: xx; Djaït, 1989: 411; al-Banna, 2003: 4-9).

The Abbasids (750-1258) replaced the Umayyads with a bloody revolution. They were not very different from the Umayyads in terms of lacking effective religious legitimacy. Both the Umayyad and the Abbasid rulers called themselves "caliphs," claiming to be the successors of the Prophet (Crone and Hinds, 1986). But the Shii ulema largely refused their legitimacy, in both the religious and political grounds, while most Sunni ulema regarded them as political rulers per se. For these Sunni ulema, the true "caliphs" with religious legitimacy were only the first four after the Prophet and before the Umayyads (Abou El Fadl, 2009: 94-95; Lapidus, 1975: 369).

The disagreements between political and religious authorities at that time were visible in the lives of not only Shii ulema, including Jafar al-Sadiq, but also such prominent Sunni ulema as the founders of four Sunni schools of law—Abu Hanifa, Malik, Shafii, and Ahmad ibn Hanbal—who refused to serve the state.[4] Because of their principled-based rejection of political rulers' demands, Jafar al-Sadiq was poisoned to death, Abu Hanifa died in prison, Malik was whipped, Shafii was detained and chained, and Ibn Hanbal was beaten in prison (al-Nadim, 1970 [987]: 494; al-Ghazali, 2015 [c. 1097]: 72-76; Afsaruddin, 2008: 96-105, 137-141).

Abu Hanifa's (d. 767) life-story shows how the early ulema insisted on their independence from political authorities even if they faced punishment. He rejected the Abbasid Caliph Mansur's personal offer of judgeship with the excuse of not being qualified. The Caliph got angry and called him a liar. Abu Hanifa replied that a liar could not be appointed as a judge. Mansur swore an oath that he would make him accept the post. Abu Hanifa similarly swore an oath that he would never accept it. Consequently, Abu Hanifa was imprisoned and then poisoned to death (Nadwi, 2010: 39).

It is true that some Sunni ulema, such as the two prominent students of Abu Hanifa—Abu Yusuf and Shaybani—served the state as judges (Lambton, 1981: 55-58). Yet these exceptions did not represent the mainstream characteristic of the ulema-state relations between the eighth and mid-eleventh centuries. Let alone receiving money and positions, some ulema refused to make even

---

[4] Shafii served as a judge in his youth, though he later regretted having done so. See Fadel, 2011: 117.

gestures. A governor in Central Asia asked Bukhari (d. 870)—who would become the most famous hadith scholar—to teach his children in his palace. Bukhari refused and replied that the ruler was welcome to send his children to his hadith circle. The annoyed ruler forced Bukhari into exile in a village, where he died (Abdul-Jabbar, 2007: 19).

Munir-ud Din Ahmed (1968: 229) analyzed the ulema's financial autonomy during this early period. In his words, "An exceedingly large number of scholars are reported to have rejected all financial help from authorities. This was done by the scholars in the first place to keep themselves free of governmental pressure." Other historians also note that many leading ulema of the time, including Ibn Hanbal and Sufyan al-Thawri, declared that it was forbidden for the ulema to take money from political rulers (Mez, 1937: 184).

Hayyim Cohen (1970: 16) conducted the most detailed analysis of this subject. He examined 3,900 ulema biographies from the eighth to the mid-eleventh century, from Egypt eastward. Cohen finds out that at that time the ulema were very different from the Christian clergy, because the ulema, except the judges and few other scholars, "functioned in an entirely private capacity, unappointed either by the authorities or by any religious institution . . . received no emoluments and had to support themselves, which they did in a variety of ways." Most ulema or their families worked in commerce and industry, particularly as the following: merchants or artisans in the textile industry (22%); those processing or dealing with food (13%); miscellaneous merchants (11%); those sold or made leather, metals, wood, or clay (9%); those dealt with ornaments (e.g., jewelers) and/or perfumes (8%); bankers, money-changers, and middlemen (5%); and booksellers, book copiers, and paper sellers (4.5%). Some ulema worked as teachers (especially tutors) (8%), or investigators of witnesses (3%). Only a small portion of them (8.5%) worked as officials.[5]

Along the same line, Eliyahu Ashtor (1976: 111) emphasizes the connection between Islamic scholarship and commerce in the early Abbasid era: "Many merchants became . . . interested in the sciences of Islam." In some cases, "their sons devoted themselves entirely to the scholarly life." Thus, "it can be seen from the study of the Arabic collections of biographies that most theologians of this period belonged to the bourgeois class, i.e. were merchants or sons of merchants." Roy Mottahedeh (1980: 135-137) analyzes parts of Iraq and Iran under the Buyid rule from the mid-tenth to mid-eleventh centuries. He stresses that the ulema wanted to distance themselves from the government. That was why "families whose ancestors had exercised *riyasah* [leadership] in the bureaucracy or the army of the central government did not produce many leading men of religious learning." Moreover, at that time the ulema were a "vaguely defined body of men" who had "little internal structure" and held multiple identities and occupations.

The autonomy of the ulema from political rulers was associated with other characteristics of Muslim societies, such as the presence of an influential class of merchants, a creative class of philosophers, and a certain level of religious freedom for Christians and Jews. None of these characteristics existed in Western European societies at that time.

Muslims, Christians, Jews, and the State

During the Umayyads and Abbasids, the lack of a hierarchical religious authority led to the emergence of numerous Sunni and Shii interpretations of Islam. In his well-known book, Shahristani (d. 1153)

---

[5] Other occupations, such as physician, lawyer, porter, mule driver, and hair-dresser, constitute the remaining 8 percent. Cohen, 1970: 36 (Table A-I). The biographies of these scholars and their families reveal 410 different occupations, only 56 of which (less than 15 %) were "connected with official services." Cohen, 1970: 17, 45-61. See also Bulliet, 2009: 1-5, 43-44.

(1984 [c. 1127]; 1986 [c. 1127]: 105-585) analyzes religions of his time. He classifies 73 different sects within Islam.

At that time, non-Muslim communities, particularly Christians and Jews, were actively participating in socio-economic life.[6] In *The Renaissance of Islam*, Adam Mez (1937: 51, 418) elaborates that these communities had involvement with even government: during the tenth century, some Christians and Jews were workings as bureaucrats in the Abbasid state. Mez also notes that in Baghdad, Muslims were joining Christians' celebrations. In the ninth century, some caliphs ordered the protected subjects (mostly Christians and Jews) to show their lower social status in certain dress codes and vehicles, such as riding on mules and donkeys, instead of horses. In practice, however, these measures were not effectively implemented. Throughout the tenth century, these rules largely remained "dormant. With the ascendancy of orthodoxy in the 11th century they were once again taken more seriously" (Mez, 1937: 50; see also Goddard, 2000: chs. 3-4).

This diversity and relative toleration was not limited to Baghdad. According to Shelomo Goitein (1966b: 247), the Geniza documents (which were found out in a synagogue in Old Cairo and provide information about Jewish merchants in Muslim lands) reveal that in Cairo, Damascus, and Jerusalem, "Jewish houses often bordered on those of Muslims or Christians or both. There was no ghetto, but, on the contrary, much opportunity for daily intercourse. Neither was there an occupational ghetto."

Religious diversity and toleration did not mean the lack of religious persecution, even for certain Muslims. For instance, during the period of the *mihna* (inquisition), between 833 and 848, three consecutive Abbasid caliphs forced state servants and the ulema to confirm the rationalist idea that the Quran was God's creation, rather than his eternal, uncreated speech.[7] Some leading ulema such as Ibn Hanbal (d. 855) refused to obey, despite threats of punishment and even execution. During the *mihna*, "the sources list a total of forty-eight persons who were subject to official interrogation" (Lapidus, 1975: 379; see also Zaman, 1997: 106-14).

Actions generally create reactions. This rationalist inquisition was backfired and it made literalist scholars, particularly Ibn Hanbal, popular. The following sections will examine how and why a literalist orthodoxy dominated the Muslim world after the mid-eleventh century. Before that, I will briefly mention the connections between religious freedom and intellectual/economic creativity.

Religious Autonomy: Intellectual and Economic Dynamism

From the eighth to the mid-eleventh century, religious autonomy, diversity, and toleration were associated with the existence of an influential bourgeoisie and productive polymaths in the Muslim world.

According to Goitein (1966a: 238-239), Muslim lands had an effective monetary economy, which provided encouraging conditions for Muslim and Jewish merchants. He cites a tenth-century writer who claimed that "[m]erchants are more powerful than viziers [ministers]" because "a bill of exchange was accepted with greater readiness than an allocation of income from taxes." He even characterizes the situation as a "bourgeois revolution." Goitein (1966a: 241) writes, "The 'bourgeois revolution' of the Middle East during the early centuries of Islam had many repercussions on world history. To

---

[6] The case of John of Damascus (675-753) shows how a Christian could become a world-renowned theologian under Muslim Umayyad rule. Similarly, in Baghdad, under the Abbasids, Yahya ibn Adi (893-974) became a famous Christian theologian, philosopher, and translator. Fakhry, 2004: 197-207.

[7] According to Mutazilis, to depict the Quran as timeless and not created was similar to how the Christians depicted Jesus. Corbin, 1986: 160; Melchert, 2006: 10.

mention just one: through it the Jews, who up to that time had been engaged mainly in agriculture and other manual occupations, were converted into a predominantly commercial people." Similarly, Maristella Botticini and Zvi Eckstein (2012: 55-56) explain in greater detail that the "full-fledged transition of the Jews from farming to crafts and trade took place" roughly between the years 750 and 900, under Umayyad, Abbasid, and Fatimid rule, where "Jews were legally permitted to own land . . . and to engage in any occupation they wished."

In the early medieval period, Muslim merchants funded many ulema and philosophers. Muslim philosophers, or polymaths, made major contributions to various fields, such as mathematics, optics, and medicine. Their contributions included the development of Arabic numerals, the invention of camera obscura, and the distinction between smallpox and measles (Joseph, 2000; Lindberg, 1976; Pormann and Savage-Smith, 2007). Muslim merchants also led commercial and agricultural flourishing (Shatzmiller, 2011; Watson, 1983), which included the innovation of such economic instruments as the check and the bill of exchange (Braudel, 1982: 556; Van Zanden, 2009: 61; Bloom and Blair, 2002: 114). Even politically, Muslim merchants were influential (Lombard, 1975: 150). In the mid-tenth century, under Abbasid rule, merchants "constituted an international credit community that the government could abuse only at considerable risk" (Mottahedeh, 1980: 118).

A major transformation began in the mid-eleventh century. The relative separation between the ulema and the state started to deteriorate, a literalist Sunni orthodoxy became increasingly influential (al-Ashari 1953 [c. 935]), and the monetary economy was gradually replaced by a new system of the state allocation of land revenues. This transformation gradually caused intellectual and economic stagnation in the Muslim world (Kuru 2019, chapters 5-7).

The Ulema-State Alliance

The mid-eleventh century transformation had economic, political, and religious dimensions. Economically, diminishing agricultural revenues in Iraq had already weakened the old regime (Bonner, 2010: 354). In the eleventh century, the new economic regime emerged with the increasing usage of *iqta*s—tax farming and land revenue assignments to the military and other state servants. In subsequent centuries, various Muslim sultanates developed and used versions of the *iqta* system (Cahen, 1953; Lambton, 1991; Hodgson, 1974b: 46-52). Politically, the state structure gained a more militaristic form. Starting with the eleventh century, focusing on military conquests became another common characteristic of Muslim sultanates (Barthold, 1977 [1900]: 272-292; Starr, 2013: 332-335). These new economic and political systems marginalized the once-influential merchant class. The emerging alliance between religious and political authorities was based on these economic and political transformations (Kuru, 2019: 93-116).

There also existed a deep religious dimension of this transformation. In the first half of the eleventh century, Abbasid caliphs in Baghdad attempted to regain political power against the Shii rulers who dominated North Africa, Egypt, Syria, and even Iraq. To change this situation, two subsequent Abbasid caliphs called for the unification of Sunni sultans, ulema, and masses. They declared a creed, which defined a "Sunni orthodoxy." Those whose views were deemed to contradict this creed, including certain Shiis, philosophers, and rationalist theologians (Mutazilis), were declared to be apostates and faced the threat of execution (Mez 1937, 206-9; Hanne 2007, 71).

In the second half of the eleventh century, the Seljuk rulers allied with the Abbasid caliphs and the ulema to consolidate the Sunni orthodoxy and to eliminate Ismaili Shiis. Muslim philosophers were also targeted due to their heterodox thoughts. Ghazali (d. 1111), a genius member of the ulema, played a leading intellectual role in the attacks against Ismaili Shiis and philosophers (al-Ghazali, 1999 [1095]: 228–231). In several books, which have been widely read from that time to the present, Ghazali declared two leading Muslim philosophers, Farabi (d. 950) and Ibn Sina (d. 1037), apostates due to their three unorthodox views—that the world is eternal, God's knowledge encompasses only the universals, and the resurrection is only spiritual. Ghazali wrote that defending these views were punishable by death (al-Ghazali, 2000 [1095]: 226; see also al-Ghazali, 2013 [1095]: 241; al-Ghazali, 2002 [c. 1105]: 110; al-Ghazali, 1999 [c. 1108]: 62–3).

The institutional basis of the ulema-state alliance was a network of madrasas. The Seljuk grand vizier Nizam al-Mulk (r. 1064-92) patronized a madrasa in Baghdad, which became the pioneer of that network. These institutions were later called after him—the Nizamiyya madrasas. These madrasas were funded by waqfs (foundations). Nevertheless, madrasas could not be simply defined as private or independent, because political rulers and officials were the founders of the madrasas' endowments. Nizamiyya madrasas promoted Sunni orthodoxy and trained a particular type of ulema that would accept the service to the state (Ephrat, 2000; Arjomand, 1999).

The Seljuk way of combining the *iqta* system, the military state, and the ulema–state alliance emerged in Central Asia, Iran, and Iraq in the second half of the eleventh century. A century later, it was spread to Syria and Egypt under the Ayyubids and then Mamluks (Ibn Khaldun, 1967 [1377]: 435; Berkey, 1992: 130-46). Later, it became dominant in vast geography from the Balkans to India under the Ottomans, Safavids, and Mughals (Lapidus, 1996; Kuran, 2011: 128-131). These sultanates were militarily powerful, but they failed to revive early Muslims' intellectual and economic dynamism because they eliminated philosophers and marginalized merchants (Lapidus, 1984; İnalcık, 1994).

I use the term "alliance" because there was a reciprocal relationship between the ulema and the state. The Ottoman Empire (1299-1922) was the case where the ulema-state alliance had the deepest institutionalization. In the Empire, the ulema had certain religious, legislative, judicial, and educational prerogatives. In some cases, the ulema even cooperated with the Janissaries in deposing sultans. Nonetheless, the sultans had executive powers, including coercion and finance, that they could use against certain members of the ulema (İnalcık, 2000 [1973]: 63-64, 169-172). In sum, the Ottoman case reveals that the relationship between the ulema and the state meant a mutually beneficial partnership, rather than a one-way state dominance over the ulema, or vice-versa.

In sum, after the eleventh century, the ulema–state alliance used religious orthodoxy and state violence to suppress contenders. Threatened by execution in this world and eternal hellfire in the hereafter, many Muslims were discouraged from intellectual exploration outside the boundaries drawn by the alliance between religious and political authorities. Nonetheless, in Western Europe, a different process began in the eleventh century in terms of the relations between these authorities.

Western Europe: The Church-State Separation

Western Europe and the Muslim World: A Brief Comparison

Between the ninth and twelfth centuries, Western Europe had inferior scientific and socioeconomic conditions in comparison to the Muslim world. Regarding literacy, Muslim libraries in such cities as Baghdad, Cairo, and Cordoba had hundreds of thousands of books, whereas Western European libraries had fewer than 600 books (al-Nadim, 1970 [987]; Mez, 1937: 172; Harris 1995, 98). Muslims started to produce paper in the eighth century, while it took five more centuries for Western Europeans to do so (Bloom 2001, 45–9, 116; Kennedy 2005, 36; Glick 2005, 279–80; Kilgour 1998, 79). In terms of urbanization, around the year 1000, Muslim Cordova had the largest population

(450,000) in Europe, including Constantinople (300,000), whereas the largest Western Christian city, Palermo, had only 75,000 people (Chandler, 1987: 467–9). Baghdad was even bigger than Cordoba (Watson, 1983: 133; Lapidus, 2002: 56). Financially, Muslims began to mint gold coin in the early ninth century, four and half century before Western Europeans achieved to do that (Braudel, 1982: 559; Maddison, 2004: 73).

A major reason for this divergence was that thinkers and merchants enjoyed a relatively high social status in Muslim lands, whereas the clergymen and the military elite dominated Western Europe. According to Norbert Elias (2000 [1939]: 221), until the mid-eleventh century, there were only "two classes of free people" in Western Europe—the clergy and the warrior nobles. This situation began to change in the mid-eleventh century. Agricultural development, in particular, and economic growth, in general, led to the development of cities and the emergence of a free and flourishing merchant class. Marc Bloch (2014 [1940]: 75-8, 307, 372) also regards the year 1050 as a turning point in Western Europe. Until that time, he explains, townspeople were marginal because they depended on commerce that was undermined by ecclesiastical and knightly classes.

Another reason why Bloch (2014 [1940]: 370) refers to the mid-eleventh century as a turning point is the transformation of the relationship between the Catholic Church and the royal authority.

The Eleventh Century Reform, or Papal Revolution

In the second half of the eleventh century, several members of the Catholic Church claimed superiority over kings, while certain kings tried to dominate the Church. Neither side had a clear purpose of church-state separation. The struggles between the clergy and the royal authority caused not only doctrinal debates but also military conflicts. Cardinal Humbert—who also played a leading role in the Great Schism between the Catholic and Orthodox Churches in 1054—was a prominent defender of the Church's supremacy over royal authority. He argued, "Just as the soul excels the body and commands it, so the priestly dignity excels the royal" (Quoted in Tierney, 1988 [1964]: 35).

The Catholic Church established some rules to limit lay rulers' interventions in the ecclesiastical appointments. In 1059, a papal decree was issued about the pope's election by cardinals. Yet, Henry IV (r. 1054-1105), king of Germany and later Holy Roman emperor, insisted to hold the authority to appoint bishops. In response, in 1075, Pope Gregory VII (r. 1073-1085) issued 27 dictates, which asserted not only the Church's institutional independence, but also its supreme status. The dictates include the following: "That the Pope is the only one whose feet are to be kissed by all princes," "That he alone can depose or reinstate bishops," and "That he may depose Emperors" (Quoted in Tierney, 1988 [1964]: 49; Southern, 1970: 102). Consequently, Henry deposed Gregory, while Gregory excommunicated Henry. The struggles between various popes and monarchs continued in the early twelfth century. For example, King Henry V, the son of Henry IV, imprisoned the pope of his time. Despite such royal resistance, the Catholic Church's rulings during this revolutionary period created its institutional autonomy and have had long-lasting effects. Hence, they have been called the "Eleventh Century Reform" or the "Gregorian Reform" (Logan, 2013: 98-107).

According to Bloch (2014 [1940]: 114), before the Gregorian Reform "the sacred and profane had been almost inextricably mingled" in Western Europe. The reform meant a rupture for the separation "between the spiritual and the temporal," which would later be celebrated as "one of the greatest innovations introduced by Christianity." Bloch (2014 [1940]: 401) emphasizes that the Church leaders' goal in "separating the two powers so completely" was "to humble the rulers of men's bodies before the rulers of their souls." Brian Tierney (1988 [1964]: 86) also elaborates that during the eleventh-century struggles, kings tried to establish a "royal theocracy," while popes tried to found a "papal theocracy." Neither side was willing to simply render unto Caesar what is Caesar's, and unto God what is God's. Nonetheless, both sides failed to subdue the other. As an unintended consequence of this mutual failure, the separation between the Church and the royal authority became institutionalized (see also Tierney 1982: 10)

Harold Berman (1983: 87-103) goes even further than Bloch and Tierney and calls the reforms during this investiture conflict, which took place between 1075 and 1122, the "Papal Revolution." Before this revolution, the Catholic clergy largely supported the royal authority in a way that resembled Caesaropapism—the Byzantine system where the clergy recognize the royal authority as supreme and as combining the secular and religious powers:

> Prior to the late eleventh century, the clergy of Western Christendom—bishops, priests, and monks—were, as a rule, much more under the authority of emperors, kings, and leading feudal lords than of popes…In addition to its political-economic subordination, the church was also subject in its internal structure to the control of leading laymen…At the same time, bishops and other prominent clergy sat in governmental bodies—local, baronial, and royal or imperial…The system was similar to that which prevailed in the Eastern Roman Empire, and which was later denounced in the West as Caesaropapism (Berman 1983: 88).

Berman (1983: 91) also gives numbers to support his depiction of church-state relations before the late eleventh century: "Of the twenty-five popes who held office during the hundred year prior to 1059 (when a church synod for the first time prohibited lay investiture), twenty-one were directly appointed by [German] emperors and five were dismissed by emperors.

Hence, there was no church-state separation in either Western or Eastern Christianity. The Orthodox Church never experienced a separation from the Byzantine state or, later, the Russian state.[8] The Catholic Church, however, was transformed during the Papal Revolution. According to Berman (1983: 83), the Church "established itself as a visible, corporate, legal entity, independent of imperial, royal, feudal, and urban authorities." Berman (1983: 538-539) even argues that this revolution was not only chronologically earlier than subsequent epochal changes such as Renaissance and the Reformation, but also more important than them for the formation of the Western legal tradition.

More recently, Jan Luiten van Zanden (2009: 48) reiterated the significance of the Papal Revolution. He stresses that with this revolution "power within the Latin West would be divided between Pope and Emperor" and this division later became deeper with the rise of cities and other entities. Consequently, Western Europe became increasingly different from other parts of the world where there was no such religion-state separation and thus power was, at least in theory, "one and undivided."

The Eleventh Century Reform had long-terms consequences. Lord Acton (1877) famously noted that the conflicts between the spiritual and the temporal power continued in subsequent centuries and this led to the rise of civil liberty in Western Europe. In his words, if the two powers had been unified,

---

[8] In the words of Steven Runciman (1977, 4), "in contrasting Church with State we are making a distinction which would have been meaningless to the Byzantines." According to Francis Fukuyama (2011, 391-392), the "Byzantine Empire from which Russia drew its model of church-state relations was caesaropapist; the eastern emperor appointed the patriarch of Constantinople and intervened on issues of doctrine." And this was never reformed: "The equivalent of the investiture conflict and the Gregorian reform never took place in the Byzantine world." See also Møller 2017.

or if one of them had subdued the other, "all Europe would have sunk down under a Byzantine or Muscovite despotism."[9]

In short, the institutionalization of church-state separation in the eleventh century became a major turning point in Western European history. In subsequent centuries, Western Europe experienced the establishment of new institutions, particularly universities and corporations, as the bases of rising intellectual and bourgeois classes.[10] With these institutional and class-based transformations, Western Europe eventually surpassed the Muslim world, in terms of scientific and economic development, as well as religious and philosophical diversity.

Conclusion

This article analyzes the existence of a certain separation between religious and political authorities in the Muslim world between the eighth and mid-eleventh centuries. Obviously, the separation between them was not absolute: there were many exceptions and entanglements. Nonetheless, religion-state separation was not absolute in the post-eleventh century Catholicism, either. From the Gregorian reforms to the modern West, church-state relations have always contested boundaries and reflected exceptions (Kuru, 2009: ch. 4).

After the mid-eleventh century, even this relative separation between religious and political authorities ended in the Muslim world. Instead, an ulema-state alliance emerged in the Seljuk Empire and later it was adapted and adopted by subsequent Muslim sultanates, including the Ayyubids, Mamluks, Ottomans, Safavids, and Mughals.

Hence, the post-eleventh century Muslim world became similar to early medieval Western Europe, in terms of religion-state relations. In both cases the clerical and military elites dominated society and inhibited the flourishing of intellectuals and merchants. Following the mid-eleventh century, however, Western Europe changed, particularly due to the struggle between the clergy and the royal authority. They tried and failed to dominate one another, which caused the institutionalization of the separation between them. This and other institutional transformations had long-lasting impacts on the increasing intellectual creativity, economic dynamism, and religious diversity in Western Europe.

My analysis reveals the weaknesses of the essentialist claim about Islam and Christianity—that Christianity essentially embraces religion-state separation whereas Islam rejects it. In both Muslim and Christian lands, religion-state relations are changeable and shaped by political actors and conditions. The alliance between the ulema and the state was not an essential part of Islam; instead, it was historically constructed. Similarly, church-state separation in Western Europe was also a result of a historical process. The Orthodox Church had a different historical experience and thus never had a separation from the state. This also shows that the separation between the Catholic Church and the state is not a simple result of the Biblical teaching.

One may still ask, why did Western Europe achieve to institutionalize religion-state separation whereas the Muslim world failed to do so after the eleventh century? To fully answer this question requires a lengthy analysis as I tried in my recent book (Kuru 2019). I can only briefly mention two points here. First, the clergy-state alliance has been the "norm" throughout the world history. What

---

[9] Lord Acton (1877) also regards this as an unintended consequence as neither the Church nor the royal authority strove for separation or liberty. The "aim of both contending parties" was in fact "absolute authority."

[10] The number of Western European universities was twenty, in 1300, it became forty-four in 1400, and it reached sixty-six in 1500. Buringh and Van Zanden, 2009: 431. See also Collins, 2000: 516.

Muslims achieved from the eighth to the eleventh century and what Western Europeans have achieved after the eleventh century (and particularly after the eighteenth century), in terms of the religion-state separation, are rare experiences. Muslim countries lost that precious accomplishment and Western countries still have that. Second, since the mid-eleventh century, the ulema have declared their alliance with the state as a religious necessity, even a Quranic order (Ibn Taymiyya 1994 [1309–14], 184, 190). Hence, it has been very difficult to challenge it in the Muslim world. Although Islam does not inherently reject religion-state separation, a particular interpretation of Islam preached by the post-eleventh century ulema does.

In general, when religious institutions are separate from the state, they contribute to the increasing socio-political diversity and de-centralization. They legitimize opposition to the government and help the existence of a balance of power between the state and other institutions. Yet, when religious institutions establish an alliance with or become subordinate to the state, they contribute to the increasing socio-political centralization. They delegitimize the opposition and sacralize the government. They also lead to the violation of religious freedom and the oppression of religious dissent. In the case of the Muslim world, the ulema-state alliance has imposed religious restrictions to not only non-Muslims but also dissenting Muslims.

This article does not promote a pessimistic understanding about the future of religious freedom in Muslim-majority countries. In fact, it argues that Islam is not an inherently monistic religion and shows that early Islamic history included examples of a certain religion-state separation. Therefore, it, in fact, promotes optimism. If Muslims decide to separate their religious and governmental institutions, they do not have to search for models exclusively in the West. They can find inspirational examples in their own early history.

References

Abdel Razek, A. (2012 [1925]). Islam and the Foundations of Political Power. Translated by M. Loutfi. Edited by A. Filali-Ansary. Edinburgh: Edinburgh University Press.

Abdul-Jabbar, G. (2007). Bukhari. New York: Oxford University Press.

Abou El Fadl, K. (2009). Rebellion and Violence in Islamic Law. New York: Cambridge University Press.

Afsaruddin, A. (2008). The First Muslims: History and Memory. Oxford, U.K.: Oneworld.

Ahmed, M. (1968). Muslim Education and the Scholars' Social Status up to the 5th Century Muslim Era (11th Century Christian Era) in the Light of Ta'rikh Baghdad. Zurich: Verlag "Der Islam."

Arjomand, S. (1999). "The law, agency, and policy in medieval Islamic society: Development of the institutions of learning from the tenth to the fifteenth century." Comparative Studies in Society and History 41, 2: 263-293.

Al-Ashari. (1953 [c. 935]). Kitab al-Luma': The Luminous Book. Translated by Richard J. McCarthy. In The Theology of al-Ashari. Beirut: Imprimerie catholique.

Ashtor, E. (1976). A Social and Economic History of the Near East in the Middle Ages. London: Collins.

Al-Banna, G. (2003). Al-Islam Din wa Ummah wa Laysa Dinan wa Dawlah. Cairo: Dar al-Fikr al-Islami.

Barthold, W. (1977 [1900]). Turkestan Down to the Mongol Invasion. Translated from Russian by T. Minorsky. London: E. J. W. Gibb Memorial Trust.

Berkey, J. (1992). The Transmission of Knowledge in Medieval Cairo: A Social History of Islamic Education. Princeton: Princeton University Press.

Berman, H. (1983). Law and Revolution: The Formation of the Western Legal Tradition. Cambridge, MA: Harvard University Press.

Berman, H. (2003). Law and Revolution II: The Impact of the Protestant Reformations on the Western Legal Tradition. Cambridge, MA: Harvard University Press.

Bloch, M. (2014 [1940]). Feudal Society. Translated from French by L. Manyon. New York: Routledge.

Bloom, J. (2001). Paper Before Print: The History and Impact of Paper in the Islamic World. New Haven: Yale University Press.

Bloom, J. and S. Blair. (2002). Islam: A Thousand Years of Faith and Power. NewHaven: Yale University Press.

Bonner, M. (2010). "The waning of empire: 861-945." In C. Robinson, ed., The New Cambridge History of Islam. Vol. 1: The Formation of the Islamic World. Sixth to Eleventh Centuries. New York: Cambridge University Press.

Botticini, M. and Z. Eckstein. (2012). The Chosen Few: How Education Shaped Jewish History, 70-1492. Princeton: Princeton University Press.

Braudel, F. (1982). Civilization and Capitalism, 15th-18th Century. Volume 2: The Wheels of Commerce. Translated from French by Sian Reynolds. New York: Harper and Row.

Bulliet, R. (2009). Cotton, Climate, and Camels: A Moment in World History. New York: Columbia University Press.

Buringh, E. and J. van Zanden. (2009). "Charting the 'rise of the West': Manuscripts and printed books in Europe. A long-term perspective from the sixth through eighteenth centuries." The Journal of Economic History 69, 2: 409-445.

Cahen, C. (1953). "L'évolution de l'iqta du IXe au XIIIe siècle: contribution à une histoire comparée des sociétés médiévales. Annales. Économies, Sociétés, Civilisations 8, 1: 25- 52.

Chandler, T. (1987). Four Thousand Years of Urban Growth: An Historical Census.Lewiston, NY: Edwin Mellen Press.

Cohen, H. (1970). "The economic background and the secular occupations of Muslim jurisprudents and traditionists in the classical period of Islam (Until the middle of the eleventh century)." Journal of the Economic and Social History of the Orient 13, 1: 16-61.

Collins, R. (2000). The Sociology of Philosophies: A Global Theory of Intellectual Change. Cambridge, MA: Harvard University Press.

Corbin, H. (1986). Histoire de la philosophie islamique. Paris: Gallimard.Crone, P. and M. Hinds. (1986). God's Caliph: Religious Authority in the First Centuries of Islam. New York: Cambridge University Press.

Djaït, H. (1989). La grande discorde: Religion et politique dans l'islam des origins. Paris: Gallimard.

Elias, N. (2000 [1939]). The Civilizing Process. Translated from German by E. Jephcott. Malden, MA: Blackwell.

Ephrat, D. (2000). A Learned Society in a Period of Transition: The Sunni 'Ulama' of Eleventh-Century Baghdad. Albany: SUNY Press.

Fadel, M. (2011). "A tragedy of politics or an apolitical tragedy?" Journal of the American Oriental Society 131, 1: 109-127.

Fakhry, M. (2004). A History of Islamic Philosophy. New York: Columbia University Press.

Fox, J. (2020). Thou Shalt Have No Other Gods before Me: Why Governments Discriminate against Religious Minorities. New York: Cambridge University Press.

Fukuyama, F. (2011). The Origins of Political Order: From Prehuman Times to the French Revolution. New York: Farrar, Straus and Giroux.

Al-Ghazali. (1999 [1095]). The Infamies of the Batinites and the Virtues of the Mustazhirites (Fada'ih al-Batiniyya wa Fada'il al-Mustazhiriyya). Partially translated and edited by R. McCarthy. In Freedom and Fulfillment. Deliverance from Error: Five Key Texts Including His Spiritual Autobiography, al-Munqidh min al-Dalal. Louisville, KY: Fons Vitae.

--------. (2000 [1095]). The Incoherence of the Philosophers [Tahafut al-Falasifa]. Translated by M. Marmura. Provo, UT: Brigham Young University.

--------. (2013 [1095]). Moderation in Belief (Al-Iqtisad fi al-I'tiqad). Translated by A. Yaqub. Chicago: University of Chicago Press.

--------. (2015 [c. 1097]). Kitab al-'Ilm: The Book of Knowledge. Book 1 of the Ihya' 'Ulum al-Din: The Revival of the Religious Sciences. Translated and edited by K. Honerkamp. Louisville: Fons Vitae.

--------. (2002 [c. 1105]). The Decisive Criterion for Distinguishing Islam from Masked Infidelity (Faysal al-Tafriqa bayna al-Islam wa al-Zandaqa). Translated and edited by S. Jackson. In On the Boundaries of Theological Tolerance in Islam: Abu Hamid al-Ghazali's Faysal al-Tafriqa. Karachi: Oxford University Press.

Glick, T. (2005). Islamic and Christian Spain in the Early Middle Ages. Boston: Brill.

Goddard, H. (2000). A History of Christian-Muslim Relations. Chicago: New Amsterdam Books.

Goitein, S. (1966a). "The Rise of the Middle-Eastern Bourgeoisie in Early Islamic Times." In S. D. Goitein, Studies in Islamic History and Institutions. Leiden: Brill.

Goitein, S. (1966b). "The Mentality of the Middle Class in Medieval Islam." In S. D. Goitein, Studies in Islamic History and Institutions. Leiden: Brill.

Hanne, E. (2007). Putting the Caliph in His Place: Power, Authority, and the Late Abbasid Caliphate. Madison, NJ: Farleigh Dickinson University Press.

Harris, M. (1995). History of Libraries in the Western World. London: The Scarecrow Press.

Hodgson, M. (1974a). The Venture of Islam: Conscience and History in a World Civilization. Vol. 1: The Classical Age of Islam. Chicago: University of Chicago Press.

Hodgson, M. (1974b). The Venture of Islam: Conscience and History in a World Civilization. Vol. 2: The Expansion of Islam in the Middle Periods. Chicago: University of Chicago Press.

Huntington, S. (1996). The Clash of Civilizations and the Remaking of World Order. New York: Simon and Schuster.

Ibn Khaldun. (1967 [1377]). The Muqaddimah: An Introduction to History. Vols. I-III. Translated by Frantz Rosenthal. New York: Pantheon Book.

Ibn Khaldun. (2005 [1377]). The Muqaddimah: An Introduction to History. Translated by Frantz Rosenthal. Abridged and edited by N. J. Dawood. Princeton: Princeton University Press.

Ibn Taymiyya, Abu al-Abbas Ahmad. (1994 [1309–14]). Al-Siyasah al-Shar'iyah fi Islah al-Ra'i wa al-Ra'iyah. Algiers: Editions ENAG.

İnalcık, H. (2000 [1973]). The Ottoman Empire: The Classic Age, 1300–1600. Translated by Norman Itzkowitz and Colin Imber. London: Phoenix.

İnalcık, H. (1994). "The Ottoman state: Economy and society, 1300-1600." In H. İnalcık with D. Quataert, eds., An Economic and Social History of the Ottoman Empire. Vol. I: 1300-1600. New York: Cambridge University Press.

Joseph, G. (2000). The Crest of the Peacock: Non-European Roots of Mathematics. Princeton: Princeton University Press.

Kennedy, H. (2005). When Baghdad Ruled the Muslim World: The Rise and Fall of Islam's Greatest Dynasty. Cambridge, MA: Da Capo Press.

Kilgour, F. (1998). The Evolution of the Book. New York: Oxford University Press.

Kuran, T. (2011). The Long Divergence: How Islamic Law Held Back the Middle East. Princeton: Princeton University Press.

Kuru, A. (2009). Secularism and State Policies toward Religion: The United States, France, and Turkey. New York: Cambridge University Press.

--------. (2019). Islam, Authoritarianism, and Underdevelopment: A Global and Historical Comparison. New York: Cambridge University Press.

--------. (2020). "Execution for a Facebook post? Why blasphemy is a capital offense in some Muslim countries." The Conversation, February 20, https://theconversation.com/execution-for-a-facebook-post-why-blasphemy-is-a-capital-offense-in-some-muslim-countries-129685.

Lambton, A. (1981). State and Government in Medieval Islam. An Introduction to the Study of Islamic Political Theory: The Jurists. New York: Oxford University Press.

--------. (1991). Landlord and Peasant in Persia: A Study of Land Tenure and Land Revenue Administration. New York: I.B. Tauris.

Lapidus, I. (1975). "The separation of state and religion in the development of early Islamic society." International Journal of Middle East Studies 6, 4: 363-85.

--------. (1984). Muslim Cities in the Later Middle Ages. New York: Cambridge University Press.

--------. (1996). "State and religion in Islamic societies." Past and Present 151, 1: 3-27.

--------. (2002). A History of Islamic Societies. New York: Cambridge University Press.

"Le Testament d'Ardasir." (1966). Arabic-French text edited and translated by M. Grignaschi. In "Quelques spécimens de la littérature sassanide conservés dans les bibliothèqes d'Istanbul." Journal Asiatique 254: 46–90.

Lewis, B. (1991). The Political Language of Islam. Chicago: University of Chicago Press.

Lindberg, D. (1976). Theories of Vision from Al-Kindi to Kepler. Chicago: University of Chicago Press.

Logan, F. Donald. (2013). A History of the Church in the Middle Ages. New York: Routledge.

Lombard, Maurice. (1975). The Golden Age of Islam. Translated from French by J. Spencer. New York: American Elsevier Publishing.

Lord Acton. (1877). "The History of Freedom in Christianity." An Address Delivered to the Members of the Bridgnorth Institute, May 28, https://www.acton.org/research/history-freedom-christianity.

Maçoudi. (1863 [947]). Les prairies d'or [Muruj al-Dhahab]. Vol. II. Arabic-French text edited and translated by C. de Meynard and P. de Courteille. Paris: L'imprimerie imperial.

Maddison, A. (2004). Growth and Interaction in the World Economy: The Roots of Modernity. Washington, D.C.: The AEI Press.

Mahoney, J. and D. Rueschemeyer. (2003). Comparative Historical Analysis in the Social Sciences. New York: Cambridge University Press.

Melchert, C. (2006). Ahmad ibn Hanbal. Oxford, U.K.: Oneworld.

Mez, A. (1937). The Renaissance of Islam. Translated from German by S. Bakhsh and D. Margoliouth. Patna, India: Jubilee Printing and Publishing House.

Møller, J. (2017). "Medieval origins of the rule of law: The Gregorian reforms as critical juncture?" Hague Journal on the Rule of Law 9: 265–282.

Morony, M. (1984). Iraq after the Muslim Conquest. Princeton: Princeton University Press.

Mottahedeh, R. (1980). Loyalty and Leadership in an Early Islamic Society. Princeton: Princeton University Press.

Al-NadiM. (1970 [987]). The Fihrist of al-Nadim: A Tenth-Century Survey of Muslim Culture. Vol I-II. Translated and edited by Bayard Dodge. New York: Columbia University Press.

Nadwi, M. (2010). Abu Hanifah: His Life, Legal Method and Legacy. Oxford: Kube and Interface Publications.

Nizam al-Mulk. (1978 [c. 1090]). The Book of Government or Rules for Kings. The Siyar al-Muluk or Siyasat-nama of Nizam al-Mulk. Translated from Persian by H. Darke. Boston: Routledge and Kegan Paul.

Pew Research Center. (2019). "A Closer Look at How Religious Restrictions Have Risen Around the World." July 15. https://www.pewforum.org/2019/07/15/a-closer-look-at-how-religious-restrictions-have-risen-around-the-world/.

Philpott, D. (2019). Religious Freedom in Islam: The Fate of a Universal Human Right in the Muslim World Today. New York: Oxford University Press.

Pormann, P. and E. Savage-Smith. (2007). Medieval Islamic Medicine. Washington, D.C.: Georgetown University Press.

Rahman, F. (1968). Islam. New York: Anchor Books.

Rosenthal, E. (1958). Political Thought in Medieval Islam: An Introductory Outline. Cambridge University Press.

Runciman, S. (1977). The Byzantine Theocracy. Cambridge: Cambridge University Press.

Shahrastani, M. (1984 [c. 1127]). Muslim Sects and Divisions. The Section on Muslim Sects in Kitab al-Milal wa '1-Nihal. Translated by A. K. Kazi and J. G. Flynn. Boston: Kegan Paul International.

--------. (1986 [c. 1127]). Livre des religions et des sects. Vol. I [Kitab al-Milal wa '1-Nihal]. Translated into French by D. Gimaret and G. Monnot. Paris: Peeters, UNESCO.

Shatzmiller, M. (2011). "Economic performance and economic growth in the early Islamic world." Journal of the Economic and Social History of the Orient 54, 2: 132-184.

Southern, R. (1970). Western Society and the Church in the Middle Ages. New York: Penguin Books.

Starr, F. (2013). Lost Enlightenment: Central Asia's Golden Age from the Arab Conquest to Tamerlane. Princeton: Princeton University Press.

Tierney, B. (1988 [1964]). The Crisis of Church and State: 1050-1300. Toronto: University of Toronto Press.

--------. (1982). Religion, Law, and the Growth of Constitutional Thought 1150-1650. Cambridge: Cambridge University Press.

Van Zanden, J. (2009). The Long Road to the Industrial Revolution: The European Economy in a Global Perspective, 1000-1800. Leiden: Brill.

Watson, A. (1983). Agricultural Innovation in the Early Islamic World: The Diffusion of Crops and Farming Techniques, 700-1100. New York: Cambridge University Press.

Zaman, M. (1997). Religion and Politics under the Early 'Abbasids: The Emergence of the Proto-Sunni Elite. Leiden: Brill.

International Journal of Religion
November 2020
Volume: 1 | Number 1 | pp. 105 – 119
ISSN: 2633-352X (Print) | ISSN: 2633-3538 (Online)
journals.tplondon.com/ijor

TRANSNATIONAL PRESS®
LONDON

First Submitted: 1 June 2020 Accepted: 31 October 2020
DOI: https://doi.org/10.33182/ijor.v1i1.1201

Secularism, Religion, and Identification beyond Binaries: The Transnational Alliances, Rapprochements, and Dissent of German Turks in Germany

Nil Mutluer[1]

Abstract

This article discusses the ways in which power-based socio-political shifts in Turkey during the AKP (Justice and Development Party) era transnationally influence the relations between and within the Muslim German Turkish communities and their organizations in Germany. Based on ethnographic fieldwork, archival research and reflexive discourse analysis, this article takes DITIB (The Turkish Islamic Union of Religious Affairs) in Germany, which is the affiliate organization of Diyanet (The Presidency of Religious Organization) in Turkey, and analyses its relations with other German Turkish organizations such as Milli Görüş (The Islamic Community of National Vision) and the Gülen Movement in Germany. Such analysis reveals the dynamics of competition between secular and religious, as well as intra-religious, actors and how their members claim their religious and socio-political rights beyond binaries.

Keywords: *Religion; Diyanet/DITIB; Milli Görüş; Gülen Movement; German Turks.*

Introduction

German Turks[2] and their socially, politically, religiously, ethnically, and culturally heterogeneous organizations reflect the dynamic transnational power relations between states, non-state organizations, and individuals. These organizations shape the socio-political relations in different localities of Germany, Turkey, and Europe. Among them, Muslim German Turks, i.e. German Turks who affiliate themselves with Sunni identity, and their religious and socio-political organizations, play a significant role in claiming their religious freedoms and socio-political rights and liberties as citizens of Germany and Turkey. The heterogeneous political and social consequences and formations of their transnationality (Faist, 2011 in Beilschmidt, 2013) shape Muslim German Turks' everyday claim-making (Adar, 2009) and identification processes (Jenkins, 2004), as well as the discourses and policies they develop in relation to the state and other organizations' policies.

This article looks at the ways in which power-based socio-political shifts in Turkey during the AKP (*Adalet ve Kalkınma Partisi*, Justice and Development Party) era transnationally influence the relations between and within the Muslim German Turkish communities and organizations in Germany. Starting in 2011, the AKP's liberal political approach during its first two governing periods gradually shifted to a radically authoritarian one. This shift became particularly pronounced with the 17-25 December 2013 corruption cases. After the coup attempt of 15 July 2016, the shift reached its zenith and became

---

[1] Nil Mutluer, PhD, Einstein Foundation Senior Scholar, Diversity and Social Conflict Department, Humboldt University, Berlin. E-mail: nilmutluer@gmail.com

[2] By German Turks, I refer to Turkish descent individuals in Germany of whom a remarkable share of were born and raised in Germany.

a well-established cornerstone of AKP rule. This has not only caused corresponding shifts in the AKP's religious political alliances, but also led to increasingly tense political relations between Germany and Turkey. In turn, this tension·has put additional pressure on the Muslim Turkish institutions and communities in Germany.

The focus of this article is on the alliances, rapprochements, and dissent not only between Muslim German Turkish communities, but also within them. This focus is informed by broader ethnographic and archival research which begun in Turkey in 2013, and in Germany in 2018, and continues to the present. The research includes several in-depth interviews, including with the presidents of *Diyanet* (The Presidency of Religious Affairs) in Ankara and DITIB (*Türkisch-Islamische Union der Anstalt für Religion e.V.,* The Turkish Islamic Union for Religious Affairs) in Cologne. In addition, the article is based on interviews with several members and volunteers of *Diyanet*, DITIB, and other religious communities both in Turkey and Germany, for example, *Milli Görüş* (*Islamische Gemeinschaft Milli Görüş,* The Islamic Community of National Vision) and *Gülen* Movements' *Süleymancılar* (*Verband der Islamischen Kulturzentren* -VIKZ, The Association of Islamic Culture Centers), AABF (*Alevitische Gemeinde Deutschland, Federation of German Alevi Associations*), German Turkish Society (*Türkische Gemeinde in Deutschland*), and KOMKAR (*Verband der Vereine aus Kurdistan in Deutschland e.V.,* Federation of Associations from Kurdistan in Germany). The interviews were conducted in Turkish and at locations of the respondents own choice, such as their offices, the respective mosques at which they worship, the cafes they frequent, or, in some cases, their homes in Ankara, Berlin, Cologne, and Istanbul. To analyze the data gathered, reflexivity and feminist critical discourse analysis are employed as analytical tools to identify the multi-dimensional shifts in social and political power relations (Ransom, 1993; Alvesson et al., 2000).

It is this methodological framework which guides the article in exploring how the politics of religious dissent shifted during the AKP period, as well as the translation of the meanings attributed to the religious and the secular in the transnational space between Turkey and Germany. This methodology also allows the paper to examine the heterogeneous discourses, policies, and practices of religious institutions and their members to continue with their transnational claim-making processes in Germany and/or Turkey.

In order to carry out this examination, I analyze the transnational identification, policy-making processes, and heterogeneous composition of German Turks and their organizations in several critical intersectional dimensions. I start by discussing the ways in which secularism (Asad, 2003; Fox, 2015) and the politics of religion, specifically Islam, have been practiced both in Turkey and Germany. Following this, I seek to identify the shifts in alliances, rapprochements, and dissent triggered by the shifts in opportunities, obstacles, interests (Jenkins 2004), and threat perceptions that Muslim German Turkish organizations and individuals feel in their everyday socio-political relations with one another and the German and Turkish states. Finally, I highlight the discourses and policies that Muslim German Turks as individuals or as groups within their organizations develop beyond the binary oppositions which political power holders produce and promote. Such a multi-dimensional intersectional analysis has the potential to foreground the meanings attributed to the secular, the religious, the national, and the democratic beyond the binaries. Furthermore, in all these interactions with one another and with the German and Turkish states, Muslim German Turks create what Mignolo calls 'border-thinking' (Mignolo, 2000), in other words, a frame of mind which not only aims to understand and express knowledge from a subaltern point of view, but also closes the gap between opposite knowledge and terminologies, creating, in Mignolo's words (2000:18), a 'dialogue with the debate on the universal/particular'.

Secularism, Religion, and Beyond

Elaborating the political doctrine of secularism and its relation with the secular and the religious as concepts in modern everyday power relations is crucial in comprehending the current transnational social and political shifts of alliances, rapprochements, and dissent between individuals, the state, and non-state actors of Muslim German Turks. In this respect, I find the respective theoretical approaches of Asad and Fox particularly inspiring, for they allow us to understand not only how and why secularism was formed in Turkey the way it was, but also how and why the relations between the secular (nation) state and religious actors have shifted in Turkey over time. Furthermore, they also offer us a conceptual framework to understand why the German state has given free rein on its own soil to a religious state institution of Turkey.

According to Asad, secularism is a political doctrine 'by which a political medium (representation of citizenship) redefines and transcends particular and differentiating practices of the self that are articulated through class, gender, and religion' (Asad, 2003: 5). The secular is that integral part of secularism which engenders modern behaviors, knowledge(s), sensibilities, and governance (Asad, 2003). Values attributed to what is understood as the secular and the religious are shaped in an intersectional way beyond the exclusionary binaries and, in many cases, secular overlaps with the religious (Asad, 2003). However, in the context of the modern nation-state, the secular and the religious have been dichotomously connected to one another. As Dressler argues, Asad's historicizing criticism of 'the work' of the secular and the religious 'in the formation of modern discourses and subjectivities has radically challenged (the essentialist perspective of) both secularist and religionist approaches to religion' (2013: 85).

Fox, for his part, focuses on the tension between the secular and the religious and develops what he calls the 'competition perspective' (2015) to understand the role of religion in politics in the modern era. According to Fox, in the 'secular-religious competition perspective', secularism poses an ideological challenge to religion in political and social areas (Fox, 2015). Yet he also makes a point of underlining the fact that 'neither religion nor secularist ideologies are monolithic' and that there are 'clearly divisions and competition within... the secular and religious camps' as well (Fox 2015, 18). In order to flesh out the competition perspective, Fox prefers a narrower concept of political secularism which he defines as 'an ideology or set of beliefs advocating that religion ought to be separate from all or some aspects of politics and/or public life' (2015: 28). Fox refers to Casanova (2000) to argue that, thus defined, political secularism is a 'statecraft principle' which separates and excludes religion from political authority.

In the case of Turkey, religion plays a significant role in the formation not only of the nation, but also of what Asad calls the secular.[3] Following the Ottoman path, founding elites of the Turkish Republic aimed to control religion's role by adopting a unifying approach centered around Islam. Forged through various secular legislation and state institutions (Gözaydın, 2009; Azak, 2010; Dressler, 2013), a Sunni (Hanefi), Muslim, Turkish identity was made the central element which gives unity to the nation. In this process, religion became so central to what is referred to as *laiklik* that it became a politically loaded concept (Cizre, 1996). As the goal of the founding elites was to tightly control the religious practices in the public sphere (Özyürek, 2006), the aim of the secularist-laicist approach has evolved to restrict and control public religious activities and institutions (Kuru, 2009; Haynes, 1997).

---

[3] In this study, I use Asad's conceptualization of the secular to understand the interrelation between religion and secularism in the formation of the nation-state. As Gözaydın (2020) argues, an in-depth analysis focusing on the archeology of the secular since the Ottoman era still needs to be done.

This approach became the reference point for the continuation of the top-down nationalist state policies, engendering the laic (Kemalist) – Islamist competition, to use Fox's terminology. This competition, in turn, resulted in fundamental values built around two poles in which laic values are considered progressive, while religious/Islamic values are considered backward (Azak, 2010). Kemalist laicism can be considered as 'both a value system and an identity that becomes manifest in the symbols of those who identified themselves with that system' and excludes the ones who are not identified with these values (Mutluer, 2016: 41).

This competition in the socio-political arena notwithstanding, there is a common-ground which both religious and secular camps share. By integrating the intersection of corporatism, populism, and nationalism as the basis of its ideology, Kemalism tried to absorb possible right-wing conservative challenges (Çiğdem, 2004). Thus, with Kemalism on one side and Turkish conservatism and Islamism on the other, both shaped their relations with secularism by embracing the political, economic, and social outcomes of modernization while rejecting its cultural and intellectual ramifications. As a result, a culture that assimilates political and social categories became the principal modern basis for both camps (Çiğdem, 2004). The main differences they have stemmed from the different values they embrace in the cultural realm and from their different positions in the power hierarchy. It is these two differences which underpin what Fox (2015) would call their 'secular-religious competitive positioning' vis-a-vis one another.

Even though laicists on one side and conservatives and Islamists on the other were locked in a secular - religious competition in Fox's sense, the common ground which they both shared allowed, particularly during the Cold War, the joining of forces in the anti-communist camp. On the one hand, secular establishment bureaucrats and elites saw Islamism/Conservatism as an antidote to what they considered to be the bigger and more serious threat of communism. On the other, the Islamists were happy to develop alliances with the establishment whenever they were allowed to do so (Özkan, 2020). Since the 1950s, Islamists and conservatives have been active in politics and invariably side with the state on the many occasions in which the state decides to crack down on the left. This 'anti-communist alliance' became particularly pronounced after the 1980 coup when state secularism started to gain a manifestly Islamic tone (Parla, 1986). The irony of the matter was that the same state bureaucracy that, particularly after the 1980 and 1997 coups, tried to forcibly oust Islamists from whatever public service positions they were occupying also allowed them to gain strength in such positions (Çiğdem, 2004; Özkan, 2020). While the 1980 coup resulted in the left's erasure (Laçiner, 2004), particularly after the 1990s Islamists and conservatives found a chance to increase their visibility and popular credibility in the political arena (Çiğdem, 2004; Yavuz, 2009). Thus, the AKP's election to power in 2002 was a victory for Islamism and conservatism which had been in the making since at least the beginning of the Cold War.

During these decades in which secular and religious actors both competed with one another and formed anti-communist alliances, there was only one state institution which was charged with the task of regulating Muslim religious affairs in Turkey, namely *Diyanet*. Since the foundation of the Turkish Republic, *Diyanet*, the Presidency of Religious Affairs, is the only institution officially allowed to regulate Sunni Muslim religious affairs and serve citizens who profess that faith. *Diyanet*'s primary purpose has been to act as 'an ideological apparatus' of the Turkish state (Öztürk, 2016). The institution was granted and used a certain degree of administrative autonomy, but politically its main function was that of a 'belt of transmission to convey to society the ideology of the governments' (Ozzano et al., 2019: 472). Depending on the governments' policies, *Diyanet*'s budget, activities, and service areas were restricted in some periods and expanded in others (Mutluer, 2014; Mutluer, 2018).

Diyanet has full control over the mosques in Turkey. There is no legal and official mosque or Sunni religious organization in Turkey which is not under the purview of *Diyanet*. This means that there is no other venue for Sunni Muslim groups to practice their religion other than at *Diyanet's* state-controlled mosques. This does not mean, however, that various religious communities have simply disappeared. Many of them, like *Milli Görüş* and the *Gülen* Movement, have carried on their underground activities and, thanks to their transnational connections, have maintain their social, economic, and political strength. Germany was one of the countries, and perhaps the most important one, in which such communities found a free rein to nurture a transnational social and economic power base.

DITIB: transnational secular-religious actor

The German Turkish transnational field has played a significant role in the formation of political Islam in both countries. The politics of Islam has been an issue for Germany since the 1950s. With its increasing Muslim migrant worker population, Germany found itself confronted with the necessity of regulating hundreds of imams, places of worship, and Islamic organizations. The intensifying transnational activities of Islamic groups of Turkish origin, like *Milli Görüş*, *Gülen* Movement, and *Süleymancılar* (Seufert 1999; Ostergaard-Nielsen, 2003; Yurdakul, 2009; Yurdakul, et.al. 2009), accentuated this. Especially after the 1979 Iranian revolution, Germany started considering political Islam as a potential security threat and increased its determination to regulate and control political Islam. Some scholars, notably Özkan (2019), argue that the perceived 'communist threat' also motivated Germany to regulate and keep political Islam as a controlled political actor. As such, the politics of Islam in Germany have been shaped in a transnational ambiguity between safeguarding the freedoms of conscience and speech of Muslim individuals and communities, and regulating Islamic organizations as controlled political actors (Ostergaard-Nielsen, 2003; Yurdakul, 2009; Yurdakul et al., 2009; Özkan, 2019).

Under these circumstances, Turkey became an attractive partner for Germany during the Cold War era as they were both positioned in the anti-communist Western camp. As a result, Germany saw Turkey and its state institution *Diyanet* as a tame and safe alternative to provide political stability and control any possible extremist activities at the grass-root level. After all, the task of *Diyanet* was described in the Article 136 of the 1982 Turkish constitution, written by the 1980 junta, as:

> "remaining over and above all political views and thoughts and performing its legally assigned duties under the guidance of the principle of secularism and adopting national solidarity and integration as its sole purpose".[4]

The 1980's *Diyanet* interpretation of Islam, often referred to as 'official/reformed secular state Islam', was seen more adaptable to the secular European public values. Germany thus gave a green light to the foundation of DITIB precisely because of its official links with the powerful state institution of Turkey, *Diyanet*.

In 1984, DITIB was founded as an umbrella organization of around 200 mosques of Turkish migrants with a special agreement between Germany and Turkey. It is directly linked with the Turkish state institution *Diyanet*. The president of DITIB is appointed by the Turkish state and holds a diplomatic status as a Religious Services Advisor (*Din Hizmetleri Müşaviri*) at the Turkish Embassy in Berlin. The imams of DITIB mosques are sent by *Diyanet*, and are funded by the Turkish state. In other words,

---

[4] https://www.resmigazete.gov.tr/eskiler/2010/03/20100319-17.htm

imams serving in DITIB mosques in Germany are public servants of the Turkish state. Today, DITIB is the biggest Muslim organization of Turkish-German citizens with its 960 mosques affiliated to 14 federal states. DITIB provides general education and cultural activities, youth and woman branches reaching out to the majority of the Turkish Sunni-Muslim community in Germany, and links to the German society with its intercultural and inter-religious dialogue activities.

DITIB follows *Diyanet* in executing services regarding Islamic (Sunni) faith and practices, in enlightening society about religion, and in carrying out the management of places of worship. However, in many cases the information given through DITIB venues goes beyond religion to include messages promoting Turkish nationalism or commenting on current political controversies. In some of my interviews with DITIB volunteers, both from Berlin and Cologne, respondents said that it was commonplace to hear messages about the armed conflict between the Turkish state and the PKK (*Partiya Karaken Kurdistan*, The Kurdistan Workers Party) in the 1990s. More recently, the official and unofficial statements of imams and DITIB officials include frequent references to such politically loaded subjects like the 2016 coup attempt in Turkey or Turkey's military incursion into the Afrin region of northern Syria in 2018. In my interviews with DITIB's officials, they made a point of emphasizing that DITIB imams never go into such political matters in their sermons. However, the Diyanet's President's public statements in Ankara on the same politically loaded subjects raises the question of how the imams, who are *Diyanet* appointed civil servants of the Turkish state, can ignore *Diyanet* president's statements (Mutluer, 2014; Mutluer, 2018) Nevertheless, among other Muslim German Turks' mosques, the DITIB's mosques in Germany still provide a relatively neutral space for Muslims who do not want to affiliate themselves with other political-religious communities.

Germany has developed regulations for its Muslim inhabitants, yet it took time for the German state to accept that Muslim migrant communities in Germany are permanent parts of the German society. It was only in 1999 that Germany started to naturalize the newborn children of the migrant population by introducing the new citizenship law, *Staatsangehörigkeitsgesetz*. In 2006, German Chancellor Angela Merkel and the then Minister of the Interior, Wolfgang Schäuble, emphasized the fact that 'Islam is a part of Germany and that the German society welcomes its 14.5 million people with a migration background' (Rosenow-Williams and Kortmann, 2013: 53). Yet in my research I heard from different Muslim German Turkish community members what has already been well documented by previous studies: although Germany's recognition of the permanence of the Muslim population is welcomed by the community and their organizations, they still feel alienated and in some cases stigmatized. As one of my interviewees said, 'Germany still confuses integration with assimilation'.[5]

This being the case, DITIB's perception of Muslim German Turks and their position in German society reflects the common ground which both Kemalists, Islamists, and conservatives all share in their understanding of Turkish secularism. Following research of scholars like Yükleyen and Yurdakul, I also observe that DITIB encourages the improvement of the socio-economic status of Muslim German Turks but also aims at 'maintaining the loyalty of Turks to the Turkish state and nation and shows no tolerance for debates that criticize the Turkish state' (2011:70). As such, being part of German society culturally and intellectually is not an idea which finds much support in DITIB. However, against the official approach of DITIB, there is a heterogeneity of discourses and practices among the grassroots of the organization and even among some DITIB officials.

---

[5] Interview dated 27 November 2019 in Cologne.

Germany has always had a cautious relationship with political Islam. DITIB has long been regarded as a 'good Muslim organization' because of its close ties with the state organization of secular Turkey, namely *Diyanet,* and its activities are more controlled in comparison to other organizations like *Milli Görüş* in Turkey (Yurdakul, 2009) or the Muslim Brotherhood in Egypt and Syria (Özkan, 2019).

Competition within Transnational Religious Actors

As argued by Fox, secular and religious are not monolithic and the competition between 'religious and secular ideologies is also complemented by struggles between subsets of these ideologies' (2015, 37). There has been an ongoing competition between the actors within these categories as well. The tensions between religious actors arises not necessarily or mainly from their religious differences, but from the competing power positions that they want to hold in in their relations with one another. This is the case with the religious organizations of Muslim German Turks. Depending on opportunities, obstacles, and interests in everyday power relations, individuals, communities, and/or state and non-state organizations identify with, or distinguish from, each other (Jenkins, 2004). As such identification processes are based on power relations, we see shifts in transnational alliances and disassociations among religious organizations (in our case DITIB, *Milli Görüş,* and the *Gülen* Movement) and/or states (in our case the German and Turkish states). The AKP's political turn from democratic conservative to authoritarian had a transnational impact on the positioning of *Milli Görüş* and the *Gülen* Movement in this power hierarchy.

Milli Görüş is the second largest Turkish association in Germany after DITIB with 15 regional associations and 323 mosques. Its organizational activities in Germany started in the1970s around the political and spiritual ideas of former Prime Minister Necmettin Erbakan, and these ideas were institutionalized as IGMG (Islamische Gemeinschaft *Milli Görüş*) in Germany in 1995. *Milli Görüş* also organized itself in a successive series of political parties in Turkey. However, each time a party was founded, it was eventually banned by the constitutional court citing activities contrary to the separation of religion and state (the main principle of Turkish state secularism) and a new party had to be formed. The political oppression in Turkey led the movement to strengthen itself transnationally (Yurdakul, 2009). Although their Islamic political ideas were banned, they still manage to influence their members in Turkey.

Milli Görüş has long been under surveillance by *Verfassungschutz* (The Federal Office of Protection of Constitution), the German intelligence agency, mainly because of its Islamist ideas (Yükleyen et al., 2011) and alleged relations with Islamist groups in the Middle East, such as the Muslim Brotherhood (Vielhaber, 2012). As a result, *Milli Görüş* was regarded as a threat to both German and Turkish societies by their respective states (Yükleyen et al., 2011). Nevertheless, the community members of *Milli Görüş* are heterogeneous in their level of social and political identification to both the German state and society. Although, in comparison to DITIB, the institution has managed to amend its institutional structure in time, *Milli Görüş* is more engaged in making their demands public, such as speaking out against religious discrimination, and it is still monitored by *Verfassungschutz* (Yurdakul, 2009; Rosenow-Williams, 2014). This situation demotivates members of *Milli Görüş* to identify themselves with the German state and society. As one of my interviewees said:

"Milli Görüş in Germany and Europe has changed in time and has become a more democratic, transparent institution. It cut its ties with fundamentalist groups. Yet still this does not seems to be enough for the German state to accept us as part of this society".[6]

From the 1980s to around the 2010s, DITIB and *Milli Görüş* were positioned as binary opposites in Germany. If DITIB was regarded as the 'good Muslim organization', *Milli Görüş* was regarded as the 'bad' one (Yurdakul, 2009). Moreover, both organizations distanced themselves from one another because of their relationship with the Turkish state. Their members refrained from going to each other's mosques and, even though some of my interviewees said that there were some religious differences between them, the distance they keep is better understood as reflective of competition in the religious camp, in Fox's sense.

Today, President Erdoğan himself comes from the tradition of *Milli Görüş*. Erdoğan was one of the disciples of Erbakan and a leading figure in the *Refah Partisi* (Prosperity Party), the political forerunner to *Milli Görüş* until late 1990s. In the early days after his resignation from the Prosperity Party, to becoming one of the leading founders of the AKP in 2002, Erdoğan publicly declared that 'he has taken off the *Milli Görüş* shirt' and started to follow a new path.[7] In its party program in 2004, the AKP positioned itself as a 'conservative democratic' political party committed to 'protecting differences within unity' (Akdoğan, 2004).

When the AKP was elected for the first time in 2002, Erdoğan appointed well-educated members of the *Gülen* Movement to key governmental positions in order to securely 'govern the country and closely monitor the military with the help of the police force' (Yavuz et.al., 2016: 136). The *Gülen* Movement had long had an 'erstwhile dark network' of influence (Watmough et al., 2018) and this was entrenched in the police force, intelligence service, and state bureaucracy after its coalition with the AKP (Yavuz, 2003; Yavuz et al., 2016). As such, Erdogan's metaphor of 'taking off the *Milli Görüş* shirt' can also be seen as a symbolic gesture signaling Erdoğan's shifting alliance from *Milli Görüş* to the *Gülen* Movement in order to consolidate his government's power.

The *Gülen* Movement's spiritual leader, Fethullah Gülen, takes Said Nursi's religious perspective as his spiritual base. In Germany during the 1990s, the *Gülen* Movement organized its activities around educational and learning centers, and the Movement's newspaper *Zaman* had a German edition. It was, and still is, far more successful than the other religious organizations of Muslim German Turks because of its loose networking ability, intercultural as well as inter-religious activities, and its structural visibility and accessibility to the German authorities (Andrews, 2011). The movement does not have its own mosques and until very recently Movement followers preferred to go to DITIB mosques. My interviewees tell me that many *Gülen* Movement members also took active roles in the management of DITIB mosques.[8] However, members of the Movement used to stay away from *Milli Görüş* mosques especially as *Milli Görüş* used to be in the bad books of the Turkish state.

The *Gülen* Movement used to be a pro-state, Turkish nationalist movement and served as an actor in the transnational soft power strategies of the AKP, particularly when it came to developing connections with German actors. Two of my interviewees from the *Gülen* Movement reminisced about how they were contacted by Turkish state officials during the AKP era to organize events for

---

[6] Interview dated on 29 November 2019 in Cologne.

[7] https://www.milliyet.com.tr/siyaset/milli-gorusle-gurur-duyuyorum-5178071

[8] Interviews between March 2019 and January 2020 in Berlin and Cologne.

Turkey or to develop transparent connections and, in some cases, public events.[9] The Movement also enjoyed the recognition and acceptance of local and national public authorities in Germany. One of the above mentioned interviewees tells me that when the Federal State authorities had a message to convey to the religious Muslim community in Germany, they did so by talking at one of their events or to the *Gülen* Movement's newspaper *Zaman*.[10]

AKP, DITIB, and the *Gülen* Movement were allies until it became public knowledge that the *Gülen* Movement and the AKP government parted company after the Movement released evidence of corruption implicating the Erdogan government (what is known as the 17 and 25 December 2013 events). This was the moment when the AKP and the *Gülen* Movement became opponents. The attempted coup, which the AKP government claims to have been masterminded by Fethullah Gülen, happened two years later on 15 June 2016. In September 2016, Diyanet demanded that DITIB imams collect intelligence about Gülen Movement members. In 2017, after this espionage affair became public, the head of the Turkish Intelligence Service, Hakan Fidan, handed a dossier to the German government with a list of people and institutions that the Turkish state had put under surveillance.[11] The list included institutions and people from the Gülen Movement, as well as from Kurdish and leftist circles. German officials subsequently communicated to the people on the list that they were in danger and should not travel to Turkey (Adamson, 2020). These steps signaled that the Turkish government sought to export a domestic political conflict 'in the form of extraterritorial repression' (Öztürk et al., 2020: 64).

Since then the financial, personnel, and organizational dependence of DITIB on Diyanet is viewed with rising skepticism by German politicians, and is increasingly considered by many as a mixture of religious practice and pursuance of Ankara's political objectives in Germany.[12] In September 2018, one week before the state visit of Erdoğan to Germany, Verfassungschutz sent a dossier to its local state agencies about DITIB and suggested for the organization to be placed under surveillance. Many local federal states refused to accede to this suggestion arguing that, at a local level, they cooperate closely with DITIB to reach out to Muslim communities and do not want to harm these relations. Because of the refusal of the Federal States, the Verfassungschutz decided not to put DITIB under surveillance for the time being.[13] Different than Milli Görüş and the Gülen Movement, when the heterogeneous grassroots composition of Muslim German Turks who use DITIB services are considered, the concern of local federal governments not to harm their relationship with the Muslim German Turkish community is understandable as different localities have different social and political dynamics.

According to some of my interviewees, the transnational pressure that the Turkish state put on the Gülen Movement since 2015 greatly harmed the Movement's institutional power and its members' everyday life. Their relations with the German authorities are on good terms as they believe that Germany tries to protect them, yet they also realize they are no longer invited to all socio-political occasions. There are cracks appearing within the Movement. Some are critical either of the

---

[9] Interview dated 8 May 2019 in Berlin and interview dated 9 May 2019 in Berlin.

[10] Interview dated 8 May 2019 in Berlin.

[11] https://www.dw.com/tr/casusluk-krizinin-kronolojisi/a-40391548

[12] Deutscher Bundestag, wissenschaftliche Dienste, Ausarbeitung: Rechtlicher Status der DITIB. p. 4, 19.07.2018.

[13] https://www.tagesschau.de/inland/ditib-beobachtung-101.html

Movement's involvement in politics or in the undemocratic policies of the AKP.[14] Some have grown critical of all the political activities of the Gülen Movement and distance themselves from it. In addition to the Turkish state's transnational surveillance and profiling activities, the Gülen Movements' members and institutions have been subjected to social lynching and vandalization of their properties, intimidation through threats to their relatives in Turkey, stigmatization, and mobbing. Individuals who were known to be a member of the Movement were forced to resign from their managerial positions at mosques or were chased away. The highest ranking DITIB officials say that there are standing instructions to prevent such things from happening but unfortunately such things happen.[15]

The relations between the AKP government and DITIB on one side, and the Gülen Movement on the other, led to the formation of a new alliance between the AKP, DITIB, and Milli Görüş in Germany. The symbolic turning point that crowns this new alliance is Diyanet's President Ali Erbaş's visit to Milli Görüş's headquarter in Cologne and a jointly organized public event at a stadium in Bremen. With this visit from one of the high ranking state bureaucrats of Ankara, Milli Görüs gained legitimacy. This transnational alliance will surely change the power dynamics within the Muslim Turkish community in Germany.

Seen from Fox's competition perspective however, this newly formed alliance between DITIB and Milli Görüş is akin to any other political alliance. As such, it is subject to the whims of shifting threat perceptions and power relations within the religious camp which can change at a moment's notice. Perhaps the most perceptive expression of this insight came from one of my interviewees, a prominent figure of the Muslim Turkish community in Germany, who has been an active member of IMGM (Islamische Gemeinschaft Milli Görüş): 'Our state either neglects us, or suffocates us.'[16] On the one hand, he sees Erdoğan and the Turkish state as a strong power that protects their 'Muslim' priorities and dignity in the international area. Yet, on the other hand, he also criticizes him and the Turkish state for regarding the Muslim migrants from Turkey as a ready-to-hand force to defend Turkey's interests. Such an approach puts Muslim Turkish migrants in a position where they always feel compelled to justify and defend Turkey's political discourse to German bureaucrats and people. These sentiments suggest that the grassroots level is more heterogeneous than the shifting alliances at the higher levels of the organizational hierarchies.

Thinking beyond Binaries

Since its foundation, DITIB has had a transnational hybrid character as its organizational structure combines both vertical/hierarchical and horizontal/grassroots elements. It is Turkish Diyanet's centrally controlled affiliate in Germany and has a hierarchical administrative structure. However, DITIB is also the umbrella organization of grassroots mosque communities. In this hybrid character, power is concentrated in DITIB's headquarters in Cologne but, for Muslim German Turks, the local branches of DITIB in different federal states, as well as the mosques in communities, can wield power through voicing their opinions and influencing the everyday socio-political decision making of the organization. The fact that influence can be wielded at the grassroots level shows that local actors have the capacity to practice the religious, the secular, as well as the democratic in intersectional ways that go beyond well-worn binary oppositions. Furthermore, in all of these interactions Muslim

---

[14] Interview dated 8 May 2019 in Berlin and interviews on April - June 2019 in Berlin, November - December 2019 in Cologne.

[15] Interview with Berlin Embassy Religious Services Advisor President of DITIB dated 3 December 2019 in Cologne.

[16] Interview dated 29 November 2019 in Cologne.

German Turks create what Mignolo calls a 'border-thinking' (2000), namely a frame of mind which bridges opposite forms of knowledge and terminologies, expressing them from a subaltern point of view and engaging them in a dialogue with the debate on the universal/particular. Grassroots Muslim German Turks interventions in politics represents the potential knowledge and perspective which is nourished by, but at the same time critical of, both German and Turkish states and societies.

The shifts within Diyanet from being decentralized and democratic to an authoritarian organization also influence DITIB's approach to its grassroots. When the AKP first came to power in Turkey, it advocated abolishing Diyanet as it saw the organization as an obstacle to religious freedoms (Mutluer, 2018). Since abolishing an institution which had an existential significance for Turkish secularism was not easy, the AKP chose to reform Diyanet and redesign it to be more responsive to grassroots demands. These steps were also welcomed by the members and volunteers of DITIB as they regarded that moment as an opportunity to have their claims heard and acted upon. They also thought that the decentralization and democratization of DITIB would eventually lead to Islam being recognized under German Law. One of my interviewees expressed the mood of that period:

> "for a time we really thought a democratic change could be possible and we could even developed a platform with the involvement of theologians, sociologists etc., where we could provide responses, if necessary reformed responses, to Muslim migrants' religious questions and needs regarding the country they live in".[17]

In 2006, the women, youth, and education branches of DITIB started to be formally institutionalized at the local level in federal states and at the central level in Cologne. In 2009, DITIB's charter was amended to allow for local branches in different Federal States to be organized with their own management structure (Gorzewski, 2015). However, DITIB members and volunteers, as well as many other Muslim German Turks, believe that the short decentralization and transparency period ended around 2014. Some of the ex- and current DITIB members feel that what came after 2014 was the opposite of decentralization; it was a new wave of centralization within DITIB. One example of this can be found in the DITIB's demand that imams and *vaizes* - women religious preachers - be involved in social activities regarding female and youth issues. Maybe not coincidentally, this policy came at a moment when the AKP attempted to redesign the family in Turkey by restructuring the role of women as 'religious', and *Diyanet* followed suit by signing a protocol with the Turkish Ministry of Family and Social Policy (Mutluer, 2018; Mutluer, 2019). At the time, this new policy of *Diyanet* was not welcomed by DITIB members and volunteers as they did not want to mix the area of the secular with the religious. As one of them said:

> "I was told to have women religious preachers in all our activities. I asked them what would be the point of having women religious preachers in social services? We are doing social work for women. Women religious preachers do not have anything to do with that type of work".[18]

As observed by Muslim German Turks who use DITIB mosques, since 2014 the DITIB headquarters used the Turkish consulate-affiliated religious affairs attachés and consulate officials to restrict the activities and stifle the voices of grassroots mosque communities. In one prominent example, told by several interviewees, during the Hessen local branch elections in 2014, the old administration was forced out of office and a new administration installed by DITIB headquarters. Following this, the

---

[17] Interview dated 28 December 2019 in Cologne.

[18] Interview dated on 9 October 2019 in Berlin.

new administration changed articles of an agreement with the Hessen Ministry of Education, without informing the Ministry. The Ministry found DITIB headquarters' intervention to be contrary to democratic transparency and suspended the agreement. This shows that both the German authorities and the grassroots communities are actors regarding their own rights, and DITIB cannot establish a centralized control over Muslim German Turks as *Diyanet* does to Turks in Turkey, even when it sought to re-centralize DITIB.[19]

The 2017 general assembly was another example of re-centralizing tendencies in DITIB. When DITIB headquarters tried to change its charter in a way that would restrict the voting rights of the grassroots mosque communities, it introduced this change in an underhand way. By making use of the language differences between the German and Turkish versions of the charter, DITIB headquarters argued that the change was necessary to bring each version in line. The voting rights of the mosque communities were mentioned in the German version but not in the Turkish and, as the issue was not allowed to be discussed openly during the assembly, the changes were approved despite some local branch delegates' objections.[20]

According to some ex-volunteers of DITIB, the re-centralization policies went so far that anyone who defended the pluralist and transparent values of the institution were blamed by public servants appointed by *Diyanet* for being thoroughly 'Almanlaşmış' (Germanized). They were further accused of forgetting Turkishness and nationalist feelings. One of my interviewees said that:

> "that period was like a 'take over'. We just wanted a transparent institution that reflects the needs of the grassroots. DITIB's grassroots are made of people like me, civilians who grew up in DITIB's mosques. But we were educated and are living in Germany as citizens of this country. We believe in transparency and democracy".[21]

The new alliance between *Milli Görüş* seems not to be welcomed by all DITIB members and volunteers. Some regard it as the direct intervention of politics into religion and an attack on DITIB's neutrality.[22] Some are also unhappy of being positioned as 'the diaspora, ready forces to apply the homeland politics'[23] by the Turkish state. Especially those who were born and educated in Germany feel themselves active members of both the Turkish and German communities, but not as a 'diaspora whose connections are cut off' as some of them highlight.[24]

According to some of the ex- and current DITIB and mosque community volunteers and members, one of the main problems of DITIB is in not meeting the needs of Turks in German society, even though the organization has the capacity to do it. It seems Diyanet's approach is much more influential in DITIB's policy development and decision making process than its grassroots. Nevertheless, the resistance, new discourse, and recent policies developed by local DITIB bodies and mosque

---

[19] Interviews between March 2019 and January 2020 in Berlin and Cologne. https://euturkhaber.com/index.php/2020/05/12/hessen-eyaletinde-ditibin-sorumlulugunda-inanca-dayali-islam-din-dersi-okutulmasina-son-verilmesi-ve-surece-dair-dusunceler/#

[20] Interviews dated 7 March 2019, 12 April 2019, 13 September 2019 in Berlin and 22-25 November 2019, 1-3 December 2019 in Cologne.

[21] Interview dated on 23 November 2019 in Cologne.

[22] Interviews dated March 2019 - January 2020 in Berlin and Cologne.

[23] Interview dated on 24 November 2019 in Cologne.

[24] Interviews dated March 2019 - January 2020 in Berlin and Cologne.

communities suggest that coming generations think beyond binaries. It seems that they would like to have more say in the management of their religion in the future.

Conclusion

The transnational space between Germany and Turkey is shaped by the 'competition' (Fox 2015) within and between religious and secular actors. During the AKP era, power-based socio-political shifts in Turkey, and the accompanying political shifts within Diyanet, influenced the relations among and within DITIB, Milli Görüş, and Gülen Movements in Germany. In order to consolidate the political power of the party he leads, Erdoğan first distanced himself from Milli Görüş and approached the Gülen Movement during the early 2000s. Subsequently, and especially after 2013 corruption scandal, Erdoğan broke this alliance with the Gülen Movement and again started courting the popular support base of Milli Görüş. These shifts in Erdoğan's alliances and rapprochements had significant repercussions in the identification processes of the members of Milli Görüş, the Gülen Movement, and DITIB in Germany.

Since its foundation in the early 1980s, up until Erdoğan's authoritarian turn in the early 2010s, DITIB in Germany was considered by German officialdom as a reliable and trustworthy religious civil society organization of Muslim Turks. They based this on DITIB's close ties with Diyanet, and hence with the secular Turkish state. By contrast, German officialdom shunned Milli Görüş, despite the organization ardently adhering to the regulatory legal and political framework of Germany. German officials branded Milli Görüş as a 'radical Islamic' organization due to its members' Islamist activities in the past and of the critical distance organization kept from DITIB, Diyanet, and the secularism understanding of the Turkish State. During this period, the Gülen Movement acted as the AKP governments' non-governmental goodwill ambassador in Germany, and even though some of its members were critical of Erdoğan's authoritarian turn, they did not stop collaborating and supporting the Turkish state. This came to an end when Erdoğan and the Gülen Movement parted company for good; a long and turbulent break-up which started in 2013, and ended with the 2016 coup attempt.

In the aftermath of the coup attempt, the Gülen Movement's fall from grace in Turkey was almost complete, but the civil relations it had cultivated with the German officialdom in the past allowed it to continue its activities in Germany, albeit with a much restricted field of play. By stark contrast to the Gülen Movement's fall from grace after 2016, Milli Görüş in Germany enjoyed a marked rise in favor with the Turkish State and its relations with DITIB, thus Diyanet and the Turkish state.

Amidst these shifts in alliances and rapprochements, my research reveals that there is an emerging new group of dissenting actors in the transnational field between Germany and Turkey. This emerging new group consists of those Muslim Turks living in Germany who have been (and in most cases who still are) affiliated with either DITIB, Milli Görüş, or the Gülen Movement, but who have grown weary of the skirmishes and competition both within and among these movements, institutions, and the German and Turkish states. These new actors identify themselves simultaneously as German and Turkish, while maintaining a healthy critical distance to both the German and Turkish state policies and practices regarding Muslim Turks living in Germany. As individuals or as members of their mosque communities and/or religious organizations, they develop another way of identifying beyond the established binaries. They are still not strong, but their well-discerned presence says something about what can be expected in the future.

The meanings attributed to the secular and religious are beyond binaries (Asad, 2003), and the values attributed to secularism are shaped by the 'secular and religious actors competition' (Fox 2015). My research suggests that new meanings and new forms of everyday identification with the secular and the religious may emerge among the dissenting group of Muslim Turks living in Germany. Their quest for another way beyond the established binaries gives rise to 'border thinking' (Mignolo, 2000), enabling them to think through, and be critical of, opposing and different knowledges at the same time.

References

Adamson, F. 2020. Non-state authoritarianism and diaspora politics. Global Networks 20, no. 1: 150-69.

Adar, S. 2019. Rethinking Political Attitudes of Migrants from Turkey and Their Germany-Born Children: Beyond Loyalty and Democratic Culture. SWP Research Paper 7, June, Berlin.

Akdoğan, Y. 2004. Adalet ve Kalkınma Partisi (Justice and Development Party). In Modern Türkiye'de Siyasi Düşünce Vol. 6: Islamicism (Political Thinking in Modern Turkey: Nationalism), ed. Y. Aktay, 620-631, Istanbul, İletişim.

Alvesson, M., Skoldberg, K. (2000). Reflexive Methodology: New Vistas for Qualitative Research. London: Sage Publications.

Andrews, M. 2011. Building Institutional Trust in Germany: Relative Success of the Gülen and Milli Görüş. Turkish Studies, 12:3, 511-524.

Asad, T. 2003. Formations of the Secular: Christianity, Islam, Modernity. Stanford, CA: Stanford University Press.

Azak, U. 2010. Islam and Secularism in Turkey: Kemalism, Religion and the Nation State. London: I.B. Taurus.

Beilschmidt, T. 2013. Religious Practices of DITIB Mosque Community Members: Perspectives from Germany. In Islamic Organizations in Europe and the USA. A Multidisciplinary Perspective, ed. M. Kortemann and K. Rosenow-Williams, 186-202. London: Palgrave Macmillan.

Casanova, J. 2009. The Secular and Secularisms. Social Research 76, no. 4: 1049-66.

Çiğdem, A. 2004. Sunuş [Introduction]. In Modern Türkiye'de siyasi düşünce: Muhafazakarlık [Political thinking in modern Turkey: Conservatism], ed. A. Çiğdem, 13-19. Istanbul: İletişim Publications.

Cizre, Ü.1996. Parameters and Strategies of Islam-State Interaction in Republican Turkey. International Journal of Middle East Studies 28, no.2: 231-51.

Dressler, M. 2013. Writing religion: the making of Turkish Alevi Islam. New York: Oxford University Press.

Faist, T., M. Fauser, and E. Reisenauer. 2011. Perspektiven der Migrationsforschung: Vom Transnationalismus zur Transnationalität. Soziale Welt – Zeitschrift für sozialwissenschaftliche Forschung und Praxis 62, no. 2: 203–20.

Fox, J. 2015. Secularism or Secularization? The Secular-Religious Competition Perspective and Beyond. In Political Secularism, Religion, and the State: A Time Series Analysis of Worldwide Data, 16-38. Cambridge: Cambridge University Press.

Gorzewski, A. 2015. Die Türkisch-Islamische Union im Wandel. Wiesbaden: Springer Fachmedien.

Gözaydın, İ. 2020. Diyanet: Türkiye Cumhuriyet'inde Dinin Tanzimi [Directorate of Religious Affairs: Religious Arrangement of the Republic of Turkey] - New Edition. Istanbul: İletişim.

Gözaydın, İ. 2009. Diyanet: Türkiye Cumhuriyet'inde Dinin Tanzimi [Directorate of Religious Affairs: Religious Arrangement of the Republic of Turkey]. Istanbul: İletişim.

Jenkins, R. 2004. Social Identity. London: Routledge.

Haynes, J. 1997. Democracy and Civil Society in the Third World: Politics and New Political Movements. Cambridge: Polity Press.

Körs, A. and A. Nagel. 2018. Local 'Formulas of Peace': Religious Diversity and State-Interfaith Governance in Germany. Social Compass 65, no. 3: 346-62.

Kortmann, M. and K. Rosenow-Williams. 2013. Islamic Umbrella Organizations and Contemporary Political Discourse on Islam in Germany: Self-Portrayals and Strategies of Interaction. Journal of Muslim Minority Affairs 33, no. 1: 41-60.

Kuru, A. 2009. Secularism and State Policies Toward Religion: the United States, France, and Turkey. Cambridge: Cambridge University Press.

Laçiner, Ö. 2004. Islamism, Socialism and Left [İslamcılık, Sosyalizm ve Sol]. In Modern Türkiye'de Siyasi Düşünce: İslamcılık [Political Thinking in Modern Turkey: Islamism], ed. A. Yasin, 469-475. Istanbul: İletişim Publications

Mignolo, W. 2000. Local Histories - Global Designs: Coloniality, Subaltern Knowledges, and Border Thinking. Princeton, NJ: Princeton University Press.

Mutluer, N. 2019. Intersectionality of Gender, Sexuality and Religion: An Analysis of Novelties and Continuities in the Case of Turkey During the AKP era. Southeast European and Black Sea Studies, 19(1).

Mutluer, N. 2018. Diyanet's Role in Building the 'Yeni (New) Milli' in the AKP era. European Journal of Turkish Studies 27: 1–24.

Mutluer, N. 2016. Kemalist Feminists in the era of AK Party. In Political Criticism Against Turkey's AK Party: Criticism, Opposition and Dissent, ed. Ü. Cizre, 40–74. London: Routledge.

Mutluer, N. 2014. Yapısal, Sosyal ve Ekonomi-Politik Yönleriyle Diyanet İşleri Başkanlığı [Structural, Social and Political-Economic Aspects of the Presidency of Religious Affairs]. In Sosyo-Ekonomik Politikalar Bağlamında Diyanet İşleri Başkanlığı [The Presidency of Religious Affairs with the Context of Social-Economic Policies], ed. S. Özçelik, 4–72. Istanbul: Helsinki Citizens Assembly Publication.

Ostergaard-Nielsen, E. 2003. Transnational Politics: Turks and Kurds in Germany. London: Routledge.

Özkan, B. 2020. The 1945 Turkish-Soviet Crisis. Russia Global Affairs 18, no. 2: 156-87.

Özkan, B. 2019. Cold War Era Relations Between West Germany and Turkish Political Islam: From an Anti-Communist Alliance to a Domestic Security Issue. Southeast European and Black Sea Studies 19, no.

Öztürk, A. Erdi, and Hakkı Taş. The Repertoire of Extraterritorial Repression: Diasporas and Home States. Migration Letters 17, no. 1 (2020): 59-69.

Öztürk, A. 2016. Turkey's Diyanet Under the AKP Rule: From Protector to Imposer of State Ideology? Southeast European and Black Sea Studies 16, no. 4: 619-35.

Özyürek, E. 2006. Nostalgia for the Modern: State Secularism and Everyday Politics in Turkey. Durham, NC: Duke University Press.

Ozzano, L. and C, Maritato. 2019. Patterns of Political Secularism in Italy and Turkey: The Vatican and the Diyanet to the Test of Politics. Politics and Religion 12, no. 3: 457-77.

Parla, T. 1986. Dinci Milliyetçilik [Religionist Nationalism]. Yeni Gündem [New Agenda], May 19.

Ransom, J. (1993). Feminism, Difference and Discourse, the Limits of Discursive Analysis for Feminists. Up Against Foucault: Explorations of Some Tensions between Foucault and Feminism. New York: Routledge, pp. 123 146.

Rosenow-Williams, K. 2014. Organising Muslims and Integrating Islam: Applying Organisational Sociology to the Study of Islamic Organisations. Journal of Ethnic and Migration Studies 40, no. 5: 759-77.

Wang, B. and J. Wang. 2016. Political Aspirations, Participations and Influence of Turkish Muslims in Germany. Journal of Middle Eastern and Islamic Studies (in Asia) 10, no. 2: 99-120.

Watmough, S. and A. Öztürk. 2018. From 'Diaspora by Design' to Transnational Political Exile: The Gülen Movement in Transition. Politics, religion & ideology 19, no. 1: 33-52.

Yavuz H. And R. Koç. 2016. The Turkish Coup Attempt: The Gülen Movement vs. the State. Middle East Policy, Volume XXIII, 4.

Yavuz, M.H. 2009. Secularism and Muslim democracy in Turkey. Cambridge: Cambridge University Press.

Yavuz, H. 2003. Islamic Political Identity. New York: Oxford University Press.

Yurdakul, G. 2009. From guest workers into Muslims: the transformation of Turkish immigrant associations in Germany. Newcastle upon Tyne: Cambridge Scholars Publishing.

Yurdakul, G. and A. Yükleyen. 2011. Islamic Activism and Immigrant Integration: Turkish Organizations in Germany. Immigrants & Minorities 29, no. 1: 64-85.

Yurdakul, G. and A. Yükleyen. 2009. Islam, Conflict, and Integration: Turkish Religious Associations in Germany. Turkish Studies 10, no. 2: 217-31.

International Journal of Religion

ISSN: 2633-352X (Print) | ISSN: 2633-3538 (Online)

journals.tplondon.com/ijor

TRANSNATIONAL PRESS®
LONDON

International Journal of Religion
November 2020
Volume: 1 | Number 1 | pp. 121 – 134
ISSN: 2633-352X (Print) | ISSN: 2633-3538 (Online)
journals.tplondon.com/ijor

TRANSNATIONAL PRESS®
LONDON

First Submitted: 8 July 2020 Accepted: 31 October 2020
DOI: https://doi.org/10.33182/ijor.v1i1.1080

Dissenting Yogis: The Mīmāṃsaka-Buddhist Battle for Epistemological Authority

Jed Forman[1]

Abstract

While dissent connotes a type of split or departure, it can bind as much as it separates. This paper traces a millennium-long history of debate between Buddhists and other religionists who championed the Vedic authority rejected by the Buddha, a camp that came to be known as "Mīmāṃsā." My analysis illustrates dissent can have the paradoxical feature of forging strong relationships through its seeming antithesis: opposition. Specifically, I explore Mīmāṃsaka-Buddhist debate on meditation. Buddhists argued that meditation could yield authoritative spiritual insight once a meditator had honed their yogic perception (yogipratyakṣa). Mīmāṃsakas rejected yogic perception, arguing only the scriptural corpus of the Vedas had authority. By undermining yogic perception, Mīmāṃsakas aimed to defang religious movements, like the Buddhists', who appealed to meditative experience as legitimate grounds for dissent. Counterintuitively, such exchanges were essential for the construction of each faction's identity and were continually mutually formative over the long history of their interaction.

Keywords: *Buddhism; Mīmāṃsā; epistemology; meditation; Yogic perception.*

Introduction

> Cain, who turns away from the God who turns away from him, already follows the line of deterritorialization, protected by a sign allowing him to escape death. The mark of Cain. A punishment worse than imperial death? The Jewish God invented the reprieve, existence in reprieve, *indefinite postponement*. But He also invented the positivity of alliance, or the covenant, as the new relation with the deity, since the subject remains alive. Abel, whose name is vanity, is nothing; Cain is the true man… It is the regime of betrayal, universal betrayal, in which the true man never ceases to betray God just as God betrays man, with the wrath of God defining the new positivity (Deleuze & Guattari 1987, p. 123).

Gilles Deleuze and Félix Guattari (1987) here describe "the line of flight." They note that in contrast to the priest, the prophet ushers in a new religion with betrayal, through a "face-off" with God. This "double turning away" between God and prophet, perhaps counterintuitively, ensures their ongoing relationship. Rather than a pure fleeing, it is the "faciality" with God that "organizes the line of flight" (p. 124). Cain's dissent against God, therefore, elevates him to the status of the preeminent prophet. As the impetus for God's covenant with humanity, he founds an ongoing relationship of betrayal. Although a seeming flight and deterritorialization from God's kingdom, Cain's actions ensure his being marked by God, the mark of Cain; after all, it is Cain and not Abel who lives on in humanity.

Deleuze and Guattari's formulation is equally applicable to the complex and seemingly paradoxical dimensions of dissent. Although dissent connotes a turning away and a rejection, the process is bi-

---

[1] Jed Forman, PhD, University of California Santa Barbara, California, United States. E-mail: jed.forman@gmail.com

directional and mutually informing: while the dissenting party's dissent occurs in reaction to the provenance of a larger regime, that regime in turn also reacts to that dissent, becoming "obsessed" with the dissenter's line of flight, and even reforms itself in contradistinction. As Geleuze and Guattari note, this is a "double turning away." Although we may think of prophets in continuity with God's message, Deleuze and Guattari conceive of prophets as the product of tension with, even betrayal of, the powers that formed them. There is thus both continuity and opposition. Dissent reveals itself as both a reaction and a continuation of those powers that it "resists." This analysis reveals that although religious dissent superficially appears to be a departure from orthodoxy, it maintains an intimate relationship with it, one that is mutually informing and ongoing.

Focused on Abrahamic traditions, Deleuze and Guattari (1987) further argue that the Book is emblematic of this line of flight, which "takes the place of the face and God, who hides his face and gives Moses the inscribed stone tablets" (p. 127). In forging a new path, the prophet writes about God away from God. In this paper, I argue that the relationship *cum* opposition between Vedic authority and Buddhism suggests an inversion of the Abrahamic transition from the face of God to the Book. While the Vedas profess that only its scripture can describe the divine, Buddhism attempts to recover the face of "God" through direct experience. The Buddhist line of flight retreats from the separation entailed by the Book and seeks to recover a direct connection to spiritual insight unmitigated by scripture. But as Geleuze and Guattari theorize, this opposition puts Buddhism and Vedic authority in an ongoing relationship, a "face-off" which mutually influences. It is in response to Buddhism that the Mīmāṃsā approach arose as an attempt to recover the authority of the Vedas. This paper analyzes a short history of this dissent, showing its role in the evolution of both Buddhist and Vedic epistemology. Specifically, their argument centers on the role of meditation and whether it can lead to veritable spiritual insight. Dissent is thus the friction that heats the forge in which both these schools developed their sophisticated theories on the soteriology (or lack thereof) of meditation.

The *Śramaṇa* Movement

Buddhism was just one of many contemporaneous religious movements that sought independent authority from the Vedas—the dominant orthodox scriptures of pre-sixth century BCE India—Jainism being another well-known example. Modern scholars collectively categorize these religions under the "*śramaṇa* movement." The term "*śramaṇa*" itself is not alien to the Vedas. It was only later repurposed to refer to groups that dissented against Vedic authority, and even this connotation may reveal a Buddhist bias.[2] Etymologically, it simply denotes "making effort." However, it is easy to anticipate how *spiritual* effort can quickly transgress orthodoxy. If spiritual effort results in spiritual acumen, this in turn may lead to entitled claims of a rival spiritual authority. The Buddha reflects a general trend of religious figures during this period who laid claim to novel spiritual authority through the graces of their own efforts.

This is beautifully allegorized in Aśvaghoṣa's (c. 80-150 CE) *Buddhacarita,* a hagiography of the Buddha's life and one of the earliest Sanskrit Buddhist works. Being confronted for the first time with old age, sickness, and death, Siddhārtha Gautama (as he was known before his awakening as the Buddha) was deeply troubled. Upon seeing a mendicant—whom we could also proleptically identify as a member of the *śramaṇa* movement—he was inspired to become a renunciate in order to escape

---

[2] Much of what we know concerning *śramaṇa* religions comes from the Buddhist *Sāmaññaphala Sutta* (Dīgha Nikāya 2), which, predictively, describes other *śramaṇa* rival movements rather disparagingly. On the other hand, Patrick Olivellle argues that in the larger religious context, "*śramaṇa*" had no connotation of being anti-Vedic. See Olivelle (1993) for a discussion (p. 14). This, of course, does not undermine the existence of several anti-Vedic movements of which Buddhism was one; it merely questions their appellation as "*śramaṇa.*"

these otherwise inevitable sufferings. However, Siddhārtha was a prince. He would have to gain permission to take leave from his father, King Śuddhodana, which would be no small request, since Siddhārtha had been groomed since birth to take over the throne.

> Bowing down with folded hands, [Gautama] said, "Grant me leave, O God of Men, to become a mendicant. I want to completely renounce [the world] and focus solely on the causes for liberation, separated from this life."

> Hearing his words, the king shook like a tree that had been struck by an elephant. With beseeching hands, shaped like a lotus, he said this in a tearful voice,

> "Stop thinking like this! This not the time for you to concentrate on dharma. They say that the practice of dharma during the confusion of early youth incurs many faults.

> "The senses of the young are curious about the world. They do not have the determination necessary for the difficulties of religious austerities. Their minds shirk from the forest, and they are especially naïve in their judgments.

> "Giving my wealth to you, Dearest Dharma, you have become wealthy, and now *my* time for [religious] dharma has come. For you, firm in your strides, it is your dharma to do this in stages, for abandoning [me], your master, would not be dharma.

> "Giving up this resolve, be satisfied with the dharma of the householder. Forest-dwelling austerities are acceptable after first enjoying the pleasures of manly youth."

> Hearing these words, the Illustrious One replied in a sparrow's voice, "If, King, you can assure me of four things, then I will not pursue forest austerities:

> "That my life will not just be for death, that disease will not separate me from health, that old age will not destroy my youth, and that misfortune will not deprive me of this wealth." (v. 528-35).[3]

Of course, the king can make no such guarantee, and so Gautama departs for the forest, his literal line of flight and deterritorialization. In this dialogue, King Śuddhodana represents Vedic orthodoxy, which calls for a delay of the spiritual path. Religious pursuits are not for the young; only once one has fulfilled certain household duties—raising a family, amassing wealth for one's progeny, and, in Gautama's case, completing his commitments as king—is it appropriate to become a mendicant. Aśvaghoṣa gestures specifically to the *āśrama* stages, the four life stages that every Brahman is meant to undergo. King Śuddhodana specifically mentions the second stage, the householder (*gṛhastha*), during which pleasure (*kama*) is the primary pursuit. The king, by contrast, has reached the appropriate age to pursue religion as a mendicant (*saṃnyāsa*). Gautama's decision to part with this expectation—to deny the burden of kingship—signals an egregious form of dissent, but one indicative of the larger *śramaṇa* movement, within which wandering ascetics became an emblem of the individual quest for spiritual truth. As Deleuze and Guattari note, Gautama's turning away from his father *cum* orthodoxy is a line of flight that not only gives rise to the Buddhist tradition, but one that conditions its ongoing relationship with that orthodoxy.

---

[3] Translations from Pali, Sanskrit, and Tibetan are my own throughout unless specified otherwise.

Gautama's journey reflects an ongoing pursuit of individual insight: even the teachings of other *śramaṇa* figures failed to satisfy him. He was a meditation student of both Ārāḍa Kālāpa and Udraka Rāmaputra, but eventually abandoned them to seek his own enlightenment under the Bodhi tree. Though not unique to Buddhism, individual insight as the foundational claim to spiritual authority—and thereby the justification for dissent against Vedic orthodoxy—became a central trope in the formation of Buddhist religiosity. Like the founders of many *śramaṇa* religions, the Buddha claimed that not only was the legitimacy of his movement based on his direct perception of the truth—in contrast to the necessity of a textual intermediary in Vedic religion—but also on the claim that his insight was replicable. This marks a paradigm shift in spiritual epistemology, for now instead of the necessity of scripture to relay truth to the adherent, this intercessional medium could be dispensed with in favor of a direct insight that is theoretically available to any ardent seeker.[4]

Suttas in the Pali canon, the oldest strata of Buddhist literature available, are rife with conversion narratives that demonstrate direct access to truth as a superior feature of the Buddhist religion. One such story concerns the Brahman Kūṭadanta. Knowing the Buddha to be learned, Kūṭadanta requests that Gautama instruct him on the proper way to perform a sacrifice. Kūṭadanta's plan is to perform a sacrifice according to well-known Vedic customs, including the slaughter of several livestock. But the Buddha suggests instead examples of increasingly more profitable forms of sacrifice, starting with replacing live sacrifices with vegetarian offerings and continuing with making these offerings to Arhats directly (those who have gained nirvana). The highest form of "sacrifice," however is to become enlightened oneself, such that "having realized the clairvoyant forms of knowledge oneself, one teaches."[5] This stock phrase occurs some 36 times in the sutta canon. Interestingly, it is usually used as an introduction for the Buddha—"the one who teaches having realized the clairvoyant forms of knowledge himself."[6] Here, however, it is used proscriptively. Thus, in lieu of following Vedic injunctions for sacrifices that will ensure a higher rebirth, the Buddha implores the Brahman Kūṭadanta to realize the truth for himself and be liberated from rebirth altogether—to become like the Buddha. Kūṭadanta's response is predictably zealous. Once he vows not only to release the animals planned for sacrifice, but provide them wide pastures to live peacefully, the Buddha begins to teach him:

> Then, lo, the Bhagavan gave the progressively sophisticated teaching to the Brahman Kūṭadanta. He gave the talk on giving, on ethics, and on the heavens. He pointed out the disadvantage, uncouthness, and impurity of desire and the profit had by renunciation. When the Buddha knew the Brahman Kūṭadanta to be of sound mind, a good heart, unbiased, with a happy disposition, and pious, he then gave him the condensed teachings of the Buddha, [the Four Noble Truths]: suffering, its cause, cessation, and its path. Just like a clean cloth free of stain may take to dye perfectly, so too did the stainless and clear dharma eye arise to the Brahman Kūṭadanta in his seat thereby [as he realized,] "Whatever arises also ceases." Then, the Brahman Kūṭadanta became someone who saw the dharma, who attained the dharma, who found the dharma, who penetrated the dharma, whose doubt was deflated,

---

[4] There is some undeniable similarity here to the Protestant Reformation, which emphasized a direct experience of God over the necessity of the church as an intermediary. However, the Western gaze on Buddhism as a Protestant-like religion has also engendered a slew of misleading projections and misreadings. See Thompson (2020) for a discussion (loc. 1886 of 3328 ff.).

[5] *sayaṃ abhiññā sacchikatvā pavedeti*

[6] See, for example, Dīgha Nikāya 12.1, para. 3 and Majjhima Nikāya 3.5, para. 1.

whose uncertainty disappeared, who gained confidence, and who need not rely on others [in order to understand] the Master's teaching (Dīgha Nikāya 5.12-3).

This last line describing those "who need not rely on others [in order to understand] the Master's teaching"[7] is part of another stock phrase that occurs ten times in the sutta canon and is usually reserved for those disciples who gain a direct realization of the Buddha's teaching. It is also most often associated (as it is here) with the "dharma eye" (*dhamma-cakkhu*), suggesting a direct perception of the dharma over and above mere intellectual comprehension. The Pali canon, however, offers no clear epistemological account of how adherents transition from mere intellectual grasp of the Buddha's teaching to this deeper realization denoted by the "clear dharma eye." But this transition is essential, for it marks the point at which the practitioner becomes an authority unto themself, no longer needing to "rely on others." Indeed, the potential of this direct realization becomes the promissory appeal of Buddhism over Vedic authority.

Intersectarian Debates

Fifth and sixth century CE India saw an explosion of intellectual exchange among religious factions. With several religious schools well-established and all vying for influence, the Indian intellectual milieu developed a sophisticated shared language with which to compete and debate, including a system of formal logic, discussions of epistemic instruments, and a copious list of agreed-upon logical fallacies. Dignāga (480-540 CE) was most likely the earliest Buddhist figure to engage in this language and was undeniably instrumental in its development. His connection to earlier Buddhist conceptions of realization is also apparent, specifically the notion that insight marks a break with reliance on others.[8] Specifically—most likely drawing from *yogācara* philosophy or *yogasūtra* terminology—he dubs those practitioners who gain this direct realization "yogis." Thus, his *Pramāṇasamuccaya* verse 1.6 states that "yogis see just the object, *unmixed with the guru's instructions* [emphasis added]."[9] Dignāga thus concurs with the suttas that true realization is marked by independent authority, not relying on others, including the instructions of one's guru. Dignāga's notion that realization involves seeing "just the object" (*artha-mātra-dṛk*) is also reflected in the Pali suttas, where there are hundreds of references to realization as "seeing things as they really are with wisdom" (Pali *yathābhūtaṃ sammappaññāya* √*pass* or √*dis*). Both phrases denote a perception with the veil of ignorance lifted, such that the object itself as it really is (Skt. *artha-mātra*, Pali *yathā-bhuta*) appears. But Dignāga elaborates on what this means technically. He explains that the ignorance that prevents our seeing reality "as it is" is our ongoing conceptual proliferations, which we superimpose on reality. Thus, the "guru's instructions" does not simply denote one's intellectual understanding of the dharma but is a synecdoche for *all conceptualization in general*. Dignāga therefore explains in his auto-commentary that "those very yogis have a perceptual vision (*darśana*) of just the object, unmixed with any conceptual understanding (*vikalpa*) from scripture."[10]

---

[7] *aparappaccayo satthusāsane*

[8] Coming almost a millennium after the suttas, Dignāga clearly also drew on Buddhist literature and figures closer to his own era in developing his theory of yogic perception, notably, likely, Asaṅga (300-370 CE), and assuredly Abhidharma works. While I do not have the space here to reconstruct that entire lineage of thought, my aim here is to show its continuity from the Pali sources up to Dignāga.

[9] yogināṃ gurunirdeśāvyavakīrṇaarthamātradṛk || (Dignāga 2005, p. 3). Dignāga (1744a) was also consulted (f. 2a): /rnal 'byor rnams kyi bla mas bstan/ /ma 'dres pa yi don tsam mthong/.

[10] *yoginām apy āgamavikalpāvyavakīrṇam arthamātradarśanaṃ pratyakṣam* / (Dignāga 2005, p. 3). Dignāga (1744b) was also consulted (f. 15b): *rnal 'byor ba rnams kyis kyang lung las rnam par rtog pa dang ma 'dres pa'i don tsam mthong ba ni mngon sum mo/* /

In this way, Dignāga elevates the mark of self-possessed authority—direct understanding without the need of the teacher—to an epistemological principle: the ability to see reality without the confusion of conceptual overlay. Although the guru may impart some necessary instructions, "seeing without the teacher" denotes both the practice and achievement of spiritual insight, where the adherent strives to see these truths autonomously and thereby become an independent authority. And it is the possibility of gaining this independent authority that furthermore justifies dissent against Vedic orthodoxy.

Buddhists still must explain how this nonconceptual direct realization of the truth can be cultivated. Without a clear delineation of praxeology, the epistemological description of yogis' perception as nonconceptual is inert, since it gives no method by which the Buddhist may come into their own authority. The tradition quickly identified adept meditation as the *sine qua non* of gaining this direct insight. Dharmakīrti (fl. 6th or 7th century CE), who greatly elaborated Dignāga's system, understood the generation of yogic perception as a specifically meditative practice in which one has a vivid encounter with the meditated object, as if it were "right in front of them." Dharmakīrti (1972) thus writes:

> One is driven crazy by desire, fear, and sorrow
> And haunted by dreams, robbers, etc.
> They see what does not exist
> As if it were right in front of them.
>
> [...]
>
> Although considered unreal, meditative bases
> Like of the ugliness [of the body], the earth, etc.
> Can arise in a nonconceptual clear appearance
> Constructed by the power of meditation.
>
> Therefore, whether existing or non-existing,
> Whatever one meditates upon intently
> Will end up forming a nonconceptual cognition
> Once that meditation is perfected. (v.3.282-285 except verse 283).

The transition from intellectual understanding to nonconceptual, direct insight, therefore involves intense habituation. By meditating on some object unabatedly, it no longer appears as an idea in the mind's eye, but as a visceral sensorial object. Dharmakīrti gives several examples of similar experiences. He cites how intense emotions are known to produce hallucinations—namely fear and grief.[11] He also cites traditional meditation examples, specifically a meditation practice known as "*kaṣina*," which involves meditating on one of the elements (i.e., earth, fire, water, or air) until one can control them. Meditation on ugliness is a practice meant to cultivate renunciation of worldly life,

---

[11] Dharmakīrti is not wrong here, especially concerning grief. See Sacks, (2012, pp. 229-54) and Castelnovo et al. (2015, pp. 266-274).

where the meditator imagines the world as full of bones.[12] Both instances are said to produce vivid appearances of the object of concentration, be it the substance of earth or skeletons.

While one can imagine what the hallucination of one's loved one provoked by grief, or a similar experience through excessive fear, or the appearance of earth or skeletons through meditation might be like, it is unclear exactly what the clear appearance of something like the Four Noble Truths might be. As we saw from the Pali strata, as the essence of the Buddha's teaching, the Four Noble Truths are the object of the "dharma-eye," and Dharmakīrti (1744) concurs their place as the object of yogic perception (f. 161a-b). What exactly does it mean to see something as abstract as the Four Noble Truths vividly, like a hallucination? Moreover, the fact that Dharmakīrti analogizes yogic perception to hallucinations does not bode well for his aim to substantiate it as epistemologically robust. If yogic perception is phenomenologically identical with hallucination, what makes it any more trustworthy than an illusion?

The Mīmāṃsā school leveraged this exact point of attack. As Deleuze and Guattari would anticipate, the Buddhist break with Vedic authority was not excepted from the general historical trend in which dissent is usually accompanied by a resurgent conservative effort from orthodoxy in resistance.[13] Such movements typically result in the creation of various forms of fundamentalism, which, though usually claiming a return to tradition and a recovery of deteriorating values, often involve novel, strict forms of religion that seek to reassert control over perceived threats to a tradition's integrity. Mīmāṃsā may be construed as fundamentalist in this limited sense, for it seems to have gain traction in reaction to the *śramaṇa* movement and (at least in its earliest strata) strictly rejects the possibility of meditative insight, something that was never explicit in the Vedas proper, just as creationism proposes a literalism to the Bible that had not been previously championed.

In considering Mīmāṃsā as a fundamentalist reaction against *śramaṇa* religion, it is not surprising then that its earliest work, the *Mīmāṃsāsūtras*, hail from a period roughly contemporaneous with the Buddha, around 450 BCE (Verpooten 1987, pp. 4 §4 and 5 §7). I examine two Mīmāṃsā works in this lineage of Buddhist critique. The first is a commentary on the *Vidhiviveka* by Maṇḍana Miśra (7th-8th century CE), who was a student of Kumārila Bhaṭṭa, who in turn wrote a sub-commentary on the *Mīmāṃsāsūtras* (see footnote 13). This commentary on the *Vidhiviveka* is entitled the "*Nyāyakaṇikā*" by the eclectic author Vācaspatimiśra (9th or 10th century CE). I also investigate a Buddhist response to this work in the *Yoginimayaprakaraṇa* by Jñānaśrīmitra (fl. 975-1025 CE). I then examine a further Mīmāṃsā critique in Sucaritamiśra's (c.1120 CE) *Kāśika,* which is a commentary on Kumārila Bhaṭṭa's work (see footnote 13). Jñānaśrīmitra's student, Ratnakīrti (11th century CE), gave a rebuttal to Sucaritamiśra in his *Sarvajñasiddhi,* which we will also discuss. Throughout my analysis, I will demonstrate that the stakes of this exchange concern the epistemic validity of meditation—whether it can produce credible knowledge. Through the lens of dissent and the longstanding feud between Mīmāṃsikas and Buddhists, the preoccupation with meditation and yogic perception becomes clear: if meditation is an authentic means of spiritual insight, it threatens the necessity of Vedic authority,

---

[12] See Bhadantācariya Buddhaghosa (1991, p. 111) and (pp. 118–264) respectively for a discussion of the *kaṣina* meditation and meditation on ugliness.

[13] As Kanchana Natarajan (1995) explains, the initiatory Mīmāṃsā work, Jaimini's *Mīmāṃsā Sūtras* in the fourth century BCE, constituted an attempt to rescue proper Vedic sacrificial technique from its declining use. Furthermore, the first principle commentary on these sutras, Śabara's *bhāṣya* during the early centuries, was written specifically in response to Buddhist attacks on Vedic dharma. Its commentary, the *Mīmāṃsāślokavārttika*—of which Sucaritamiśra's (c.1120 CE) *Kāśika* is a sub-commentary—written by Kumārila Bhaṭṭa (fl. 700 CE)—of whom Maṇḍanamiśra was a disciple—was also in defense against Buddhist attacks (pp. xviii-xx). My paper explores both the *Kāśika* and a commentary on Maṇḍanamiśra's work, highlighting an almost millennium long rivalry between Buddhists and Mīmāṃsikas.

since these truths can be realized directly without the need of an intermediary medium like Vedic scripture.

Does Meditation Correspond with Anything?

As we noted earlier, Dharmakīrti's analogies for meditation and yogic perception involve a glaring weakness. If yogic perception is like a hallucination, what guarantee is there that it corresponds with any real object? If it does not, it cannot be knowledge producing or trustworthy. Vācaspatimiśra (1978) attacks this very ambiguity in Dharmakīrti's formulation, arguing that yogic perception cannot correspond to reality. His *Nyāyakaṇika* first gives his consensus of why meditative objects cannot correspond with anything real. "That momentariness [as described by the Four Noble Truths] has no correspondence (*avyabhicāra*) with this [meditative] object, neither through a shared identity nor causally. The process of having a peak experience in meditation thus assuredly is distinct from engagement with [real] objects" (p. 105). As stated earlier, the Four Noble Truths are the object of yogic perception. The Mahāyana Buddhist tradition came to recognize 16 aspects of the Four Noble Truths, four aspects per truth, which are realized in quick succession.[14] The first of four aspects in the Truth of Suffering, the first Truth, is impermanence (*anitya*): the Buddhist realizes that life is conditioned by suffering because all things are momentary, in constant flux, and thus doomed to decay—nothing ever lasts. The fact of impermanence is supposedly realized in yogic perception. But Vācaspatimiśra notes that even if he were to concede that phenomena are impermanent, impermanence or momentariness (*qua* quality) is distinct from those objects, just as beauty is distinct from beautiful objects. Not only, thus, do impermanent objects not share an identity with impermanence, but neither is impermanence causally related to impermanent phenomena, since it is an epiphenomenal abstraction. According to Buddhists, these are the only two ontologically robust relationships two objects can have—identity or causal connection—and both appear untenable between impermanent objects and impermanence. Furthermore, if, according to Buddhists, all existing things are impermanent, how can impermanence—which as a quality is abstract and static— itself be impermanent? If it is not, it is a phantasm, an illusion, or a mental superimposition—but it is not real. Thus, meditation on impermanence entails concentration on a non-existent object and has no connection with real objects. It thus cannot be knowledge producing.

Vācaspatimiśra's *Nyāyakaṇika* admits, however, that impermanence and impermanent objects are not wholly unrelated. He notes that the Buddhist may counter that their relationship is like the inference of fire from smoke. Just as the inferential understanding of fire based on seeing smoke has a robust relationship to actual fire, so too does the inference of things' impermanence relate to actual impermanent objects. Impermanence, therefore, has as robust a relationship with reality as the inference of fire. The reader, however, may be able to anticipate why this is not a satisfying comparison. Dharmakīrti seems to couch yogic perception as generating a hallucination of impermanence. Even if we grant impermanence is real, the hallucination of a real object does not vitiate its being a mere hallucination. Intuitively, we would think there is a difference between hallucinating about an existing object—which only has a happenstance connection to reality—and *actually* seeing it. Vācaspatimiśra (1978) argues as much in response to his imagined Buddhist interlocutor.

---

[14] The *Abhisamayālaṅkāra* is one of the earliest records of this idea: "The [four] truths are distinctive, since they are unique in being unfathomable, etc. / Their unique quality is fixed upon [in meditation] for sixteen moments." *acintyādiviśeṣeṇa viśiṣṭaiḥ satyagocaraiḥ / viśeṣalakṣaṇaṃ ṣaḍbhirdaśabhiścoditaṃ kṣaṇaiḥ //* (Asaṅga 1977, v. 4.23).

But how does the fact one can establish the presence of fire through inference guarantee the authenticity of the vivid cognition of fire in mediation? If you reply yes, [meditation on fire is epistemically valid], you would have to say that while someone was ascending a mountain, the apprehension of its clarity in meditation would equally correspond [with the object] as actual sensory contact with that fire, and this is absurd. (pp. 105-6).

Vācaspatimiśra gives an excellent retort. The Buddhist interlocutor claims that yogic perception on impermanence—though like a hallucination—has an inferential relationship with impermanent objects. But Vācaspatimiśra rightly asks why a hallucination of an inferred object would undermine it as a hallucination. If there were no difference between the hallucination of an object and actually perceiving it, then vivid meditation on a fire merely inferred from smoke would absurdly be the same as seeing it directly, even when one's line of sight is blocked by a hill. Although that meditation produces the apparition of an object that actually exists, it does not directly represent that object in the manner seeing it would, and so it cannot be valid.

Jñānaśrīmitra was aware of Vācaspatimiśra's text and directly quotes it at several points in his *Yoginirṇayaprakaraṇa*, a text solely devoted to fleshing out the Buddhist interpretation of yogic perception. There, he offers a retort to Vācaspatimiśra's critique and attempts to recover the continuity between yogic perception and its object in a more explicit manner than afforded by Dharmakīrti. As we will see, he builds off Dharmakīrti's unique understanding of correspondence to explain how the appearance cultivated in yogic perception corresponds with a real object. Jñānaśrīmitra essentially understands Vācaspatimiśra to have charged the Buddhists with violating parsimony. That is, if yogic perception is valid despite being generated like a hallucination, it would then have to be categorically different from normal perception.

Jñānaśrīmitra (1987) counters that Vācaspatimiśra has failed to account for how we practically confirm that correct inference has occurred. In contrast to the inference of spiritual truths, "the inference of fire merely establishes the capacity to burn and cook." But this inference does not correspond *prima facie*, but only pragmatically "when one approaches the place [where that fire is]" and encounters *actual* burning and cooking. Otherwise, "cultivation [of that inference] is in vain if that place remains out of reach" (p. 323). In other words, Jñānaśrīmitra deconstructs what it means to validly correspond with an object. When we infer the presence of an object, we do so with a certain goal and purpose. In the case of the fire, we expect that it will be able to cook and burn, and it is to the degree that these expectations are met that we can say our original inference of fire was correct. This can only be fulfilled once one "approaches the place" of that burning and confirms their expectations.

Meditation is the same, Jñānaśrīmitra argues. Just as the inference of fire is only valid if it fulfils the intention of cooking and burning, so too is a meditation valid only if it leads to spiritual liberation. Furthermore, "before the meditation is complete, its appearance is mistaken with reference to that object" (p. 323). Only when the meditation culminates in realization is its epistemicity validated. There is no test for correspondence other than this. In light of this criterion, Vācaspatimiśra has made a false comparison when he argues that if the object of yogic perception legitimately corresponds, then the vivid meditative appearance of fire would be no different from its perception. Why? Because the appearance of fire *in meditation* cannot cook and burn, and thus does not fulfill purposeful intention. The vivid appearance of the Four Noble Truths in mediation, however, *does* fulfill the intention for liberation. Thus, just as our inference of fire is confirmed only "when one approaches that place" and finds a fire that can cook and burn, the inference of the Four Noble Truths is confirmed through yogic perception's ability to produce liberation via meditation. There is no "absurdum of there being a different type of perception" specific to yogic perception (p. 323).

More than this, Jñānaśrīmitra even concedes that meditation "is mistaken with regard to that object" before this intention is achieved. But this is not the specific fault of meditation, but general to the process of inference. Because Dharmakīrti argues that all inference involves conceptual processes that obscure reality, all intentional inferential cognition begins in error.[15] Jñānaśrīmitra and Dharmakīrti therefore both argue that the initial inference upon which one bases their intentional action—whether that is further meditation or walking toward smoke—entails an error (*bhrānti*). In both cases, however, once that inferentially motivated action is brought to completion, the validity of that inference is confirmed, either by the encounter with actual burning or actual spiritual advancement away from suffering. Thus, they reject correspondence *simpliciter* as the criterion for ontological continuity between a conceptual representation and its object. Rather, correspondence is confirmed pragmatically as the degree to which an inference can fulfill intention, which is idiosyncratic to the intentional object. Dharmakīrti thus says "a valid cognition corresponds (*avisaṃvādi*) in the sense that it engenders causally effective (*arthakriyā*) knowledge."[16]

This pragmatism[17] differs significantly from Mīmāṃsā realism, which argues that successful completion of intentions does not sufficiently establish the validity of an initial cognition. For example, after losing my keys, I may have a dream in which I remember I left them at a friend's house. Even though I may come to find those keys at my friend's house later, it seems counterintuitive to say that therefore my dream of my keys was effectively a *perception* of my keys. But Buddhist of Dharmakīrti and Jñānaśrīmitra's ilk insist that such realist intuitions—which suggest correspondence must be more robust than pragmatic fulfillment of goals—are flawed, and so their framework here is consistent with their larger idealist project. In some ways, therefore, the exchange between Jñānaśrīmitra and Vācaspatimiśra reveals a talking past one another, each holding different ontological assumptions that inform their epistemological lines of argumentation—one realist, the other idealist.

Is Meditation Redundant?

The previous debate concerned whether meditation is a valid form of knowledge given its tenuous relationship with real objects. The line of attack in Sucaritamiśra's *Kāśika* is slightly different. He argues that even if we grant that the appearance of an object in meditation cogently corresponds to a real object, we must wonder whether this appearance affords us any new information. Dharmakīrti himself argues, "An understanding (*saṃvṛta*) that apprehends that which has already been apprehended is not accepted [as a valid cognition]. Instrumental thinking is primarily to engage with [deciphering anew] what objects are to be avoided or acquired."[18] In line with his pragmatist paradigm, Dharmakīrti stipulates that any robust knowledge producing instrument (*pramāṇa*) must afford new information about how to stay away from what we do not want or obtain what we do. If it merely tells us something we already know, like a memory, then it is not an epistemic instrument.

---

[15] "When concepts superimpose a linguistic sign, which is another object [from the percept proper], there is a cause for error, since it never accords with perception." *saṃketasaṃśrayānyārthasamāropavikalpane / na pratyakṣānunivṛttitvāt kadācid bhrāntikāraṇam //* (Dharmakīrti, 1968, p. 186 v. 290).

[16] *pramāṇamavisaṃvādi jñānamarthakriyāsthitiḥ /* (Dharmakīrti 1972, v. 2.1).

[17] There are tempting parallels here with William James's pragmatism into which I will not digress in this paper.

[18] *gṛhītagrahaṇān neṣṭaṃ sāṃvṛtaṃ dhīpramāṇatā / pravṛttestatpradhānatvād heyopādeyavastuni //* (Dharmakīrti 1972, v. 2.3).

If meditation does not afford new information of this sort, then yogic perception cannot be an epistemic instrument in the manner Buddhists claim. It is this potential weakness that Sucaritamiśra (1929) exploits.

> The strength of one's meditation is said to be the cause that produces the yogi's knowledge. But that [knowledge] cannot come from meditation on an object that was already conceived, nor is it an understanding that arises accidentally [with no cause at all]. All things that are produced have a cause. Thus, why does that which is already understood through a different valid epistemic instrument have to be cultivated through meditation?

As Sucaritamiśra points out, meditation cannot simply rehash what is already known: it cannot be meditation on something that is already conceived. Otherwise, per Dharmakīrti, it is not knowledge producing. Nor can meditation arise *ex nihilo*. As Jñānaśrīmitra identified, it is motivated from purposeful intention. But if meditation is simply a process of familiarizing oneself with an intentional object that "is already understood through a different valid epistemic instrument"—and it must be, since if prior to meditation that meditative object is not verified through such an instrument, then the meditator is merely self-inducing a false hallucination—then meditation would seem by Dharmakīrti's own definition to "apprehend that which has already been apprehended," and thus not be epistemically warranted. Sucaritamiśra continues:

> And what even is that epistemic instrument? It is not inference. There is no earlier comprehension of what is dharma and what is not […] Only an object that is something to avoid or acquire is the thing that is desired to be known. And thus, if that object is already established, then meditation is useless. Even the Compassionate One [the Buddha] should [be able to] explain his scriptural dharma diligently for the sake of his students. He should not have to exhaust [himself] with the experience of meditation. (p. 217).

In other words, how could pre-meditative verification of the meditative object be possible? Buddhists argue that yogic perception is uniquely a perception of the meditative object. Thus, there must be a pre-meditative inference. But this cannot be the case, since spiritual truth (*dharma*) and what is untrue (*adharma*) is exactly *what is to be discovered* in yogic perception. If inference has already determined dharma and adharma, then yogic perception is redundant. Sucaritamiśra uses Dharmakīrti's own reasoning against the Buddhist: if inference has already determined what "to avoid or acquire," since this is the criterion of validity, "then meditation is useless," since it adds nothing to that determination.

Ratnakīrti, Jñānaśrīmitra's student, provides the Buddhist response to Sucaritamiśra's argument against meditation *qua* redundancy. Like Sucaritamiśra, Ratnakīrti (1957) also tries to overturn his opponent's argument on its own terms. That is, he attempts to show why the Mīmāṃsā rejection of meditation's validity would be problematic for its own system. Ratnakīrti asks, "What do you even mean by the words 'dharma' and 'adharma'?" He gives two possibilities of what Sucaritamiśra could mean: (1) the Mīmāṃsa understanding of spiritual truths like the existence of heaven, or (2) the Buddhist understanding of reality as momentary. If Sucaritamiśra is criticizing Buddhist conceptions of meditation as incapable of establishing (1), then he has failed to evaluate Buddhism on its own terms, since this is not the concern of Buddhist praxis. Ratnakīrti explains that Buddhism, by contrast, is concerned with *practical* omniscience. "Practical omniscience is established by the *direct* knowledge of samsara and nirvana and all that attends it," namely, the Four Noble Truths. As Ratnakīrti explains, only *direct*—that is non-inferential—knowledge is sufficient for achieving one's spiritual goals. A mere inference of the truth will not suffice.

The question, then, is whether this perception of the truth at the culmination of meditation is preceded by perception or inference. There must be some epistemic instrument that obtains the meditative object *before* meditation, else there is nothing to meditate upon. And Ratnakīrti concurs, "Indeed, [the Four Noble Truths] must be apprehended either by perception or inference, since there is no other type of epistemic instrument that exists." Furthermore, "For those [developing their] fixation on momentariness, etc., it is not perception." If the perception of the object occurred before meditation, mediation *would* be redundant indeed. It must, therefore, first, be grasped by inference. However, Ratnakīrti takes issue with Sucaritamiśra's assumption that this object's inference is tantamount to its perception, rendering no need for meditation. The perceptual experience afforded by meditation is qualitatively different "because inference does not come in contact with the true object" (pp. 18-9).

Ratnakīrti argues that inference of this meditative object *before* meditation is not equivalent to its direct perception *in* meditation, and thus, meditation cannot be redundant. This is because, as Dharmakīrti argued, inferential understanding of spiritual truth obscures that truth by virtue of being conceptual. The superior perceptual clarity of the object culminated in mediation affords liberation in a manner that conceptuality cannot. This reiterates Buddhist pragmatism over realism: while on a realist understanding of epistemology the fact that the vivid object in mediation and the pre-meditative inference upon which it is based represent the same object should make them epistemically identical, Buddhist pragmatism forgoes correspondence and only asks what cognitions *do*. The added liberative value of yogic perception *vis-à-vis* its exceptionally clear meditative object warrants its distinction from inference, within which that object is still seen through a glass darkly.

Lastly, Ratnakīrti's juxtaposition of two possible meanings of "dharma" uses Sucaritamiśra's position against him. If he means (1), then Sucaritamiśra has effectively undercut his own school's position, arguing that the Mīmāṁsa view on dharma has no epistemic warrant. But even if he means (2), by arguing the Buddhist has no epistemic resource to substantiate dharma, he has effectively evacuated any such resource for the Mīmāṁsa to substantiate their own claims about dharma. He has shot himself in the foot.

Conclusion

While the debate here concerns elite meditative practices, we should not, therefore, assume that its ramifications are only for the spiritually elite. Max Weber (1946) made a similar insight concerning science in the modern age, arguing that while most people may not be elite scientists, scientific rationalization has a profound effect on culture writ large. The culture of the scientific age is disenchanted, Weber argued, but not because we know everything—or even know more than those who have come before this age—and have thereby, somehow, exterminated the unknown. Rather, it is because science promises the potential that everything *could* be known with enough experimental effort, a metaphysics in which all objects are in essence *knowable*. This erodes the presence of mystery, since there are no longer ineffable and inherently inaccessible truths. Only the as-of-yet discovered.

Similarly, I argue that Buddhist dissent against the Vedas resulted in a similar disenchantment, dissolving the notion that the justification for these scriptural prescriptions was beyond human understanding and impenetrably mysterious. With the advent of meditative technology, Buddhists and other *śramaṇists* dissolved an authoritative power predicated on the unknowable, such that, like the promise of scientific rationalism, these types of spiritual truths *could* be known directly. Though *this* potential does not disenchant in the Weberian sense of draining meaning from the world, it does undermine the power structures that rely on maintaining mystery, namely the religious sects that insist a spiritual life can only be led vicariously through the dictates of the Vedas, much in the same way that science, Weber argues, has deflated religion of its influence—a process that came to be coined "secularization."

Later theorists, notably Peter Berger (1967), argued, however, that the secularization that arose with the rise of science was not as detached from its religious roots as it may appear. In fact, secular disenchantment may be a natural outgrowth of a culture founded on Protestant values, which made spiritual matters a personal rather than collective concern. This truncates God into a purely subjective phenomenon, which evacuates the role of the sacred in the world, in the vacuum of which secular concerns take precedent (p. 111). This description undeniably resonates with Geleuze and Guattari's analysis of deterritorialization, in which the "face-off" between God and the prophet forms a covenant, despite each one's turning away from the other. For Berger, we have all individually become prophets, at ends with a far-off God, the distance from whom is irrecoverable. But that distance created is not a departure, for it informs the subjectivity of the now "secularized" individual, an individual formed through the Protestant insistence on a personal relationship with God, which, counterintuitively, makes God more removed and the resulting deterritorialized subjectivity more prominent. God is also transformed: just as Christ is removed from the Protestant cross, just as the Protestant rejects the worship of Mary as the mother to an immanent, living God, so too does the divine become further transcendentalized, further removed, further Othered. Thus, the otherness of God—which *à la* Weber (1946) manifests in the secular age as the pursuit of "infinite progress" (p. 139)—is ironically intimately connected to the secularized subject, a relationship that is in fact ongoing and maintains this individualized, deterritorialized subjectivity.

Our analysis of Buddhist dissent against the Vedas reveals a similar mutual re-forming. Just as the Protestant approach toward God lead to her Othering, it was not until the Buddhist argued that spiritual truth was accessible by any ardent seeker that the Mīmāṃsā came into being to double down on that truth's *in*accessibility. Originally, the Vedic attitude toward mediation was likely nebulous; the meditative practices of the Upaniṣads, for example, were seen as perfectly continuous with Vedic authority. It was only when meditation was used as an epistemological tool by Buddhists to question that authority did allegiance to the Vedas entail, at least from a Mīmāṃsā point of view, a rejection of mediation's value full stop. But as the history traced in this paper reveals, the growing sophistication of each opponent's epistemology occurred in their tandem, each reacting to each other in an ever-increasing arms race of well-developed arguments. As Geleuze and Guattari suggest, this face-off was thus never a separation, but indicative of an at least millennium-long relationship, demonstrating that dissent is rarely a singular moment connoting a split, but an ongoing process of interaction that binds as firmly as it separates.

References

Asaṅga & Tripathi, R. (Ed.). (1977). Abhisamayālaṅkāra Sphuṭārtha. Sarnath: Central Institute of Higher Tibetan Studies.

Aśvaghoṣa & Johnston, E. H. (Ed.). (1935). The Buddhacarita: or, Acts of the Buddha; Part I. Sanskrit Text. Calcutta: Baptist Mission Press.

Berger, P. (1967). The Sacred Canopy: Elements of a Sociological Theory of Religion. New York: Doubleday.

Bhadantācariya Buddhaghosa. (1991). The Path of Purification (Visuddhimagga) (Bhikkhu Ñāṇamoli, Trans.). Kandy, Sri Lanka: Buddhist Publication Society.

Castelnovo, A., Cavallotti, S., Gambini, O., & D'Agostino, A. (2015). Post-Bereavement Hallucinatory Experiences: A Critical Overview of Population and Clinical Studies. Journal of Affective Disorders, 186.

Deleuze, G., & Guattari, F. (1987). A Thousand Plateaus: Capitalism and Schizophrenia. Minneapolis: University' of Minnesota Press.

Dharmakīrti. (1744). "Pramāṇaviniścaya. Tshad ma rnam par nges pa." In: Sde dge btan 'gyur (Toh. no. 4211, Tshad ma, ce). Derge: Sde dge par khang.

Dharmakīrti & Miyasaka, Y. (Ed.). (1972). Pramāṇavarttika-kārikā: (Sanskrit and Tibetan). Acta Indologica, 2.

Dharmakīrti & Shastri, D. (Ed.). (1968). Pramāṇavārttika. Varanasi: Bauddha Bharati.

Dignāga. (1744a). "Pramāṇasamuccaya. Tshad ma kun las btus pa." In: Sde dge btan 'gyur (Toh. no. 4203, Tshad ma, ce). Derge: Sde dge par khang.

— . (1744b). "Pramāṇasamuccayavṛtti. Tshad ma kun las btus pa'i 'grel pa." In: Sde dge btan 'gyur (Toh. no. 4204, Tshad ma, ce). Derge: Sde dge par khang.

Dignāga & Steinkellner, E. (2005). Dignāga's Pramāṇasamuccaya, Chapter 1: A Hypothetical Reconstruction of the Sanskrit Text with the Help of the Two Tibetan Translations on the Basis of the hitherto Known Sanskrit Fragments and the Linguistic Materials Gained from Jinendrabuddhi's Ṭīkā. Vienna: Österreichische Akademie der Wissenschaften.

Jñānaśrīmitra, & Thakur, A. (Ed.). (1987). Jñānaśrīmitranibandhavāli: Buddhist Philosophical Works of Jñānaśrīmitra. Patna, Bihar: Kashi Prasad Jayaswal Research Institute.

Natarajan, K. (1995). The Vidhiviveka of Maṇḍana Miśra: Understanding Vedic Injunctions. Delhi, India: Sri Satguru Publications.

Olivelle, P. (1993). The Āśrama System: The History and Hermeneutics of a Religious Institution. Oxford: Oxford University Press.

Ratnakīrti, & Thakur, A. (Ed.). (1975). Ratnakīrtinibandhavāli: Buddhist Philosophical Works of Ratnakīrti. Patna, Bihar: Kashi Prasad Jayaswal Research Institute.

Sacks, O. (2012). Hallucinations. New York: Alfred A. Knopf.

Sucaritamiśra & Śāstrī, K. S. (Ed.). (1929). The Mīmamsaslokavartika with the Commentary Kasika of Sucaritamiśra. Trivandrum, Kerala: Superintendent Government Press.

Thompson, E. (2020). Why I Am Not a Buddhist. [Kindle Version]. New Haven: Yale University Press.

Vācaspatimiśra, Maṇḍanamiśra, & Goswami, M. L. (Ed.). (1978). Vidhiviveka of Śrī Maṇḍana Miśra with the Commentary Nyāyakanikā [sic.] of Vāchaspati Misra [sic.]. Varanasi: Tara Publications.

Verpoorten, J. (1987). Mīmāṃsā Literature. Wiesbaden: Otto Harrassowitz.

Weber, M. (1946). From Max Weber: Essays in Sociology (H. Gerth , & C. W. Mills, Trans.). Oxford: Oxford University Press.

International Journal of Religion
November 2020
Volume: 1 | Number 1 | pp. 135 – 149
ISSN: 2633-352X (Print) | ISSN: 2633-3538 (Online)
journals.tplondon.com/ijor

TRANSNATIONAL PRESS®
LONDON

First Submitted: 31 July 2020 Accepted: 1 November 2020
DOI: https://doi.org/10.33182/ijor.v1i1.1104

Tar & Feathers: Agnotology, Dissent, and Queer Mormon History

Nerida Bullock[1]

Abstract

In 2014 the Church of Jesus Christ of Latter-day Saints (LDS Church) updated their official website to include information about the polygamy/polyandry practiced by Joseph Smith, their founder and prophet, and his many wives. The admission by the LDS Church reconciles the tension between information that had become readily available online since the 1990s and church-sanctioned narratives that obscured Smith's polygamy while concurrently focusing on the polygyny of Brigham Young, Smith's successor. This paper entwines queer theory with Robert Proctor's concept of agnotology—a term used to describe the epistemology of ignorance, to consider dissent from two interrelated perspectives: 1) how dissent from feminists and historians within the LDS Church challenged (mis)constructions of Mormon history, and; 2) how the Mormon practice of polygamy in the late nineteenth century dissented from Western sexual mores that conflated monogamy with Whiteness, democracy and social progression in the newly formed American Republic.

Keywords: *Mormon polygamy; Agnotology; Polyandry; Queer theology; ignorance; Joseph Smith; The Church of Jesus Christ of Latter-day Saint.*

Introduction

In 1945, acclaimed historian Fawn Brodie published a secular biography on the enigmatic founder of the Church of Jesus Christ of Latter-day Saints (LDS Church), Joseph Smith.[2] To secular historians and book critics, *No Man Knows My History* (1945) is considered one of the best scholarly books on early Mormonism of all times (Bringhurst, 1997, 1989; Reston, 2012). However, to devout Mormons, Brodie's non-hagiographic historical biography of Smith is a malicious atrocity that good Mormons do best to avoid (Hill, 1972: 73). Brodie, a member of the LDS Church, drew the ire of church leaders for producing an account of Smith's life that rejected the *priori* assumption that Smith was a modern-day prophet of God. Her psychohistory of Smith was a strong statement of *dissent* that challenged the carefully cultivated historic renderings of Smith's life as disseminated by the LDS Church. One of the many extraordinary claims Brodie made, was that Smith had been married to more than forty women—a claim that contrasted sharply with LDS Church-sanctioned narratives that obscured Smith's polygamist practices while simultaneously focusing on the polygamy of Smith's successor, Brigham Young and other early members of the faith.

The LDS Church has a complicated history of polygamy—a practice of marrying multiple spouses simultaneously. Although it has always been common knowledge that many early members of the faith practiced polygamy both secretively and openly, Smith's polygamy had long been a matter of

[1] Nerida Bullock, PhD Student and SSHRC Doctoral Fellow, Department of Gender, Sexuality and Women's Studies, Simon Fraser University, Burnaby, BC, Canada. E-mail: nbullock@sfu.ca

[2] The abbreviation "LDS Church" will be used to refer to The Church of Jesus Christ of Latter-day Saints, "Mormons" to refer to members of the church, "Mormonism" to refer to the faith throughout this paper.

speculation and rumor. The construction of a misleading narrative through denial and omission commenced with Smith himself, who publicly denied his practice of "celestial marriage" to all but his closest associates until his death at the age of thirty-eight in 1844. Responding to a growing number of public accusations of sexual impropriety one month prior to his assassination, Smith is quoted as saying, "... what a thing it is for a man to be accused of committing adultery, and having seven wives, when I can only find one. I am the same man, and as innocent as I was fourteen years ago; and I can prove them all perjurers" (Roberts, 1912: 411). After Smith's death, the LDS Church continued to conceal Smith's plural marriages going so far as to publish tracts denying polygamy which were disseminated by proselyting missionaries in Europe (Gordon, 2002: 23). The ambiguity surrounding Smith's polygamy continued until 2014, when the LDS Church quietly updated its official website to include a description of "plural marriage" as practiced by Smith (The Church of Jesus Christ of Latter-day Saints, 2014; Egan, 2015; Goodstein, 2014). The LDS Church website now affirms Brodie's findings that Smith had been concurrently married to numerous women between the ages of fourteen to fifty-six.[3]

Included in this "new" information is the historically significant, somewhat perplexing and often overlooked fact that Smith's practice of "celestial marriage" was not limited to men having multiple wives (polygyny), but also included women having multiple husbands (polyandry). As stated by the LDS Church, "Joseph Smith was sealed [married] to a number of women who were already married. [...] In Nauvoo, most if not all of the first husbands seem to have continued living in the same household with their wives during Joseph's lifetime" (The Church of Jesus Christ of Latter-day Saints, 2014: para. 20-21). The fact that some of Smith's polygamist wives were concurrently married to other men and that these women maintained their spousal relations with their first husbands is a curiously queer admission that presents exciting scholarship opportunities.

The question must be asked, what purpose did the creation of ignorance through the suppression of history surrounding Smith's "plural-marriages" serve and what were the consequences for those who produced dissenting scholarship? Entwining a queer mindset with Robert Proctor's concept of agnotology—a term used to describe the epistemology of ignorance, facilitates a consideration of religious dissent from two interrelated and mutually reinforcing perspectives: 1) how *dissent* from feminists and historians within the LDS Church challenged (mis)constructions of Mormon history, and; 2) how the practice of polygamy by Smith and other early Mormons *dissents* from Western sexual mores that conflate racialized notions of family formation with social progression. Both genealogies of *dissent* illustrate how the convergence of racial and moral superiority in Western culture, predicated upon Christian monogamous sensibilities, motivated the active concealment of Smith's non-conforming sexuality by LDS Church leadership until 2014.

The LDS Church has taken great care to control the historic accounts of early Mormonism including its founder, Smith—a feat of progressive difficultly since the 1990s. The online proliferation of information about early Mormonism has encouraged the free exchange of knowledge and the dissemination of historical records beyond the reach of church authority. Counter-publics have emerged where (ex)members of the LDS Church engage in theology, feminism, history, and matters avoided in orthodox Mormon settings (Bartlett, 2018). The 2014 LDS Church website "update" is likely the result of what is now easily accessible online to faithful church members and outsiders alike—material that refutes the "historical face lift" (Eagan, 2014: para. 3) that evolved over the

---

[3] Brodie identified forty-nine women likely married to Smith (1945: 335-336), however the LDS Church website states that the total number of Smith's wives is unknown (2014: para. 18).

church's one-hundred-ninety years of history. Understanding the purposeful creation of ignorance regarding early LDS Church history contributes to the larger study of agnotology and presents opportunities to consider Mormon theology through a queer lens.

Constructing Ignorance

"There is a temptation for the writer or the teacher of Church history to want to tell everything, whether it is worthy or faith promoting or not. Some things that are true are not very useful." (Packer, 1981: 5)

Boyd K. Packer, Quorum of the Twelve Apostles[4]
The Church of Jesus Christ of Latter-day Saints

The purposeful creation of ignorance surrounding the conjugal practices of early LDS Church members, particularly Smith, is an interesting case study of agnotology, a termed coined by Robert Proctor to describe the epistemology of ignorance (2008). Knowledge production cannot be divorced from epistemologies of ignorance—what is known and unknown about Mormon history is the product of power, gender, race, economics, science, etc., and must be understood in relation to the cultural politics of ignorance. Reflecting on the various manifestations of ignorance making in Mormon histories exposes a variety of internal and external power regimes. As explained by Proctor, "ignorance has a history and a complex political and sexual geography and does a lot of other odd and arresting work that bears exploring" (2008: 2). Engaging with questions as to "why some knowledges are suppressed, lost, ignored, or abandoned, while others are embraced […] reveals how ignorance is often not merely the absence of knowledge but an outcome of cultural struggles" (Schiebinger, 2008: 152). Tuana suggests that an important consideration of an epistemology of ignorance is the recognition that ignorance is not a simple act of "omission or passive gap but is, in many cases an active production" that is often linked to issues of "authority, trust, doubt, silencing and so forth" (2008: 109, 140).

An illustrative example of ignorance by purposeful omission is a story taught to school-aged children about Smith being *tarred and feathered* by an angry mob because of his religious beliefs.[5] An abbreviated version of the story goes as follows (The Church of Jesus Christ of Latter-day Saints, 1997):

Soon after the church was organized, some members began to apostatize—they quit attending church meetings, opposed Joseph Smith and persecuted the Saints. One such person was Ezra Booth who wrote public letters to local newspapers questioning the church. Although Booth was excommunicated from the church, his published letters stirred up suspicion against local Mormons. One night, a group of men who believed Ezra Booth's letters, got drunk and attacked the home of Smith. They dragged Smith outside, choked him, tore off his clothes, spread hot tar over his body and covered him with feathers [abbreviated from original].

---

[4] The Quorum of the Twelve Apostles is the second highest level of LDS Church authority acting directly under the First Presidency (the President and his two counsellors). Members of the Quorum are "called of God" through the First Presidency and are considered representatives of God.

[5] Pine tar, used in 18th & 19th century shipbuilding, was only heated to 140 degrees Fahrenheit, and consequently was unlikely to cause permanent injury. Mobs performed the act of tarring and feathering as a form of public humiliation meant to deter the victim (and others) from arousing community disdain (Bell, 2013; Levy, 2011; Irvin, 2003).

Brodie's biography of Smith includes an account of the same *tar and feathering* incident with details omitted from the official LDS Church narrative. According to Brodie (1945: 119):

> Smith, his wife Emma and their adopted twins were residing under the hospitality of John Johnson in Kirkland, Ohio. Rebellion against Smith was growing locally and one night, a group of intoxicated men including Eli Johnson, the son of Smith's host, smashed their way into the home, dragging Smith into the night. The mob stripped him, beat him and covered his body with tar and feathers. Eli Johnson demanded that Joseph be castrated, accusing Smith of intimacy with his fourteen-year-old sister, Nancy Marinda [who would later become one of Joseph's polyandrous wives]. The doctor who was part of the mob declined performing the castration, and Eli Johnson subsequently decided he was content with seeing the prophet beaten [abbreviated from original].

The omission of Smith's intimacy with Nancy Marinda Johnson in church-sanctioned narratives is indicative of purposeful efforts by the LDS Church to obscure historic details, most notably the sexual proclivities of Smith, that sit in tension with Western gender and sexual mores.

It is not surprising that LDS Church officials and general membership would struggle to reconcile Smith's divine role in founding the Mormon faith with his secret conjugal practices that defied hetero-normative monogamous sensibilities of the nineteenth and twentieth centuries. Proctor suggests that "secrets are as old as human thought and perhaps older still, judging from the fantastic variety of animal techniques of deception ranging from insect camouflage to predators stashing their prey to the myriad disguises of herbivores" (2008: 9). Ignorance, in the case of Smith's secretive marital practices, was not passive, it was an ongoing *active* engagement— a strategy propagated with *intent* by Smith, himself, and later by LDS Church officials. Historian Benjamin E. Park (2020) published an account of early Mormon history in Nauvoo, Illinois that carefully documents the efforts taken by Smith and those closest to him, in keeping his polygamy a secret.[6] Aspects of LDS Church history deemed too controversial have long been omitted from church sanctioned narratives in order to circumvent a real or imagined danger. As Proctor suggests, acts of omission and/or censorship happen when "certain people don't want you to know certain things" and the whole point of secrecy is to "hide, to feint, to distract, to deny access, and monopolize information" (2008: 8, 19).

"Cultural occlusion—what not to know and how not to know it" (Laats, 2016: 176), plays a role in official Mormon historic narratives. Adam Laats' exploration of American-Christian historical texts in private Christian schools, found that authors and editors knowingly create content that departs from mainstream historical accounts in "order to advance a culturally distinct body of knowledge and way of knowing about the past" (2016: 176). Similarly, the LDS Church has cultivated distinct historical narratives that might be better understood as transmissions of *heritage* as opposed to *history*. Citing David Lowenthal, Laats suggests that heritage and history have different goals: heritage is a "declaration of faith," whereas history is to "understand the past on its own terms" (2016:176-177). The tension between *heritage* and *history* articulates the ongoing conflict that exists between dissenting Mormon historians and the hierarchal leadership to which they answer. Lance Chase, a historian at Brigham Young University-Hawaii (owned by the LDS Church) states, "Mormon religious orthodoxy asks the Mormon historian: 'Why expose the foibles of Church leaders and the consequent embarrassing results for Church members? How do your efforts serve in any way to promote faith?

---

[6] Even Smith's wife, Emma, was purposefully kept ignorant about the practice of polygamy and took great care in defending her husband against what she believed to be false rumors about her husband's polygamy. It is likely that Smith had over twenty wives by the time Emma became aware of Smith's polygamy (Park, 2020: 102, 104, 150, 151).

Why not stick with stories that build faith rather than destroy it'" (1997: 5). Mormon heritage prioritizes "faith promotion" over historic accuracy to foster a shared sense of the divine. However, crisis lurks when historical facts challenge carefully constructed communal narratives, such as the case of Smith's polygamy/polyandry.

Historians such as Brodie, who transgress Mormon orthodoxy to produce dissenting research are a key aspect of this agnotological puzzle. Brodie was born into the Mormon faith, and supposedly used her familial connection to her uncle, David O. McKay (who would become the nineth President of the LDS Church) to access historic records in the LDS Church archive. Brodie was no longer active within the Mormon faith when her biography of Smith was published in 1945.[7] After publication she was excommunicated from the LDS Church in 1946 (Bringhurst, 1989a; 1989b; The New York Times, 1981). It is important to note that in 1946 there was no voluntary system of membership withdrawal—one could not formally leave the LDS Church without being subjected to the excommunication process (Mauss, 2015: 388; Haglund, 2012: para. 8). The LDS Church has a complicated history of excommunicating dissenters, and then dismissing their dissent as the bitter musings of those who have been excommunicated— a case in point, Ezra Booth, who played a role in the *tar and feathering* story. The threat of excommunication has been a guiding force in curtailing intellectual inquiries that dissent from official church history. Excommunicating those who produce and publicly share dissenting scholarship empowers LDS Church leaders to frame these projects as the "product of apostates, or those that have fallen away from Mormonism" (Basquiat, 2001: 16).

In secular circles, Brodie's biography of Smith received largely positive reviews such as from Dale L. Morgan, a fellow historian, who characterized Brodie's book as "the finest job of scholarship yet done in Mormon History" (as quoted in Bringhurst, 1989 b: 3). However, within the church, it was deemed to be a work of poisonous, anti-Mormon slander, and members were advised to stick to 'faith-promoting material'—"a euphemism for church-approved material" (Basquiat, 2001: 17). Apostle John A. Widtsoe wrote in a church publication, "… the book is a flat failure. […] It will be of no interest to Latter-day Saints who have correct knowledge of the history of Joseph Smith" (as quoted in Bringhurst, 1989 b: 4). High-ranking LDS Church apologist, Hugh Nibley from Brigham Young University wrote a bitter counter-piece entitled *No Ma'am, That's Not History* that took aim at Brodie's methodology and findings (Nibley, 1946; Bringhurst, 1997). It should be noted that Brodie would later publish another critically acclaimed yet controversial biography—*Thomas Jefferson, An Intimate History* (1974) which spent thirteen weeks on the *New York Times* best-sellers list. Brodie's biography of Jefferson was the first book to prove the longstanding sexual relationship between Jefferson and his slave Sally Hemmings, thus garnering the fury of the "Jefferson establishment" which had long denied such rumors (Wallach, 2002; Fawn McKay Brodie Papers, para. 7). Both biographies of Smith and Jefferson dissented from widely held historic narratives that erased intimacies transgressive of White, heteronormative sensibilities. Jefferson transgressed codes of miscegenation and Smith transgressed codes of monogamy.

Mauss has argued that during the first half of the twentieth century, the LDS Church rarely took action against Mormons who produced dissenting intellectual works (2015: 390-91). Brodie's

---

[7] Social science can never be disassociated from the social circumstances of its construction, and Brodie's work and mine are no exception. Brodie described writing *No Man Knows My History* as a cathartic effort "to come to terms with my childhood" (Brodie as quoted in Bringhurst, 1997: 106). I find it satisfying that fifty years after its publication, I first read Brodie's book with the same goal in mind. Feminists such as Donna Haraway (1988) and Sandra Harding (1989) have long argued that *all* knowledge is situated knowledge and an ethical feminist praxis demands: 1) a relinquishing of the false promise of transcendence (the view from above); and 2) an acknowledgement of our partial view.

excommunication was an outlier amongst other dissenters.[8] However during the second half of the century, the excommunication of intellectuals, particularly feminists and historians who produced research that sat in tension with official "faith-promoting" narratives, exponentially grew (2015: 388). From the 1970's and onward, the impact of feminism and critical race theory within academia coalesced with a heightened interest in Mormon history. Within the LDS Church populace, a community of intellectuals engaged with such matters emerged. Intellectual inquiries such as reclaiming the divine feminine within Mormonism—a feminist project inherently linked to the early days of the Mormon faith when women held the priesthood were of interest to historians and feminists alike (Basquiat, 2001). Church leaders admonished intellectuals "to stop discussing publicly and in print certain doctrines and historical events that the hierarchy considered especially sensitive, embarrassing, or not open to discussion" (Mauss, 2015: 388). In 1992 Apostle Boyd K. Packer gave a public address at a religious educator's symposium warning that the Church faced *danger* from three groups: gays, feminists and 'so-called scholars or intellectuals' (Basquiat, 2001; Stacks, 2013). According to Haglund, that same year, feminist intellectual, Lavina Fielding Anderson, presented a paper at the Sunstone Symposium (an event for scholars and intellects of Mormon faith that was not sanctioned by the church) on the "growing conflict between [LDS Church] leaders and intellectuals" referring to an "internal espionage system" that "maintained secret files" on dissenting intellectuals (2012: para. 35). The existence of the "Strengthening Church Members Committee" (Anderson, 2016: 189; Mauss, 2015: 395; Roberts, 1994: 59) was confirmed less than a year later in 1993, when church officials publicly sanctioned six dissenting Mormons (including Anderson) whose transgressions comprised two categories: historic research that transgressed church-sanctioned narratives, and feminist critique of Mormon theology. (Bushman, 2020: 162; Hanks, 2017; New York Times, 1993; Johnson, 1993).[9]

Throughout the 1990s and early 2000s, the threat of excommunication hung over the heads of Mormon historians, feminists and other intellectuals who found themselves producing scholarship inherently at odds with church-sanctioned histories (Hanks, 2017; Anderson, 2016; Mauss, 2015). Historian Lance Chase (1997: 12) wrote,

> […] given today's climate within the Church, this compulsion and the profession itself can be very hazardous for the Church historian. He may choose to avoid L.D.S. Church history all together, he may choose to write only faith promoting history, or given today's climate, he may occasionally risk his church membership by writing what his research tells him really happened.

During this precarious time LDS Church leadership seemed particularly concerned "that without being spoon-fed 'truth' in a controlled setting, members might become convinced of new truths […] incompatible with those promoted by the church" (Roberts, 1994: 55). In the pursuit of purposeful agnotology, historical documents that did not support current interpretation of gospel doctrine were "conveniently swept under the rug or, to be more specific, locked up in the church vaults" (Basquiat, 2001: 15). However, with the proliferation of online resources, the church was forced to shift focus from the oppression of sensitive histories to their guarded assimilation. It "is not always easy to put

---

[8] Bringhurst (1989 b) suggests that David O. Mckay, Brodie's uncle who would become the nineth president of the LDS Church initiated the excommunication process on charges of apostasy with specific reference to the contents of *No Man Knows My History*.

[9] Five were excommunicated, and one was disfellowshipped. Being disfellowshipped is a less severe punishment wherein church membership is retained, but one is unable to participate fully.

some genies 'back in the bottle.' Knowledge escapes, that we'd rather have confined" (Proctor, 2008: 20).

Maxine Hanks, a Mormon feminist theologian who was one of the six dissenting Mormons publicly sanctioned in 1993 has illustrated how LDS Church efforts to censor and limit feminist/historical scholarship in the 1990s shifted in the mid 2000s from "fear to embrace, inaccessibility to availability, censorship to transparency. Topics we couldn't talk about in public and documents we couldn't see ten years earlier were going online" (2017: 177). Additional historic works documenting the non-monogamous marriages of Smith have been published since Brodie's 1945 biography collaborating many of her findings including Smith's polyandry (Park, 2020; Hales, 2014; Hales, 2012; Bushman, 2005; Compton, 1997; Van Wagoner, 1985). This research was conducted in spite of the fact that access to the LDS Church archive has been and continues to be, highly controlled. In response to a growing field of knowledge production and dissemination through online platforms, the tight grip the LDS Church has held on its history has been relaxed and LDS Church leadership has shifted to a more accommodating position towards internal and external scholars.[10] As Mauss states (2015: 397),

> New studies of polygamy (including polyandry) in early Mormonism, of race relations in the LDS experience, controversial new biographies of church presidents, and many other books and articles independently published by LDS intellectuals which might once have resulted in church discipline, were published in the new century with complete impunity.

Additionally, the *Joseph Smith Papers Project*, a collaborative initiative by Brigham Young University and the LDS Church to provide access to a digital database of historical documents related to Smith's life commenced in 2001.[11] These records have provided scholars the opportunity to explore what was once considered to be controversial (and consequently concealed) aspects of Smith's life (Park, 2018; Hanks, 2017; Minkema, 2015).

It is important to note that although public sanctions of dissenting intellectuals through disfellowship or excommunication has abated and the LDS Church has made conciliatory gestures towards historical transparency, the doors to the extensive and privately held church archives have not been thrown open. Keith A. Erekson, who serves as the director of the Church History Library has stated that private institutions such as the LDS Church, are under no obligation to make their archived collections accessible to the public and subsequently can restrict access to information ambiguously deemed "sacred" (2020: 120, 124). John Sillito, who boasts a forty-year career as an archivist at the University of Utah and the LDS Church Historical Department recently called "for a more open approach to the kinds of records available to the scholar—at the Church History Library and elsewhere" (2020: 116).

All cultures (and institutions) will "choose some representations over others" (Basquiat, 2010: 15), however, in the case of the LDS Church, the narration of the past has been painstakingly [mis]constructed. Putting Brodie's dissenting biography of Smith in conversation with the 2014 LDS

---

[10] In 2011 the LDS Church noted an unprecedented number of members terminating their membership due to political conflicts (internal and external) and growing doubts about fundamental truth claims of the religion (Mauss, 2015: 397). I am included in this exodus. In 2009 I initiated the process of having my name removed from the LDS Church membership records in response to the church's efforts to pass Proposition 8 in 2008, a California State constitutional amendment overturning the legalization of same-sex marriage. Although I am no longer a practising Mormon, the faith, culture and heritage are my birthright and I consider myself what Bartlett terms, a heterodox Mormon (2018: 145-147).

[11] https://www.josephsmithpapers.org

Church acknowledgement of Smith's non-monogamy, advances two important questions: What was/is dangerous about the Mormon historical archive; and why was/is it necessary for LDS Church officials to construct a sanitized narrative of Smith's life? Under conditions where ignorance is purposefully cultivated, such as in the case of Smith, it is of benefit to consider what types of knowledge are deemed dangerous and by which groups of people they are so judged (Tuana, 2006: 9).

Thinking of Mormon history as queer facilitates an understanding that "the Church's twentieth-century campaign for assimilation into and acceptance by U.S. society took the form not only of giving up polygamy, but of closely promoting and adhering to national norms around marriage, patriarchal gender relations, and reproductive sexuality" (Mohrman, 2020: 529). The embodied LDS Church practice of polygamy was in and of itself an act of *dissent* against Western sexual normativities. Within the context of the early nineteenth century, the Mormon practices of polygamy/polyandry was amongst three religiously inspired experiments in alternative sexual and marital configurations that grew out of the revival-spirit that swept through western New York State in the 1820s. Shaker celibacy, complex marriage of the Onedia Community and the Mormon practice of plural marriage shared a common desire to build communities based upon the ideal of heaven on earth—an ideal which included attempts to radically redefine conventional notions of family and community (Foster, 1981). Such attempts to reconfigure the family unit threatened power regimes reliant upon power-sensitive dichotomies such as: primitive/civilized; man/woman; adult/child; and public/private. These dichotomies were used in larger projects of imperial expansion and settler colonialism, which coded any sexuality in defiance of Christian heteronormativity as markers of *savagery* and/or *barbarianism*.

Queer History

Pinning down a precise definition of queer is impossible, as queer theory actively resists a precise definition (Greenough, 2020: 45). Yet identifying some dominant themes articulated amongst most queer theorists can point us in the right direction. Queer theory is about disrupting taken-for-granted social conventions. It is about challenging and subverting the normative to show that what we think of as "stable" (such as gender, sexuality or race) is in fact, fluid (Browne and Nash, 2010: 4). It is about challenging power-structures such as capitalism, heterosexuality, marriage and religion and considering how these structures reinforce systems of oppression. Alison Rooke suggests that "queer as a body of theory is not limited to thinking about gendered and sexual subjectivities. Rather it is a philosophical commitment to contesting the logics of normativity" (2010: 29). Queer theory has a particular interest in challenging dominant regimes of sexuality and considering how these regimes have ordered and structured society. It is also characterized as fluid and dynamic, "motivating queer researchers to work against disciplinary legitimation and rigid categorization" (Jones and Adams, 2010: 204).

Adopting the strategy of a "queer-view mirror" allows us to retrospectively consider the past through the lens of the present (Greenough, 2020: 42). Katherine Mohrman has argued that the current conservativism of the LDS Church which embraces capitalism, heteronormativity, and the heteropatriarchal family is "a response to a queer past that has been too resilient to be completely eradicated from popular memory, history, and the archive itself" (2015: 145). Smith's propensity for unsettling social and political normativities is evident in multiple arenas: his practice of polygamy/polyandry; his experiments in communal living and cooperative property ownership; his transgressions of the public/private divide; and his theocratic inclinations that conflated church and state (Park, 2020; 2018; Talbot, 2013; Bushman, 2005). Smith managed to disrupt an impressive array of taken-for-granted social conventions of the nineteenth century in a rather queer (strange and/or odd) way. Greenough explains that "queer theologies disrupt any 'normal' or 'natural' readings of Christianity in its theological forms, including tradition, scripture, worship, fellowship, dogmas, and beliefs" (2020: 34). The absorption of the LDS Church into the larger American body politic and its claims of religious legitimacy was predicated upon the need to distance itself from a rather queer past. To be accepted in the American body politic, the LDS Church has actively suppressed its queerness by maintaining a "notoriously tight grip [...] over the production of academic work about its own history" (Mohram, 2015: 146) resulting in a carefully constructed ignorance ripe for *dissent*.

In the early to mid-nineteenth century when Smith was experimenting with communal living and non-monogamy within Mormon settlements, a cultural shift was taking place in Western societies wherein "the image of the natural, patriarchal family in alliance with pseudoscientific social Darwinism, came to constitute the organizing trope for marshaling a bewildering array of cultures into a single, global narrative ordered and managed by Europeans" (McClintock, 1995: 45). Political debates on polygamy were often grounded in a linear temporal progression of civilization which suggests that societies progress from savagery (polygamy) into civility (monogamy). Layered upon these ideas of temporal progression were scientific constructs, most notable social Darwinism that explained in pseudo-scientific terms the supposed superiority of White Europeans. As Angela Willey argues, the convergence of social Darwinism, colonialism, anthropological studies, and an insistence of social progression created a temporal and geographic 'otherness' that "allowed claims about marriage practices and sexual mores across cultures to stand in as evolutionary claims" (2016: 30). *Civilized* Christian monogamy was positioned as 'evolved' being associated with (White) Western culture. *Uncivilized* non-monogamy was characterized as primitive, racialized and associated with Islam. Early sexologist Krafft-Ebing theorized European superiority in *Psychopathia Sexualis* as being predicated upon *civilized* human love—the romantic love between one man and one woman (as discussed in Willey, 2016: 30-31). When considering the case of Mormon polygamy in the territory of Utah, Francis Lieber, one of the most influential political theorists of the nineteenth century stated, "[Monogamy] is one of the elementary distinctions—historical and actual—between European and Asiatic humanity . . . It is one of the pre-existing conditions of our existence as civilized white men . . . Strike it out, and you destroy our very being; and when we say *our* we mean our race" (as quoted in Cotts, 2002: 115). Thus, monogamy became bound up "implicitly and explicitly with racialized notions of superiority, within the cultural, political, and economic logics that animated a colonial worldview" (Willey, 2016: 30).

In the United States, public discourse on the (White) practice of polygamy took place "at the height of the abolitionist and suffrage movements of the 1850s, shadowed the Civil War (1861-65) and the emancipation of some 4 million enslaved African Americans following the passage of the Thirteenth Amendment in January 1865" (Denike, 2014: 153). In fact, discussions of polygamy and slavery were often intertwined in what the Republican presidential candidate of 1856 called the "twin relics of barbarism" (Denike, 2014; Talbot, 2013; Crowley, 2011; Gordon, 2002). Anti-polygamy sentiment in the mid to late nineteenth century employed the discursive language of treason to describe the polygamous family formations of White Mormon populations (Ertman, 2010). As Denike reveals, "snapshots of anti-polygamy sentiment make clear that to speak of the difference between monogamy and polygamy was to speak of the racial difference in a very specific way" (2014: 145). Polygamist Mormons were racialized and considered a threat to proper social, political, religious, cultural, and moral order (Denike, 2010b). Pseudo-scientific social Darwinism justified imperial logics and the erasure of First Peoples through violence and forced assimilation. Concurrently, the fear of degeneration—"the possibility of racial decline from white fatherhood to a primordial black degeneracy incarnated in the black mother" (McClintock, 1995: 49) arose. White Mormons practising polygamy posed a threat of degeneracy to the newly formed White Republic of the United States (Denike, 2010 a). Although Biblical examples of polygamy exist (Abraham, being a prime example and the one to which Smith often referred) there was a collective consciousness that Christianity had evolved beyond polygamous practices while the *uncivilized* had not. As Denike explains, "the making of 'the' nation as white, in the face of all its heterogenous Aboriginal and immigrant communities, relied heavily on discourses and practices of racial purity whose theoretical justifications both mobilized and exacerbated anti-polygamy sentiment" (2014: 155).

Smith's new religion ruptured societal scripts beyond race, sexuality and family formation. Under Smith's leadership, Mormons experimented with a form of Christian communism wherein "members deeded their property" to the Church and received the "right to use it" back from the church (Ertman, 2010: 299). Smith also provoked political discomfort with his theocratic tendencies which blurred the lines between church and state (Park, 2020; 2018). All of these tensions became known in political circles as the "Mormon question," as illustrated by Christine Talbot (2013: 1-2),

> Polygamy generated decades of cultural conflict that contemporaries referred to, broadly, as "the Mormon question." The conflict was more than a simple condemnation of sexual and marital practices unacceptable to Victorian norms. […] Over the nineteenth century, white middle-class northern Protestants regarded the separation of public and private spheres as central to the meaning of Americanness. […] Polygamy destabilized these public/private divides in ways that dissociated family and gender relations from American citizenship.

Mormon transgressions against racialized family formations, property ownership and theocracy often resulted in violence and persecution, two cases in point being the 1838 extermination order of Mormons issued by the governor of Missouri (Park, 2020: 30; Gordon, 2002: 107) and the assassination of Smith by an angry mob. Over the next fifty years, anti-polygamy angst would culminate in the passing of the *Edmunds-Tucker Act* in 1887 by United States Congress which forced the LDS Church to abandon polygamy (Cott, 2000: 119). The insistence on the right to practice polygamy in the name of religion made Mormons unworthy of constitutional protections—they were "too far afield" of what constituted good citizenry (Crowley, 2011: 217). The *Edmunds-Tucker Act* contained twenty-six sections that would eradicate polygamy, constrain theocracy in the Utah territory and link monogamy with American citizenry. For example, one section repealed woman's suffrage in Utah and another section required men to swear an oath in support of the Constitution and laws of the United States, stating that one would "not, directly or indirectly, aid or abet, counsel or advise, any other person to commit" crimes of polygamy (*Edmunds-Tucker Act* as discussed in Crowley, 2011: 244). The United States government systematically linked the rights of citizenship, namely the right to vote, hold office or to serve on a jury to sexual and social monogamy. However, the most effective section of the *Edmunds-Tucker Act* was section thirteen that directed the United States Attorney General to institute proceedings to forfeit and escheat to the United States government property of the corporation of the LDS Church (Crowley, 2011: 251; Gordon, 2002: 196-197). The church held significant assets, and their interest in protecting those assets in conjunction with continued efforts to gain statehood for the Utah territory would ultimately result in church leadership denouncing the practice of polygamy (Cott, 2000: 118-20). In 1890 after several years of unsuccessfully resisting the provisions of the *Edmunds-Tucker Act* by legal pursuit, LDS Church President Wilford Woodruff publicly declared that church members were to refrain from contracting any marriage forbidden by the law of the land (Woodruff, 1890).

The convergence of racialized and moralized identities of superiority in Western culture is a legitimate motivational factor for the active suppression by the LDS Church, of knowledge about Smith's non-monogamous doctrinal teachings and embodied practice. Polygamy in the LDS Church *dissented* from western sexual mores that assumed the superiority of White nations and Christian monogamous marriage. Within a context of racialized discourse that closely identified heteronormative, monogamous marriage as being a fundamental building block of the newly formed American Republic, the survival of the LDS Church was predicated upon distancing itself from its non-normative [queer] theologies, practices and culture. If "ignorance is often not merely the absence of knowledge but an outcome of cultural struggles" (Schiebinger, 2008: 152) then we must consider the multiple cultural struggles that resulted in the agnotology of LDS Church history. At play is an almost dizzying array of historic conditions and tensions: slavery, colonization, Western Christianity, social Darwinism, prescriptive gender roles, normative family formations, moral crusaders, economics, politics and law. The very survival of the LDS Church was predicated upon disassociating itself from practices that dissented from those commonly held in the Christian/White American Republic.

These tensions are further heightened by the secrecy that shrouded Smith's practise of polygamy and the fact that a third of Smith's wives were simultaneously married to other men (Compton, 1997; Brodie, 1945: 336). "Polyandry is one of the major problems found in Smith's polygamy and many questions surround it. Why did he at first primarily prefer polyandrous marriages? [...] In the past, polyandry has often been ignored or glossed over, but if these women merit serious attention, the topic cannot be overlooked" (Compton, 1997: 15). The fact that women actively, and by most accounts, willingly practiced polyandry, and that Smith formed intimate relationships concurrently with multiple women provides an astonishingly simple reason for the intentional efforts by the LDS Church to obscure sensitive elements of its early history. The polyandry of early Mormon women is difficult to massage into the patriarchal establishment of the modern faith and touches on issues of female sexuality that have largely been invisible.

Conclusion

Tuana reminds us that "female sexuality is a particularly fertile area for tracking the intersections of power/knowledge-ignorance" (2008: 111). It is beyond the scope of this paper to offer a detailed understanding of polyandry as practiced in secret by Smith and his many wives between 1832 up until his violent death in 1844—although the possibilities of this archival research undertaken from a queer theoretical perspective is deliciously tantalizing. But the practice of polyandry does explain the political effort by LDS Church authorities to hold in secret Smith's unorthodox sexual practices. His ideas about alternative family formations defied Western narratives of cultural progression wherein non-monogamy was associated with the *barbaric* and *uncivilized*. Having it widely known that Smith sanctioned and participated in not only polygamy, but polyandry as well, complicates narratives enmeshed with LDS Church heritage and disrupts doctrinal practices which have come to be accepted by faithful Mormons. It also subjects the Mormon faith to an additional layer of scrutiny that would challenge both insiders and outsiders alike. The practice of polygamy/polyandry violates Western moral sensibilities and contradicts gendered sexual assumptions that situate marriage and female sexuality within a reproductive framework.

Chris Greenough has made a compelling case for using queer theologies to "destabilize the structures of power which have been tied up in the religion" by asking questions about whose voices and experiences have been excluded (2020: 5). Early members of the Mormon faith, including the polyandrous wives of Smith, adopted practices and principles that clearly defied prevailing normativities. They experimented with "utopian" ideals by offering alternative paradigms of "community" that rearticulated sexual connection and marriage. The historic legacy of Mormonism is a treasure trove for queer theorists who would like to consider the practice of polygamy as it relates to challenges of Western sexual mores, religious dogma and political power structures. Perhaps we have entered a new academic era in which the study of early Mormon polygamy can move beyond essentialist inscriptions of the women who participated in these non-normative marital arrangements. It would be reasonable to assume that the tight control by LDS Church authorities of the queer historical archive is predicated upon the assumption that its contents pose multiple dangers— to the "testimonies" of faithful members; to gender-based power structures within the church; to external criticism; and proselytizing endeavors. The purposeful ignorance and lack of exploration of certain aspect of early Mormonism, as in the case of the *Tar and Feathering* story, perpetuates and reinforces the privileging of heterosexual male sexuality within the larger faith and conflates the divine with sexual restraint. This privileging is deeply enshrined within current Mormon politics and is the primary *loci* for fundamentalist sects that have taken root outside of formal LDS Church authority. I suggest that a re-reading of Mormon history from a queer perspective is ripe with possibilities—the most notable of which would be to make that which has been made invisible (polyandrous women) once again, visible.

Acknowledgement

This paper draws on research supported by the Social Sciences and Humanities Research Council of Canada. I am grateful to Janice Stewart from the Institute for Gender, Race, Sexuality and Social Justice at the University of British Columbia for encouraging me to embrace my religious heritage in my scholarship. I would also like to thank Travers from Simon Fraser University for generously providing ongoing guidance and the anonymous reviewers for their helpful suggestions.

References

Anderson, L. F. (2016). "The LDS Intellectual Community and Church Leadership: A Contemporary Chronology". In J. Brooks, R. H. Steenblik and H. Wheelwright, (eds.) *Mormon feminism: Essential writings*. Oxford: Oxford University Press.

Bartlett, R. S. (2018) The Implications of Digital Technologies for the LDS Church and for Orthodox, Heterodox, and Post-Mormon Identity. PhD Dissertation, University of Colorado. Retrieved October 27, 2020, from https://scholar.colorado.edu/concern/graduate_thesis_or_dissertations/8p58pd049

Basquiat, J. H. (2001). Reproducing Patriarchy and Erasing Feminism: The Selective Construction of History within the Mormon Community. *Journal of Feminist Studies in Religion*. 17 (2): 5-37.

Bell, J. L. (2013). "5 Myths of Tarring and Feathering." Journal of the American Revolution. Retrieved October 17, 2020 from https://allthingsliberty.com/2013/12/5-myths-tarring-feathering/.

Bringhurst, N. G. (1997). "Fawn M. Brodie and Deborah Laake: Two Perspectives on Mormon Feminist Dissent." In *John Whitmer Historical Association Journal* 17 (25th Anniversary: 1972-1997): 95-112.

Bringhurst, N. G. (1989 a). "Fawn Brodie and Her Quest for Independence." In *Dialogue: A Journal of Mormon Thought*, 22 (2): 79-95.

Bringhurst, N. (1989 b). Applause, Attack, and Ambivalence—Varied Responses to Fawn M. Brodie's "No Man Knows My History". *Utah Historical Quarterly*, 57 (1): 46-63.

Brodie, F. M. (1945). *No Man Knows My History: The Life of Joseph Smith* (First Vintage Book Edition, 1995). New York: Vintage Books, Random House.

Brodie, F. M. (1974). *Thomas Jefferson: An Intimate History*. New York, NY: Norton.

Browne, K., and Nash, C. J. (2010). "Queer Methods and Methodologies: An Introduction." In K. Browne and C. J. Nash (eds.) *Queer Methods and Methodologies: Intersecting Queer Theories and Social Science Research*, Farnham, UK: Ashgate.

Bushman, C. L. (2020). "Mormon Feminism After 1970" In A. Hoyt and T. G. Petrey (eds.) *The Routledge Handbook of Mormonism and Gender,* New York, NY: Routledge.

Bushman, R. L. (2005). *Joseph Smith: Rough Stone Rolling.* New York: Alfred A. Knopf.

Carter, S. (2008). *The Importance of Being Monogamous: Marriage and Nation Building in Western Canada in 1915.* Edmonton: Athabasca University Press.

Chase, L. D. (1997). When I Have Fears: The Perils of A Fin De Siecle Mormon Historian. *Fides et historia* 29 (3): 5-13.

The Church of Jesus Christ of Latter-day Saints. (1997)."Joseph Smith is Tarred and Feathered." Primary 5: Doctrine and Covenants and Church History Teaching Manual, 110-114. Retrieved July 29, 2020 from, https://www.churchofjesuschrist.org/manual/primary-5-doctrine-and-covenants-and-church-history/lesson-21?lang=eng&clang=ase

The Church of Jesus Christ of Latter-day Saints. (2014). "Plural Marriage in Kirkland and Nauvoo". Retrieved January 16, 2018 from, https://www.lds.org/topics/plural-marriage-in-kirtland-and-nauvoo?lang=eng&old=true .

Compton, T. M. (1997). In Sacred Loneliness: The Plural Wives of Joseph Smith. Salt Lake City: Signature Books.

Cott, N. 2000. *Public vows: A history of marriage and the nation.* Harvard University Press.

Crowley, J. W. (2011). "Mormon Polygamy and the Construction of American Citizenship, 1852-1910." PhD Dissertation, Duke University. Retrieved July 30, 2020, from https://dukespace.lib.duke.edu/ dspace/ handle/10161/3950

Denike, M. (2014). "Polygamy and Race-Thinking: A Genealogy." In G. Calder and L. Beaman (eds.) *Polygamy's rights and wrongs: Harm, family and law.* Vancouver: UBC Press.

Denike, M. (2010 a). *The Racialization of White Man's Polygamy.* Hypatia, 25 (4): 852-874.

Denike, M. (2010 b). "What's Queer about Polygamy?" In R. Lecky and K. Brooks, (eds). *Queer Theory: Law, Culture, Empire.* London: Routledge.

Egan, T. (2014, November 29). Sex and the Saints. *The New York Times,* Retrieved January 16, 2018, from https://www.nytimes.com/2014/11/30/opinion/sunday/timothy-egan-sex-and-the-saints.html.

Erekson, K. A. (2020). A New Era of Research Access in the Church History Library. *Journal of Mormon History,* 46 (4): 117-129.

Ertman, M. M. (2010). Race Treason: The Untold Story of America's Ban on Polygamy. *Columbia Journal of Gender and Law* 19 (2): 287-366.

Fawn McKay Brodie papers. (1932-1983). J. Willard Marriott Library Collection. Retrieved July 30, 2020 from, http://archiveswest.orbiscascade.org/ark:/80444/xv55810/pdf.

Foster, L. (1981). *Religion and Sexuality: Three American Communal Experiments of the Nineteenth Century.* Oxford: Oxford University Press.

Goodstein, L. (2014, November 10). It's Official: Mormon Founder Had Up to 40 Wives. *The New York Times.* Retrieved January 16, 2018, from https://www.nytimes.com/2014/11/11/us/its-official-mormon-founder-had-up-to-40-wives.html?ref=us&_r=0 .

Gordon, S. (2002). *The Mormon Question Polygamy and Constitutional Conflict in Nineteenth-Century America. (Studies in Legal History).* Chapel Hill: University of North Carolina Press.

Greenough, C. (2020). *Queer Theologies.* New York, NY: Routledge.

Hales, B. C. (2014). Identifying Joseph Smith's Plural Wives. *Journal of Mormon History,* 40 (3): 155-168.

Hales, B. C. (2012). Joseph Smith's Personal Polygamy. *Journal of Mormon History,* 38 (2): 163-228.

Haglund, D. (2012, November 1). The Case of the Mormon Historian. Slate. Retrieved January 16, 2018, from http://www.slate.com/articles/life/faithbased/2012/11/d_michael_quinn_and_mormon_excommunication_the_complicated_life_of_a_mormon.html .

Hanks, M. (2017). Shifting Boundaries of Feminist Theology: What Have We Learned? *Dialogue: A Journal of Mormon Thought,* 50 (1): 167-182.

Haraway, D. (1988). Situated Knowledges: The Science Question in Feminism and the Privilege of Partial Perspective. *Feminist Studies* 14 (3): 575-599.

Harding, S. (1986). *The Science Question in Feminism.* Ithaca: Cornell University Press.

Hill, M. S. (1972). Brodie Revisited: A Reappraisal. *Dialogue: A Journal of Mormon Thought,* 7 (4): 72-85.

Irvin, B. H. (2003). Tar, Feathers, and the Enemies of American Liberties, 1768-1776. *The New England Quarterly,* 76 (2): 197-238.

Laats, A. (2016). Religion. In A. J. Angulo (ed) *Miseducation: A History of Ignorance-Making in America and Abroad.* Baltimore: Johns Hopkins University Press.

Levy, B. (2011). Tar and Feathers. *The Journal of the Historical Society* (Boston, Mass.), 11 (1), 85–110.

Mauss, A. L. (2015). Authority and Dissent in Mormonism. In T. L. Givens and P. L. Barlow (eds.) *The Oxford Handbook of Mormonism*. Oxford: Oxford University Press.

McClintock, A. (1995). *Imperial Leather: Race, Gender and Sexuality in the Colonial Conquest*. New York, NY: Routledge.

Minkema, K. (2015). The Joseph Smith Papers by Dean C. Jessee, Ronald K. Esplin, Richard Lyman Bushman, and Matthew J. Grow, and: Documents, Volume 1: July 1828–June 1831 ed. by Michael Hubbard McKay, Gerrit J. Dirkmaat, Grant Underwood, Robert J. Woodford, and William G. Hartley, and: Documents, Volume 2: July 1831–January ed. by Matthew C. Godfrey, Mark Ashurst-McGee, Grant Underwood, Robert J. Woodford, and William G. Hartley (review). *Journal of the Early Republic*, 35 (1): 157-159.

Mohrman, K. (2015). Queering the LDS Archive. *Radical History Review*, 2015 (122): 143-159.

Mohrman, K. (2020). "Queer Mormons" In A. Hoyt and T. G. Petrey (eds.), *The Routledge Handbook of Mormonism and Gender*, New York, NY: Routledge.

The New York Times Obituary. (1981, January 13). Fawn Brodie, Jefferson Biographer. *The New York Times*. Retrieved May 24, 2020, from http://www.nytimes.com/1981/01/13/obituaries/fawn-brodie-jefferson-biographer.html

The New York Times. (1993, September 19). Mormons Penalize Dissent Members. *The New York Times*. Retrieved July 29, 2020, fromhttps://www.nytimes.com/1993/09/19/us/mormons-penalize-dissident-members.html

Nibley, H. (1946). *No Ma'am, That's Not History: A Brief Review of Mrs. Brodie's Reluctant Vindication of a Prophet She Seeks to Expose*. Salt Lake City: Bookcraft.

Johnson, D. (1993, October 2). As Mormon Church Grows, So Does Dissent From Feminists and Scholars. *The New York Times*. Retrieved May 20, 2020, from https://www.nytimes.com/1993/10/02/us/as-mormon-church-grows-so-does-dissent-from-feminists-and-scholars.html?pagewanted=all&src=pm.

Jones, S. H., and Adams, T. E. (2010). "Autoethnography is a Queer Method". In K. Browne and C. J. Nash (eds.) *Queer Methods and Methodologies: Intersecting Queer Theories and Social Science Research*, Farnham, UK: Ashgate.

Packer, B. K. (1981). The Mantle is Far, Far Greater Than the Intellect. Address given at the Fifth Annual Church Educational Systems Religious Educators' Symposium, 22 August 1981. Published in BYU Studies Quarterly Journal 21 (3). Retrieved January 16, 2018, from https://byustudies.byu.edu/content/mantle-far-far-greater-intellect.

Park, B. (2020). *Kingdom of Nauvoo: The rise and fall of a religious empire on the American frontier*. New York, NY: Liveright Publishing Corporation.

Park, B. (2018) Joseph Smith's Kingdom of God: The Council of Fifty and the Mormon Challenge to American Democratic Politics. *Church History*, 87 (4): 1029-1055.

Proctor, R. N. (2008). "Agnotology: A Missing Term to Describe the Cultural Production of Ignorance (and Its Study)". In R. N. Proctor and L. Schiebinger (eds.) *Agnotology: The Making & Unmaking of Ignorance*. Stanford: Stanford University Press.

Reston, J. (2012, July 30). The Mormon Excommunication of Fawn Brodie: Why Banishing the Famous Biographer Reverberates 65 Years. *Washington Independent Review of Books*. Retrieved January 16, 2018, from http://www.washingtonindependentreviewofbooks.com/features/the-mormon-excommunication-of-fawn-brodie-why-banishing-the-famous-biograph.

Roberts, B. H. (ed.) (1912). *History of the Church of Jesus Christ of Latter-Day Saints, Volume 6*. Salt Lake City: Deseret News.

Roberts, A. D. (1994). "Academic Freedom at Brigham Young University: Free Inquiry in Religious Context". In G. Smith (ed.) *Religion, Feminism and Freedom of Conscience: A Mormon/Humanist Dialogue*. Salt Lake City: Prometheus Books.

Rooke, A. (2010). "Queer in the Field: On Emotions, Temporality and Performativity in Ethnography". In K. Browne and C. J. Nash (eds.) *Queer Methods and Methodologies: Intersecting Queer Theories and Social Science Research*, Farnham, UK: Ashgate.

Schiebinger, L. (2008). "West Indian Abortifacients and the Making of Ignorance". In R. N. Proctor, and L. Schiebinger (eds.) *Agnotology: The Making & Unmaking of Ignorance*. Stanford: Stanford University Press.

Stack, P. F. (2013, October 1). Healthy or hurtful? Twenty years later, Mormon 'Purge' still debated. The Salt Lake Tribune. Retrieved May 24, 2020, from https://archive.sltrib.com/article.php?id=56920802&itype=CMSID.

Stillito, J. (2020). A Matter of Trust: Archival Access and the Historical Record. *Journal of Mormon History*, 46 (4): 110-117.

Talbot, Christine. (2013). *A Foreign Kingdom: Mormons and Polygamy in American Political Culture, 1852-1890*. Chicago: University of Illinois Press.

Tuana, N. (2008). "Coming to Understand: Orgasm and the Epistemology of Ignorance". In R. N. Proctor and L. Schiebinger (eds.) *Agnotology: The Making & Unmaking of Ignorance*. Stanford: Stanford University Press.

Tuana, N. (2006). The Speculum of Ignorance: The Women's Health Movement and Epistemologies of Ignorance. *Hypathia*, 21 (3): 1-19.

Van Wagoner, R. (1985). Mormon Polyandry in Nauvoo. *Dialogue: A Journal of Mormon Thought*, 18 (3): 67-83.

Wallach, J. J. (2002). The Vindication of Fawn Brodie. *The Massachusetts Review,* 43 (2): 277-295.

Willey, A. (2016). *Undoing Monogamy: The Politics of Science and the Possibilities of Biology*. Durham: Duke University Press.

Woodruff, W. (1890, September 25). Official Declaration 1. Deseret Evening News. Retrieved October 25, 2020 from, https://www.churchofjesuschrist.org/study/scriptures/dc-testament/od/1?lang=eng

International Journal of Religion

ISSN: 2633-352X (Print) | ISSN: 2633-3538 (Online)

journals.tplondon.com/ijor

TRANSNATIONAL PRESS®
LONDON

International Journal of Religion
November 2020
Volume: 1 | Number 1 | pp. 151 – 165
ISSN: 2633-352X (Print) | ISSN: 2633-3538 (Online)
journals.tplondon.com/ijor

TRANSNATIONAL PRESS®
LONDON

First Submitted: 31 July 2020 Accepted: 1 November 2020
DOI: https://doi.org/10.33182/ijor.v1i1.1101

New Religious-Nationalist Trends among Jewish Settlers in the Halutza Sands

Hayim Katsman[1]

Abstract

This article describes the religious worldview of the residents of three rural villages, established since 2010 in Southern Israel. Focusing on religious authority, the article traces the complex relationship between rabbis to their communities which is rarely a simple "top-down" traditional authority model. On the contrary, both the rabbis and their communities are aware of the fragility of their relationship, and therefore created a complex belief system in which the rabbis' recommendation is sought, but not necessarily considered binding. In addition, the article describes the "Datlshim" (Hebrew acronym for "Ex-religious"). This liminal identity characterizes individuals who grew up within these religious communities but decided to dissent in their adulthood. They do not feel committed to, and sometimes openly reject Jewish religious code. The article contributes to the scholarly understanding of religious authority, as well as the diversity within the religious-Zionist community in Israel, which has become increasingly influential is Israeli politics and society.

Keywords: *Israel, religion; religious authority; religious-Zionism; secularization; religionization.*

Introduction

The young religious family that wanted to move to a village in southern Israel had no intention to provoke such a controversy. Indeed, all members on the village selection committee shared the impression that the family was friendly and showed genuine commitment to village values. However, some committee members were concerned by the fact that the wife's nose was pierced. While nose piercing is permitted according to Halacha (Jewish religious code), it is not socially acceptable among the more conservative Orthodox circles. The committee could not reach an agreement. They decided to consult with the village rabbi, who ruled that they can accept the family. Nevertheless, some members were still not convinced. As a final resort, they took the issue to their top rabbinic authority, the head of the prestigious "Har HaMor" Yeshiva, with which many of village members are affiliated. The rabbi listened to both sides, and eventually also ruled that they can accept the family. The opposers started arguing with him, questioning the ruling of their own ultimate religious authority, but the rabbi was steadfast. Eventually, the committee decided to reject the family.

This incident, which was described to me by members of one religious community in which I was interviewing, demonstrates one of the oldest problems in the study of religion. In the Platonic dialogue "*Euthyphro*," Socrates searches for the definition of 'the holy/pious' [ὅσιος]. In response to Euthyphro's attempt to define the pious as 'what is loved by the Gods,' Socrates asks: "Is the pious being loved by the gods because it is pious, or is it pious because it is being loved by the gods?" (Plato, 2002, p. 12). In other words, is the conception of holiness arbitrary, simply denoting what the

---

[1] Hayim Katsman, PhD, University of Washington, United States. E-mail: katsmanh@uw.edu

gods (represented by religious authority) have defined as 'holy'? Or perhaps is holiness that which we human beings decide through a social process?

Similar debates appear also in the Jewish tradition already in the 5th century Babylonian Talmud,[2] and Modern theorists of religion still seem to be struggling with Euthypro's dilemma. The foundational thinkers of the social sciences gravitated towards one side of Euthyphro's dilemma. Rooted in modernity and secularization, they viewed religion as a social construct. Endorsing the scientific method as their epistemological framework, Durkheim (1915) defined religion as a system of social knowledge, and Geertz saw religion as merely a "system of symbols… formulating conceptions of a general order of existence" (cited in Asad, 1993, p. 29). Later thinkers, such as Asad and Mahmood, problematized that notion from the other side of Euthyphro's dilemma. They emphasized the importance of adherence to religious rites as a precondition for constituting the knowledge within the believer (Mahmood, 2005; Asad, 1993).

Religion in Israel

Understanding the different approaches to Euthypro's dilemma sheds light on the ongoing debates regarding the public role of religion and religious authority. Religion has fascinated sociologists since the emergence of the social sciences as an academic discipline, and there are ongoing debates regarding secularization and the changing role of religion in the public sphere (Casanova, 1994; Butler et. al, 2011). However, as Casanova famously states: "There is no consensus, perhaps there will never be, as to what counts as religion" (Casanova, 1994, p. 26). Therefore, it is necessary to "unpack" what it is we talk about when we talk about religion.

The problem of understanding social processes of secularization and religionization magnifies in Israel, where the Jewish religion serves as a strong force in civil religion and national legitimation (Liebman & Don-Yehiya, 1983; Abulof, 2014). A mix of ideological, political and practical considerations kept religion as a strong force in the Israeli public sphere (Kimmerling, 2001; Katsman and Ben-Porat, 2019). Despite the inability to separate religion and state in Israel, the Israeli Labor movement was able to create a secular hegemony, in which the public role of religion was limited to certain domains. However, the gradual decline of the Labor-Zionist secular hegemony since 1977 has created anxiety among the secular public from the increasing social and political influence of the religious-Zionist movement. This anxiety has intensified over the last decade. Maniv & Benziman noted the rapid increase in public discussions of "religionization" [*Hadatah*] in Israeli media during the 2010s, pointing to an increase of 1000% in the use of the term over just three years (Maniv & Benziman, 2020).

Following the public debate, there are some attempts by researchers of Israel to account for this phenomenon and analyze different modes of religionization in Israeli society. In 2012 the *Israel Studies Review* published a roundtable discussion on the subject, in which scholars presented the empirical evidence for the phenomenon (Israel Studies Review, 2012). Israeli sociologist Yagil Levy went even further, arguing that the Israeli military has undergone a process of 'theocratization,' in which military orders are being subjected to religious authority (Levy, 2014; 2015). Recently, Yoav Peled & Horit Herman-Peled published a comprehensive account of religionization processes in the Israeli society (Peled & Herman-Peled, 2019). In their book, they provide an elaborate historical analysis of the

---

[2] The discussion on "The Oven of 'Akhnai" (Bava Metzia, 59a-b) is probably the most well-known example.

process, as well as demonstrating how almost every domain of the Israeli society has been affected by religionization.

In contrast to this body of work, Guy Ben-Porat argues that the Israeli society has actually been secularizing since the 1990s. Ben-Porat does not deny the increasing public role of Judaism in Israel, but rather makes an analytical distinction between 'secularism' as an ideology and 'secularization' as a social phenomenon. Following Mark Chaves (1994), Ben-Porat defines secularization as "the decline of religious authority and challenges to existing religious institutions" (Ben-Porat, 2013, p. 12). Applying Joel Migdal's state-in-society approach (Migdal, 2001), he traces these developments that took place not as official state policies but rather as the result of individual's decisions frequently based on economic considerations. Focusing on four issues - Regulation on marriage, civil burial, the ban on selling pork and commerce on the Sabbath, Ben-Porat demonstrates that religious authority is in-fact declining and an increasing number of Israelis are choosing are ignoring, and in some cases actively opposing, traditional religious authorities (Ben-Porat, 2013).

How can we reconcile these two opposing views? Is it possible that Israel is religionizing despite the decline of religious authority? Most authors point to the religious-Zionist sector as the primary agent of religionization in the Israeli society (Peled & Herman-Peled, 2019; Levy, 2015; Maniv & Benziman, 2020). However, my research on the religious-Zionist community in Israel reveals a more complex picture. On the one hand, as I will demonstrate in this article, religious authority is indeed in decline, and dissent is visible even among the most conservative religious-Zionist circles. On the other hand, this does not necessarily mean that individuals are undergoing "secularization." Returning to the anecdote of the family with the nose-pierced woman, we can see that a religious consideration could be used in order to reject a more traditional religious authority. However, as Euthyphro's dilemma teaches us, this is not necessarily "secularization," but rather a different understanding of what religion is.

In the next sections I will describe some findings from fieldwork carried out within three conservative religious-Zionist communities, recently established in the southern Israeli desert. I will present the unique context of their establishment, which gives us an insight on the different trends of contemporary religious settlements in Israel.[3] I will then go on to present my findings on the various approaches to religious authority among the village members, which will then shed light on the debate regarding secularization and religious authority.

Historical and organizational background

On July 15th, 2001, Israeli prime-minister Ariel Sharon brought to the cabinet a governmental decision announcing a plan to establish five new villages in the Halutza sands. The primary objective behind this decision was an attempt to prevent the evacuation of these lands as part of a future peace agreement between Israel and the Palestinians. The Halutza sands are within the 1967 borders, but due to their close proximity to the Gaza strip the Israeli representatives in the "Geneva Initiative" negotiations intended them for a "land swap" in exchange for the settlement blocs in the West Bank.[4]

---

[3] Since 1967, the settlement efforts of the religious-Zionist community focused primarily on establishing settlements in the lands occupied during the 1967 war. The settlements described in this are unique since they were established within the "Green Line," i.e. within the state of Israel and not within the Occupied Palestinian Territories.

[4] The Palestinians rejected this proposal during the negotiations, arguing that it is desert land. The final Geneva Initiative document does not include the Halutza sands in the areas intended for land swap (Klein, 2006).

The blunt political incentive behind this decision raised opposition from left-leaning MKs. Those wondered why the government does not allocate these funds to strengthen the existing desert dwellers. According to MK Taleb al-San'a, this decision is not only meant to prevent peace but rather also an attempt to 'Judaize' the space. San'a mentioned the struggle of the Al-'Azame Bedouin tribe which has requested to establish a permanent village in that area, in order to resettle a village they were evacuated from in the 1948 war. In the past, he says, the government objected the establishment of a new village in the Halutza sands for 'security concerns,' claiming the area was a military 'firing zone.' "When the government wants to establish a Jewish settlement, the firing zones are annulled immediately" said San'a bitterly.[5]

Government offices moved on in planning and zoning the villages despite the political opposition, yet it was unclear who would eventually live there. Discussing this plan in his 2003 book, Israeli geographer Elisha Efrat wrote that "there is a doubt if the Halutza sands could provide the infrastructure for massive settlement … it seems, that settlement in that area is a futile and pointless step" (Efrat, 2003, p. 99). Indeed, for years the government was not successful in attracting people to settle the villages. The solution came eventually only in 2005, just after Ariel Sharon completed his plan to evacuate 8,000 Jewish settlers who lived within the densely populated Palestinian Gaza Strip, known as the "disengagement plan." Two of the uprooted communities reached an agreement with Sharon to settle in the planned villages. The same people who were evacuated from their homes in Gaza by the decision of Ariel Sharon were also those who went on to materialize his vision of settlement in the Halutza sands. The irony in this development did not go unnoticed. On the contrary, many residents find pride in this.

Today, there are three thriving religious communities in the Halutza sands. While all three communities are religious-Zionist, each has unique characteristics. The variation is a result of the different historical trajectories of their establishment, and they preserve their cultural difference through a vetting process for new members. The villages also vary in their formal organization structure: Naveh and Bnei-Netzarim were established as a "*Moshav*," and Shlomit is officially a "community settlement" [*Yishuv Kehilati*].

Originally, the idea of *moshav* was conceived in the 1920s as a smallholders' cooperative community. In accordance with the Socialist-Zionist ideology, the *moshav* was based on communal values. The agricultural land is collectively owned by the *moshav*, but each household is considered an independent economic unit and entitled to an equal share of the land which it is expected to cultivate. Due to government economic policies and a general decline in agricultural income, today residents in *moshavim* hold various occupations and most of them lease their agricultural land to larger farms (Sofer & Applebaum, 2006).[6]

A "community village" is a newer type of settlement, which was conceived and developed under the right-wing "Herut" government after 1977 in order to settle the West Bank. As a result, the community settlement is based on liberal-individualistic values and usually has no agricultural lands and no collective ownership. Nonetheless, despite the different economic models, both community types have a general assembly, an executive board and committees which enable them to democratically reach collective decisions and preserve the sense of a community. Perhaps most

---

[5] http://knesset.gov.il/tql/knesset_new/knesset15/HTML_28_03_2012_09-20-03-AM/20010718@225-01JUL18@047.html

[6] Since the residents of the Moshav received the land in order to cultivate it, leasing it is formally illegal. However, it is a known secret and in most cases the state turns a blind eye towards this violation as long as the land is not used for other purposes other than agriculture.

importantly, these communities have an "absorption committee" [*va'adat Klita*], which is intended to preserve social homogeneity within the community by vetting potential members (Newman, 1984).

Naveh

The settlement of 'Atzmona was initially established in 1979 in Sinai, as a protest against the Camp-David accords.[7] In 1982 the Israeli government evacuated 'Atzmona's residents and resettled them in the Gaza Strip. In 2005, just before the evacuation of all Jewish settlements in Gaza ('Gush Katif'), some settlers from 'Atzmona reached a secret agreement with the government.[8] According to the agreement, they were to evacuate their village peacefully and would be given the opportunity to reestablish their community in one of the intended villages in the Halutza sands.[9] After the evacuation there was a split within the community – 65 families established a protest city of tents near the Southern city Netivot, and eventually agreed to settle in Shomriya, closer to Israel's center. A smaller group, approximately 30 families, moved to temporary housing in Yated in order to prepare for their move to the future village nearby in Halutza. At the time, they say, there was nothing in Halutza. The road just came to an end and all you could see was sand. Only after four years of intensive development was the village ready for the initial families to move in.

Since 'Atzmona's rabbi moved to Shomriya, the remaining community was in search of a spiritual leader. During the period in Yated, they asked Rabbi Mordechai (Motti) Hass, head of a religious institution in the West Bank settlement Elli and a close disciple of Rabbi Zvi Tau (head of "Har HaMor" yeshiva in Jerusalem), to be the spiritual leader of their community. Rabbi Hass had a unique vision for the creation of an ideal ultra-religious-Zionist community in light of rabbi Kook's theology, and he moved to Yated with a group of his followers from Elli with the intent to materialize it. Very soon, the original settlers from 'Atzmona stepped aside from the leadership (some left Naveh), and rabbi Hass and his followers became the dominant figures in the community's leadership.

Naveh is a *moshav* of approximately 130 households.[10] There is a consensus among residents in the area that it is the most religiously conservative among the three villages.[11] Unlike most residents in the other villages (and in the religious-Zionist community in general), all of my male interviewees from Naveh undertook extensive religious studies in a yeshiva, at least into their late 20s. The majority of them studied in "institutions of line" [*Yeshivot HaKav*].[12] Although it is formally registered as a moshav, its economic structure is intended to support the residents' Torah learning and therefore deviates from the standard model. Above all, the agricultural lands are not allocated to the residents, but rather held and cultivated by a communal agricultural association. The village's collective agricultural association employs workers, some of them from the village, to manage the collective

---

[7] On 17 September , 1978, Israel and Egypt signed a peace agreement. According to the agreement, Israel was to withdraw its troops and evacuate all settlements from the Sinai Peninsula, which it occupied from Egypt during the 1967 war.

[8] This is a sensitive issue among the evacuees, and I have heard various stories about it. Some people deny that an agreement was reached before the evacuation.

[9] Some people told me that it was the farmers from the village who pushed to accept this agreement, since they already had agricultural land in the area.

[10] Eventually, it is planned to reach 350 households.

[11] Some even say it is the most conservative religious-Zionist community nationwide.

[12] These are extremely conservative and nationalist institutions, that are affiliated with the spiritual leadership of Rabbi Tzvi Tau from 'Har HaMor' yeshiva.

property and cultivate the lands. This arrangement does not necessarily stem from an egalitarian worldview but rather in order to enable most residents to focus on the study and teaching of the Torah. To that end, Naveh runs a network of religious educational institutions, most notably the "Otzem" Mechina (pre-military preparatory institution). "Otzem" was initially established in Atzmona by Israel's former Minister of Education, Rabbi Rafi Peretz, who currently lives in Naveh. The Mechina is considered prestigious among religious-Zionist circles and draws religious youngsters who want to strengthen their religious identity prior to enlistment. In addition, in Naveh there are two religious elementary schools and two high schools (separate institutions for boys and girls), as well as an intensive-study yeshiva for high school graduates. All educational institutions are privately funded and are therefore not subjected to curriculum requirements of the Ministry of Education.[13] Most institutions are not yet economically self-sustainable and are funded by the village's economic revenues and donations. Many members of the community are employed in these institutions. Private entrepreneurship is not common in the village.

Bnei-Netzarim

Similarly, Bnei-Netzarim was also established as a result of a split within a community of evacuees from Gush Katif in the Gaza Strip. Netzarim was initially established in 1972 as a military base in the outskirts of Gaza city and was populated by temporary groups. The Jewish enclave later changed to a religious Kibbutz (communal agricultural community) in 1984, but was not able to attract many families who would bear the risk of living in the area. Finally, in the early 1990s a group of students from Merkaz Harav yeshiva joined, and the Kibbutz turned into a community settlement in 1992. After the Oslo agreements, Netzarim was completely isolated from the other Jewish settlements in Gaza, and travel to or from the village required an armored military convoy.[14] The settlers of Netzarim refused to negotiate with the government before the 2005 evacuation, hoping that the plan would not be executed. Therefore, they had no living arrangement after the evacuation and were placed temporarily in the students' housing of the Ariel College in the West Bank. While in Ariel, a debate emerged within the community. Learning about the plans of their friends from 'Atzmona to establish new settlements in Halutza, some wanted to join them, while others preferred to stay in Ariel. This debate tore the community apart and they decided to have a vote, resulting in only a slight majority of those who wanted to move to Halutza. Therefore, the community sadly decided to split, allowing each household to decide individually if it wanted to stay in Ariel or move to Halutza and establish a new village.

After the decision was made, those who chose Halutza moved to temporary housing in Yevul, where they waited for their village to be built. In contrast to Naveh, the original settlers of Netzarim are still dominant in the community leadership, and they see themselves as a direct continuation of the original community in Gaza. Some residents told me that arguing for a certain policy because "that is how it was in Netzarim" is common in village assemblies. This idea of continuity is also indicated by the name of the village ("Bnei-Netzarim" is Hebrew for "children of Netzarim").

---

[13] In the 2011, 2013 and 2016 math proficiency tests, the boys' elementary school was ranked in the lowest decile.

[14] On May 4, 1994, Israel and the Palestinians signed an agreement in which Israel would reorganize its military presence in the Gaza Strip. The new arrangement limited the Israeli military's ability to guarantee the security of drivers on the road connecting Netzarim to the other Gaza settlements. As a result, if they wanted to visit other Gaza settlements they had to leave the Gaza strip completely and enter it from the other border crossings.

As of 2019, out of 45 families from Netzarim that initially moved to the Yevul, only 22 were still living in Bnei-Netzarim. All in all, approximately 130 families live in the village.[15] Bnei-Netzarim is also considered to be extremely religious, but it allows more heterogeneity than Naveh. All my male interviewees from the village went to "yeshivas of the line," but only a few of them continued with their studies into their late 20s.[16] The model in Bnei-Netzarim is closer to the original idea of the moshav, and many individuals cultivate their agricultural lands. The village's lands that were not claimed by individual farmers are leased to large agriculture companies by the village's collective agricultural association, which generates revenues for the community. My impression was that the majority of members in Bnei-Netzarim are teachers, entrepreneurs, or college-educated professionals. A small minority receive a stipend for full-time studying of the Torah. Today, individuals who want to join the village and claim agricultural land must go through a trial period. The village allows them to rent their land for two years and provides them with training and mentorship. After this trial period, the new members can claim their land permanently and officially join the agricultural association. The logic behind this system, as was explained to me by members, is that the village wants to avoid the sight of abandoned greenhouses, which became common in many moshavim.

Similar to Naveh, Bnei-Netzarim operates several educational institutions. All these educational institutions are supported by the village but also rely heavily on Zionist donors' money. The village does not accept donations from Christian organizations.[17] Compared to Naveh, it is more common to see signs thanking donors across the village. Unlike Naveh, however, in Bnei-Netzarim the gender-separated elementary schools are public. Therefore, they are required to accept religious students from all the surrounding villages and curriculum is subjected to the Ministry of Education's requirements. A private men-only religious high school with dormitories [*Yeshiva-Tichonit*] also operates in the village, in which students work in agriculture for half a day and study (mostly religious studies) for the rest of the day. Like Naveh, in Bnei-Netzarim there is a yeshiva for high school graduates. Other than the educational institutions, the village operates a guest house for conferences and workshops. Within the village there is also a large regional health clinic, a privately-owned small grocery store, a yoga studio and some small businesses.

Naveh and Bnei-Netzarim partner in some economic initiatives, most notably they both hold shares in one of the largest solar-energy fields in Israel. This investment generates a stable revenue to both villages.

Shlomit

The third village, Shlomit, has a quite different character from Naveh and Bnei-Netzarim, and its establishment followed a unique trajectory. Shlomit was initially planned to be a small town, which will eventually populate 500 families and serve as a social and commercial center for the region.[18] The state did not intentionally plan the village for a religious-Zionist community. For a long time, the state was not able to find enough people (secular or religious) who would agree to settle this

---

[15] Like Naveh, also Bnei-Netzarim is planned to reach 350 households.

[16] "The line" refers to a specific tone within the Hardal subculture, which follows Rabbi Tau. The most notable institution of "the line" is Tau's Har HaMor Yeshiva, and the yeshivas in Mitzpe Ramon and Hebron are also affiliated with "the line." The name comes from the ideological rigidness in the institutions, which requires students to adhere to Rabbi Tau's ideological "line."

[17] A member of the community told me that once they even insisted on returning a significant donation, after retroactively finding out that it was from a Christian source.

[18] There are discussions of extending the village to 1500 families, but those plans have not yet been submitted.

undeveloped area. Eventually, the initial Gar'in (settlement group) for Shlomit consisted mostly from graduates of the "Otzem" mechina (religious pre-military preparatory institution), who were all young religious couples with one child or more. These first families moved to Shlomit only in 2011, after Naveh and Bnei-Netzarim were already established in their current location.[19] In contrast to Naveh and Bnei-Netzarim, the people of Shlomit did not have a predetermined religious or symbolic vision for the village in their minds. Primarily, they were interested in living within a national-religious community with like-minded neighbors. At first, residents hoped that also secular Jews would join the village, but those did not show interest. Today the village is officially open to accepting couples from the entire range of the religious-Zionist spectrum, but the majority of residents turned out to be affiliated with the more conservative "Hardal" (Hebrew acronym for "national-ultra-Orthodox") subculture.

As of 2019, only 70 families lived in Shlomit. Due to the relatively low housing prices it has been growing quickly and intensive construction was visible. The community in Shlomit is relatively younger than the neighboring villages (mostly under 35) and consists of college-educated professionals. From a religious point of view, Shlomit is the most heterogenous village among the three. All of my interviewees continued their Torah studies after high school, but many of them also served in the military for the full 3-year term.[20] Being a "community village," Shlomit does not possess any agricultural land and its only source of revenue is "community taxes" paid by residents and donations. As a result, Shlomit lacks the means for independent development, and the public areas in the village are far less developed in comparison to the neighboring villages.[21] Many of the roads are not paved, and only a few streets have sidewalks. Shlomit's synagogue was still in a temporary building and is the least impressive among the three villages. There is one daycare in Shlomit, but older children are educated outside of the village, mostly in the Bnei-Netzarim elementary school.

Religious Authority and the Observance of Halacha

Scholars consider the religious-Zionist sector, and even more so the conservative 'Hardal' subculture which these three communities are affiliated with, to be ideologically rigid (Herman et. al., 2014; Pfefer, 2007). However, my research finds a great ideological heterogeneity even within this subculture. What does characterize this subculture, though, is the attempt to create social boundaries of their community by presenting their ideology and actions as the only legitimate interpretation of Halacha. According to the largest survey conducted within the religious-Zionist community, 95.6% of those who self-identify as 'Hardal' and 80.1% of 'national-religious' agreed with the statement "Commitment to Halacha is an integral part of my identity" (Beit-Hillel, 2014). Some individuals confessed to me that they are not always able to follow every commandment, but they are committed to the aspiration to do so. When they are confronted with religious disagreements within their own

---

[19] https://www.ynet.co.il/articles/0,7340,L-4116115,00.html

[20] In the "Hesder" yeshivas most students defer their service and enlist for a shortened term of 16 months. In the "yeshivas of the line" it is common for students to defer even longer and enlist only for 6-9 months.

[21] This might also be a result of inadequate planning. A resident told me that the village was initially planned by an architect who used an urban neighborhood as a model, and therefore lacks planned public spaces.

community, they insist that the source of disagreement is a shared desire to truly interpret God's will. Those who are not committed to Halacha face harsh social repercussions.[22]

But who has the authority to determine God's will? In traditional Judaism, this was the role of the rabbis. They were the community's leaders, and they guided their community also with regard to social and political matters. This is still the case within the ultra-Orthodox society, where the sages promote the idea of "Daat Torah" [*the Torah view*] (Brown, 2014). A survey conducted among religious-Zionists in 2014 found that most religious-Zionists hold that belief as well. According to the survey, 54% of religious-Zionists (and 87% of Hardal) attribute high importance to the rulings of rabbis on national-political matters (Herman et. al., 2014).

My findings, which are based on in-depth interviews, reveal a more complex picture.[23] Despite their commitment to Halacha, the modern education they received brought them to adopt some of the normative claims of secularization theory. Secularization theory differentiates "the sacred" from other worldly spheres of human activity such as economics and politics (Casanova, 1994). Accordingly, I found that religious-Zionists consider the authoritative role of the rabbi to be confined only to matters regarding interpretation of Halacha. The rabbi may have an opinion on public matters, or provide individual counseling, but his advice on these matters is not considered binding. Those who follow them unquestionably do it out of their own will. Moreover, many of the individuals openly stated that they do not always agree with, or follow, rabbis' religious rulings. This does not vary with regard to the level of religiosity, but is ubiquitous across the religious-Zionist community. In many cases those who have a stronger religious background will have enough confidence to research a matter on their own instead of asking the rabbi for guidance. However, since they do consider the rabbis' opinion on matters of Halacha as binding, in many cases they will not ask the rabbi for a religious ruling, in order to not explicitly disobey it:

> I have a friend here that is a "*ba'al teshuva*."[24] After he became religious he lived in a "Mizrochnik" village.[25] He couldn't understand their behavior – Why do they not adhere to explicit rulings of Halacha?! It took him time to understand that there are nuances. I was just speaking with him. His rabbi told him to vote for *Shas* (an ultra-Orthodox political party), so he is voting for *Shas*. I respect that, but I believe that each one of us has a mind. Just like I go to the doctor when I have a medical question, I consult a lawyer when I have a legal question, so I would ask a rabbi when I have a question about Halacha. [...] Once I ask the rabbi, though, I am obligated. That is a matter of black-and-white for me. I don't play games with Halacha. Let's take traveling abroad for example.[26] Me and my wife now traveled abroad for the first time. I used to oppose that as an ideal. I don't anymore. Maybe I'm less idealistic. We really wanted to do it, so we did it. Now, can I tell you that it's 100%

---

[22] One of my interviewees was forced to divorce and leave their community after they confessed that they do not consider themselves obligated to Halacha.

[23] Since my interviews took place only 5 years after both surveys, it is not likely that the opinions changed so drastically over that time period.

[24] A term to describe someone who was not born religious but joined the religious community later in life.

[25] A term used to describe "classical," non-"Hardal" religious-Zionism. Refers to the first religious-Zionist political party - the "Mizrachi."

[26] Most religious scholars prohibit leaving the Land of Israel for vacation.

in accordance with Halacha? I know some rabbis will say it's OK and some will say it's not. So I didn't ask. I know there are rabbis who permit - so I did it.

Growing up within the Israeli society, which since the 1980s has become more individualistic, members of these communities want to make their own decisions. They expect their rabbi to give them guidance, not authority:

> In public matters, it is important that the rabbi gives a general direction, but he cannot coerce. […] Not everything is a matter that you need to ask the rabbi about. At the beginning of our marriage we had many questions about *Niddah*.[27] My husband often went to the village rabbi and asked him. One evening the rabbi told him "come sit with me for a moment, you don't need to ask every little thing." You have Halacha books, you don't have to run and ask the rabbi. He taught him – "this is prohibited, this is not." The knowledge is yours. That is a rabbi's greatness. Not to have the people dependent on you.

Some of my interviewees said they have completely lost their faith in rabbis' counseling. One woman told me how she consulted with her rabbi about her abusive and violent husband. The rabbi suggested that she change her behavior in order to accommodate his needs and achieve domestic peace [*Shlom Bayit*]. After several months of this not working, and the violence persisting, a friend insisted that she contact the state social services. Eventually, she got a divorce, but her husband remained in the community and she was the one forced to leave. Since then, she told me, she has lost her faith in rabbis. Another woman told me how her own personal experience taught her not to rely on rabbis:

> Personally, I identify myself with the Hardal subculture, but with regard to my faith in religious-Zionist rabbis… let's say that I have a problem with what religious-Zionists colloquially call "faith in the sages" [*Emunat Chachamim*] I do not like the religious-Zionist rabbinic leadership. Every time I tried to rebuild my faith in rabbis something came and brought it down. A rabbi transgressed… Even rabbi Druckman, who I consider our rabbi, and I highly appreciate his contribution to the Israeli society.[28] With one advice that he gave me he was wrong. I don't 'burn' someone because of one mistake, but this experience taught me that I need to trust my own deliberation and not rely on rabbis.

I was surprised by these statements and wondered how the rabbis understand their role. Interestingly, they seem aware of these sentiments among their congregations, and they try to rule accordingly. The rabbi of one of the villages told me that he himself will not feel obligated to follow a public ruling of his own rabbi if he did not specifically request a ruling. This rabbi also described to me how he understands his role within the community:

> I make a clear distinction. If I am asked about Halacha I say "this is what the Halacha says." With regard to public matters I state my opinion as a general recommendation, try to illuminate some aspects… They recently consulted with me about the upcoming elections for village leadership. So we sat and discussed this matter. They are really interested in what I have to say, but not as a binding decision. I really try as much as possible to avoid being

---

[27] Niddah refers to a woman during menstruation, or in the period following it before the immersion in a ritual bath. During the period that a woman is considered "Niddah," any physical contact with her husband is prohibited.

[28] Rabbi Haim Druckman, a prominent religious-Zionist rabbi, head of the "Or-Etzion" yeshiva.

the one making the decision. I actually run away from this. This is also not healthy for the person asking. I believe that one's freedom of mind is important.

These findings are important, since the majority of writing on religious-Zionism overemphasizes the importance of the rabbis' opinions. In some cases, scholars consider rabbinic discourse, represented in their books, public statements and responsa, to represent the view of the religious-Zionist public (Hellinger et. al. 2018). An illustrative example for this is the debate over disobeying a military command to evacuate a Jewish village. Most religious-Zionist rabbis have ruled that a soldier must disobey an order to evacuate a Jewish settlement (Roth, 2014). In practice, though, only 63 soldiers explicitly disobeyed orders during the 2005 Gaza evacuation. In a survey conducted among religious-Zionists in 2014, only 23% stated that "you must disobey" an evacuation order, showing that they do not consider rabbis' ruling as binding (Herman et. al., 2014). We can conclude, therefore, that we cannot view public rabbinic rulings as representing the opinions within the religious-Zionist community. Moreover, the fact that there is a decline in religious authority does not indicate secularization. Even the most religious individuals I met presented ambivalent views regarding their rabbinic authority, without feeling that this compromises their religiosity.

Datlashim - "I like the religion, not the religious people"

In this context, it is also important to discuss a group that is frequently overlooked in research on the religious-Zionism. During my interviews I also encountered a significant number of *"Datlashim"* (plural of *'Datlash'* - Hebrew acronym for "ex-religious"), who are part of an increasing trend in the religious-Zionist society. According to recent research, more than half of religious-Zionists are less religious than the house they grew up in (Rosner & Fuchs, 2018). However, socially, they cannot be excluded from the research on the religious-Zionist community (Katsman, 2020). The *Datlashim* I interviewed tend reject the binary self- identification as "religious" or "secular." The *Datlashim* do not feel committed to, and sometimes openly reject, Halacha, though some of them still adhere to certain aspects. At the same time, they do not break ties with their community, and in most cases still identify with it ideologically (Gal-Getz, 2011). Most *Datlashim* in the region are young (18-28), and were raised within these communities. The children in Shlomit are still too young, so there are currently no *Datlashim* in the village. Naveh is not tolerant towards *Datlashim*, and most of them prefer not to stay in the village. Therefore, all the *Datlashim* I interviewed were from Bnei-Netzarim. Some still lived with their families, and others moved to live and work in other secular villages in the area, while maintaining a close connection with their family and village.

The *Datlashim* all shared feelings of resentment towards their religious leadership and the coercion they experienced within their communities during their teenage years. These feelings are mostly directed at people of the village who tried to control their physical appearance and the relations between sexes. They considered this hypocritical. They were brought up to value compassion and justice, but in the end, they felt they were judged superficially by the length of their skirts or the color of their hair.

> I was a youth counsellor at 'Bnei Akiva,' but eventually I quit.[29] I had a boyfriend from the village and I didn't want to hide and lie about it. When I started wearing pants in the village

---

[29] Bnei-Akiva is the largest religious-Zionist youth movement. Counsellors are high school age.

I didn't hear comments but there were constant stares.[30] I once took a walk with a friend, and the next day he showed me that he got a text - "How can you hang out with this outcast girl?" [...] I was really hurt by this, that this is all they see in me.

Another woman told me how tensions regarding the way she dressed brought her to realize that she is no longer part of the community.

I met with the education committee and the village Rebbetzin (rabbi's wife). [...] They started preaching to me about modest dressing. They told me: "You must understand, when people see you like this it shatters their dream. People came here because they want to live in a certain place. It's like a man will wear a skirt, it's strange." [...] Until then, I didn't think that there is anything wrong with the way I dressed, so now I need to think about this?! The way men view me? I understood that I don't belong. I'm outside of the line, and that sucks.

While they left their communities, and no longer feel obligated to Halacha, some *Datlashim* still seek a certain connection to Judaism, on their own terms. Some describe a spiritual connection to God and some admit they still partially observe Halacha, though they do not feel committed to adhere to every aspect of it. They feel free to pick and choose which commandments they want to follow. I asked one *Datlash* who expressed this ambivalent feeling if he if he considers himself religious. "I'm Jewish, brother," he said smiling. When I asked if he sees himself becoming religious again in the future he replied:

I'll tell you what it is. I like the religion, not the religious people. That's the problem. I try. I put up *Mezuzot*[31] in my house, I wear *Tefilin*[32] when I feel like it, not every day. Sometimes I recite the "*Shema*" before I go to bed.[33] Sabbath is still difficult. [...] I will eat in a non-kosher restaurant, but I will not eat a cheeseburger. I never ate shrimp.[34] But my house is Kosher in case my brother or father will want to come over.

While none of the *Datlashim* expressed commitment to Halacha, most of them still identified with the Zionist nationalist ideology they grew up in. Politically, they tend to identify with right-wing and even religious parties, and most of them are still committed to the idea of the sacredness of the land of Israel:

I think I can never get "The Land of Israel" out of my system. I don't know if I want to or not. Everything about it thrills me, excites me. It got to a point that I said "enough! I don't want to feel this way anymore!" I always say that the Land of Israel is the actual (religious-Zionist) religion. That is the big thing. God. [...] Last year I started college. Academia is the biggest lie there is, and it drives me crazy that I'm a part of it. [...] It is so leftist! They tell you to "think outside the box," but what they really mean is "think inside our box." [...]

---

[30] Most Jewish Orthodox communities consider wearing pants immodest, and women are expected to wear long skirts (the acceptable length varies).

[31] Orthodox Jews interpret Jewish law to require a piece of parchment with verses from Deuteronomy to be place on every doorstep in the house (except bathrooms).

[32] A pair of small black leather boxes containing scrolls of parchment inscribed with verses from the Torah. Orthodox Jews see high importance in wearing these every weekday morning during prayer.

[33] A verse from Deutronmy 6:4-9, which is recited by Orthodox Jews three times a day: During morning prayer, evening prayer, and before going to bed.

[34] Shrimp and cheeseburger are forbidden foods for Jews who only eat Kosher.

This whole thing was a shock to me, because in my own village I am the one called "the leftist" […] I am studying this course on the history of the Middle-East, the lecturer is Arab. She showed us a film on the War of Independence from the Arab point of view. A lot of shooting, IDF soldiers constantly killing Arabs. I didn't know what to do, at some point I couldn't stay. I left the classroom.

These findings suggest that we must reconsider our understanding of the centrality of Halacha in the national-religious sector. As I have shown, even within the Hardal society rabbis' rulings on public and political matters are not considered binding. Some may choose to follow their public rulings, but the society (and rabbis themselves) do not perceive this as an obligation. Even with regard to interpretation of Halacha, where they do have authority, their interpretation is considered binding only when explicitly asked to provide a ruling. In addition, there is a significant population that grew up within the national-religious education system that does not feel committed to Halacha whatsoever. They do not define themselves as religious, but stay within the national-religious sphere of influence. They still hold to many aspects of the value system they grew up on and identify with the right-wing political camp.

Conclusion

The religiosity of religious-Zionist settlers in the Halutza Sands provides a complex image of adherence to religion in contemporary Israel. Scholars of the Israeli society are concerned by the 'religionization' of many domains in the Israeli society, fearing their eventual subjection to religious authority. However, my research demonstrates that even the most conservative segments of the Israeli religious-Zionist community do not necessarily accept religious authority unquestioningly. On the contrary, they partially accept the normative premises of secularization theory, and confine religious authority to matters strictly related to Halacha. They will consider religious reasoning on public matters, but in no way will accept it as binding.

At the same time, the fact that religious authority is in decline does not mean that religion is in decline altogether. As Euthypro's dilemma teaches us, there are two ways in which we can understand religion. Instead of interpreting religion as blindly following religious authority, Euthyphro's dilemma shows us that also individuals and societies have the power of constructing what religion is. The individuals I interviewed for this article believe that their religion requires them to have an independent mind and think for themselves. Even the supposed dissenters, the *Datlsahim*, are still connected to the Jewish religion, despite their complete disregard to formal religious authority.

Despite the predictions of secularization theory, religion is a stronger force than ever worldwide, whether these are formal traditional forms of religion or 'new age' spiritualities. This article offers a contribution to making sense of this phenomenon through the study and understanding of the contemporary religious-Zionist community in Israel. As this article demonstrates, understanding religious authority, dissent, and the self-perception of believers is crucial in the study of religion. This analysis of the different understanding of what constitutes 'religion' can be applied in various cases globally, and will hopefully contribute to the future international study of religion.

Acknowledgments

The author wishes to thank the residents of Naveh, Bnei-Netzarim and Shlomit for their openness and willingness to participate in this study. The author also wishes to thank Joel Migdal, Liora Halperin, Jim Wellman and Christian Novetzke for their insightful comments on earlier drafts of this article. Finally, this research could not have happened without the generous financial support of the Stroum Center for Jewish Studies at the university of Washington, Seattle; and the Grizzley garage in Moshav Dekel, Israel.

References

Abulof, U. (2014). The Roles of Religion in National Legitimation: Judaism and Zionism's Elusive Quest for Legitimacy. Journal for the Scientific Study of Religion, 53(3), 515-533.

Asad, T. (1993). Genealogies of Religion: Discipline and Reasons of Power in Christianity and Islam. Baltimore: Johns Hopkins University Press.

Beit Hillel. (2014). Results of The Big Religious-Zionist Survey. Jerusalem: Beit Hillel. (Hebrew).

Ben-Porat, G. (2013). Between state and synagogue: The secularization of contemporary Israel (No. 42). Cambridge University Press.

Brown, Benjamin. (2005) "The Doctrine of Daat Torah: Three Stages." In: Amir, Y. (Ed.): The Path of the Spirit: the Eliezer Schweid Jubilee: Volume two. Jerusalem: Van-Leer Institute. 537-600.

Butler, J., Habermas, J., Taylor, C., & West, C. (2011). The power of religion in the public sphere. Columbia University Press.

Casanova, J. (2011). Public religions in the modern world. University of Chicago Press.

Chaves, M. (1994). Secularization as declining religious authority. Social forces, 72(3), 749-774.

Durkheim, E. (1915). The Elementary Forms of the Religious Life: A study in religious sociology. London: New York: G. Allen & Unwin; Macmillan.

E, Elisha. (2003). National Planning and Development in Israel in the 21st Century. Tel-Aviv: Ramot – Tel Aviv University. (Hebrew).

Gal-Getz-P. (2011) Hadatlashim. Tel-Aviv: Am-Oved.

Hellinger, M., Hershkowitz, I., & Susser, B. (2018). Religious Zionism and the Settlement Project: Ideology, Politics, and Civil Disobedience. New York: SUNY Press.

Herman, T., Be'ery, G., Heller, E., Cohen, C., Lebel, Y., Mozes, H., & Neuman, K. (2014). The national-religious sector in Israel 2014. Main Findings. Jerusalem: Israel Democracy Institute.

Israel Studies Review (2012) "The 'Religionization' of Israeli Society," 27 (1): v–208.

Levy, Y. (2014). The theocratization of the Israeli military. Armed Forces & Society, 40(2), 269-294.

Levy, Y. (2015). The Divine Commander: The Theocratization of the Israeli Military. Tel Aviv: Am Oved and Sapir Academic College. (Hebrew).

Liebman, C. S., Libman, Y., & Don-Yihya, E. (1983). Civil religion in Israel: Traditional Judaism and political culture in the Jewish state. Univ of California Press.

Mahmood, S. (2005). Politics of Piety: The Islamic Revival and the Feminist Subject. Princeton, N.J.: Princeton University Press.

Maniv, O., & Benziman, Y. (2020). National-Religionization (and not Religious-Religionization) in Policies of Israel's Ministry of Education. Israel Studies, 25(2), 115-137.

Newman, D. (1984). The Development of the Yishuv Kehilati in Judea and Samaria: Political Process and Settlement form. Tijdschrift voor economische en sociale geografie, 75(2), 140-150.
https://onlinelibrary.wiley.com/doi/abs/10.1111/j.1467-9663.1984.tb00984.x

Pfefer, A. (2007). The Origins and Future Course of the National-Haredi Public. Jerusalem: The Floersheimer Institute for Policy Studies.

Peled, Y. and Herman-Peled, H. (2019). The religionization of Israeli society. Abingdon, Oxon: Routledge.

Rosner, S. & Fuchs, C. (2018). #IsraeliJudaism, a Cultural Revolution. Israel: Kineret Zmora-Bitan, Dvir.

Roth, Anat. (2014) Not at any Cost: From Gush Katif to Amona: The Story behind the Struggle over the Land of Israel, Tel-Aviv: Yediot Aharonot. (Hebrew)

Sofer, M., & Applebaum, L. (2006). The rural space in Israel in search of renewed identity: The case of the moshav. Journal of Rural Studies, 22(3), 323-336.

Katsman, H. (2020). The Hyphen Cannot Hold: Contemporary Trends in Religious-Zionism. Israel Studies Review. 35(2).

Katsman, H. and Ben-Porat, G. (2019). "Israel: Religion and Political Parties." In: Haynes, J. (Ed.): Routledge Handbook of Religion and Political Parties. Abingdon, Oxon: Routledge.

Kimmerling, B. (2001). The Invention and Decline of Israeliness: State, Society, and the Military. Berkeley: University of California Press.

Klein, M. (2006). The Geneva Initiative: An Inside View. Jerusalem: Carmel.

www.ingramcontent.com/pod-product-compliance
Lightning Source LLC
Chambersburg PA
CBHW081740270326
41932CB00020B/3343